HARRY

HARRY

A WILDERNESS DOG SAGA

Chris Czajkowski

HARBOUR
PUBLISHING

Harbour Publishing Co. Ltd.
P.O. Box 219, Madeira Park, BC, V0N 2H0
www.harbourpublishing.com

Photos from author's collection unless otherwise stated
Edited by Joanna Reid
Cover design by Anna Comfort O'Keeffe
Text design by Shed Simas / Onça Design
Printed and bound in Canada

Harbour Publishing acknowledges the support of the Canada Council for the Arts, which last year invested $153 million to bring the arts to Canadians throughout the country. We also gratefully acknowledge financial support from the Government of Canada and from the Province of British Columbia through the BC Arts Council and the Book Publishing Tax Credit.

Library and Archives Canada Cataloguing in Publication

Czajkowski, Chris, author
        Harry : a wilderness dog saga / Chris Czajkowski.

Issued in print and electronic formats.
ISBN 978-1-55017-809-8 (softcover).--ISBN 978-1-55017-810-4 (HTML)

        1. Dogs--British Columbia--Biography. 2. Czajkowski, Chris.
3. Outdoor life--British Columbia. 4. Human-animal relationships--
British Columbia. I. Title.

SF426.2.C92 2017   636.70092'9   C2017-903154-6
                                               C2017-903155-4

CONTENTS

TIMELINE

	1981	Lonesome joins the pack
Lonesome Lake cabin started	1983	
Nuk Tessli started	1988	
Cabin-in-the-Bog acquired	1990	Sport joins the pack
	1995	Lonesome leaves, Taya joins the pack
	1996	Sport leaves, Max joins the pack
	2000	Taya leaves, Ginger joins the pack
	2002	Ginger leaves, Bucky joins the pack
	2004	Raffi joins the pack
River Cabin at Ginty Creek started	2006	Bucky leaves the pack
	2007	Nahanni joins the pack
House started at Ginty Creek	2008	Raffi leaves, Badger joins the pack
	2009	Nahanni leaves, Harry joins the pack
Move into house at Ginty Creek	2010	

PREFACE

THE WILDERNESS DOG SAGA COVERS A PERIOD OF APPROXIMATELY THIRTY years. All the events actually happened. The narrative jumps around a little in time and space—ten different dogs joined and left the pack during that period, and Chris lived in four separate locations. My editor said she was a bit confused about the logistics and she said she wanted some clarification. When I tried to write it in words I became confused myself! I thought the best way to deal with it was to provide the following map and the timeline on p. 6.

— Harry, Ginty Creek, 2017

West Chilcotin

Part One
THE SAGA

1

HARRY

PARADISE YARD

THE FIRST TIME I MET CHRIS I WAS WEARING A DIAPER. NOT THE BEST way for a young, good-looking guy to be presented to a new, female pack mate, even though she was pretty old. It was not as if I needed the diaper even though I was getting a bit desperate—I had been shut in a crate for several hours by that time—but I would have cut off my right paw rather than disgrace myself. Chris, though, understood my needs perfectly. She opened the cage door, clipped on a lead, pulled the sticky-sounding tabs off the diaper and whisked it off over my tail, and led me across a short stretch of bare roadway to a large, pristine snowbank. What bliss to paint that snowy whiteness completely yellow!

That taken care of, I was able to take a proper look at Chris. Like several of the people I had been shunted past in the previous few days, she was getting a bit long in the tooth. Unlike the others, though, Chris was very roughly dressed. She had those round glass things covering her eyes; she wore baggy pants with a patch on one knee and a bulky coat that, despite the nip in the wind, was unzipped to show a heavy sweater. Her feet were enormous. Puppies often have big feet, but that shows they still have some growing to do. Surely this old lady, who was already on the big side as far as human females went, had finished growing long ago. It was only later, after she had taken her shoes off, that I discovered some of this apparent size was due to a thick layer of insulation in them. Unlike us, humans must supplement their skin, covering with all manner of outward garments, as they would otherwise freeze to death very quickly in cold climates.

This place was certainly colder than the other places I had been used to. I had seen snow before, but never at this time of year. Here it was a solid white sheet that covered everything, except the ground we were standing on. When I had started my journey that morning, it had been much warmer and pouring with rain. What a strange world we live in where you go into a box in one place and come out a short time later in a completely different one.

I don't really remember my parents. I spent most of my child-hood alone, and was generally hungry. Now that I have seen more of the world, I can describe my place of birth as a dry area with a lot of scrubby grass and bushes. Low, shabby houses straggled along a hillside above a big, wide river, and dogs of every shape and colour, mostly quite big, wandered around without restraint. I developed quite a knack for filching bits of food here and there, but was often yelled at and beaten by humans, or snapped at by canines. Unless I was really hungry, it was usually easier to do without. I tended to hang about near a house where no one gave me any grief. They didn't feed or water me, but at least I wasn't abused.

Cars occasionally puttered along the narrow road in front of the house. One came by several times. It was a white car with coloured stripes painted along the side. Near the rear end was a small picture of a man holding a flag while sitting on a galloping horse. A woman who always wore dark clothes drove this car; she would slow down and give me a hard look every time she went past. One day another vehicle cruised along the road, and this one stopped. Out climbed a different person. She wore loose, light clothes, and her hair flew about her head like an ungroomed Poodle's. Her somewhat fearful appearance, however, was instantly eclipsed by the aroma coming out of her pockets. Food. It was of a type I had never seen before, bone-shaped and almost as hard, but tasting vaguely of bread. The woman threw a piece onto the ground in front of me. I wolfed it down. Another piece followed. The third, she held in her hand. I was a bit suspicious at first, as most human hands were not kind to me, but the food had stimulated my appetite and I could not resist. As my jaws closed around it, a blue rope somehow found its way around my neck. I didn't notice it until it was too late. I jumped back in alarm, but the woman was talking a lot of gobbledygook humanspeak in a gentle way, and she still smelled of food, so I followed. She took me to her car. I wasn't too happy about that either, but I really didn't have the energy to resist. There were plenty of motor vehicles lying about my home area—some living and some abandoned and dead—but the thought of getting inside one of these stinking metal boxes was a bit nerve-racking. However, the woman continued to speak to me in a non-threatening way and gave me another bone thing and several cautious but reassuring touches with her hands, which was something I found I rather enjoyed.

The interior of the car had plastic seating and smelled of oil, but there were healthy doggy scents in there, too. We drove down to the river, crossed on a little ferry and then climbed the bank and wove our way into the hills. After a short while, we came to a large open space with a shack and a trailer at one end. A whole bevy of miscellaneous dogs came galloping to meet us—about as many as I had toes on two paws. I was quite frightened at first; where I'd come from, I'd received many a nip trying to grab a few mouthfuls of food. I need not have worried, however. These canines were all boisterous and friendly, and obviously loved this woman. They were also all very well fed.

At first I was given meals in a separate place from the other dogs: a whole bowl of food all to myself, even though I probably could have done quite well grabbing enough to eat, as food was plentiful and I could run a lot faster than any of the others. It wasn't long before I was having fun with this motley pack. All had been homeless, it appeared, most in similar circumstances to my own, but all were friendly and contented with where they had ended up. They called their new home "Paradise Yard."

The friendly lady kept telling me how pretty I looked with my black nose and eyeliner, and my soft, golden fur. I knew I was good-looking, but that didn't stop my enjoyment of hearing such praise repeated, particularly as such humanspeak was usually accompanied by a scratch behind the ears, which proved to be quite a delectable sensation.

"Because you have such long hair," she one day decided, "I am going to call you Harry." I thought "HandsomeGoldenSuperdogWho-RunsLikeTheWind" would have been a name more fitting, but hey! She was the one who fed me, and if "Harry" made her happy, I was prepared to go along with it. Later I found out that a world-famous prince is also called Harry and that made me feel better. He even has head-fur much the same colour as mine.

There was only one other house close to ours. The man who lived in it cohabited with many animals, but most of these were birds called Chicken. They didn't fly around like the other feathered animals I had experienced, but sat about in a big cage. They made a lot of squawking noises and stunk to high heaven. One day one of my new buddies and I dug a hole under the fence and went in to see what all the fuss was about. The noise from the birds escalated a hundredfold when we wriggled through, and oh, what fun we had galloping around and sending these stupid creatures into hysterics. There were feathers everywhere. My buddy was a bit tubby, and was somewhat bamboozled by all the noise and kerfuffle, but my leap was true, and I got one in my jaws. What a strange and exciting sensation to have my mouth full of warm, squirming flesh! The feathers got up my nose and tickled a bit, but the squirming did not last long, and soon I was aware of the intoxicating taste of blood and fresh meat. I had little time to enjoy that sensation, however, because along came my new human friend and the Man Who Lived with Chicken. Both were about as noisy and hysterical as the birds, and my buddy and I were grabbed and yanked away from our prize in no uncertain terms. The humans were looking pretty angry, which was a bit puzzling, as I'd seen them catch Chicken sometimes. I expected a beating, but, when she had calmed down, my human just looked sorrowful. She turned to the Man Who Lived with Chicken and said, in humanspeak (which I was beginning to understand quite well) that she would pay for the damage.

I did not know it at the time, but that marked the beginning of the end of my idyll in Paradise Yard. I had arrived when the old leaves were falling off the trees and now the bare twigs were just starting to put out new buds. In that time I had grown to full adult size, although I was still pretty skinny. During the winter, the Lady of Paradise Yard had put up notices with a picture of me at the nearest store, to see if anyone considered me theirs. (Humans are often under the misconception that they actually own us dogs, when in fact it's the other way around. Furry four-legs, especially canines, have no trouble at all manipulating humans exactly the way they want them to go. If that's not ownership, I don't know what is. But I digress.)

I could have told her that the notices were a waste of time, as I had no human friends across the river, and true enough, no one claimed me. I would have been perfectly happy to stay in Paradise Yard forever. My new friend, however, had been told that she was going to have to move. The big field had been bought by someone else and no one was going to be allowed to live on it. The Lady felt she had far too many dogs to take to her new home, and the Chicken incident precipitated her decision. She approached a rescue organization called Second Chance for Puppies, and she put me in her car and drove me for a long time down a very busy road until we arrived at a place called Vancouver.

The change from my original home to Paradise Yard had been a big one, but it was nothing like the transition to Vancouver. I was now in an enormous city. The Lady of Paradise Yard shed water from her eyes as she handed me to another woman (what strange ways humans have of expressing emotions). The new lady was called Pamela.

This place stank worse than Chicken's house. The smells were very different, though, and almost totally alien to me: exhaust from all manner of different vehicles, a huge variety of food from humans' eating places, garbage, millions of humans of all sizes and colours, clothes and buildings constructed of materials I was unused to. I was kept in Pamela's house and small yard, but two or three times a day she would clip a strap to my collar and walk me round the neighbourhood. Many dogs lived in the area, although they were kept shut inside most of the time so I rarely saw them. P-mail, however, lingered around every fence post and corner. You can bet I added to the messages whenever I got the chance.

There were two main kinds of dogs in this city. Some were well kept with fur prettied up in an artificial way. They often wore human-style coats on top of their own! They turned their noses up at any kind of dirt. Others were rougher and mangier; they scrounged a living on the streets along with a few scrawny cats. I could identify with them, as their lives were much the same as mine had been during my early years. Some street dogs, however, lay quietly beside a human who sat or slept on a blanket right on the sidewalk. These dogs were always calm and contented; their people were dressed in rags and had real human smells—unlike the scent of much of the rest of the human population, whose odour is usually heavily disguised by a variety of aromas, not always pleasant to my discerning nose.

As well as the smells, there was the noise: the roar, hum and grumble of a thousand machines. It never, ever stopped. Even during the early hours of the morning, you could always hear the mumble of constant metallic movement. Sometimes it was accented by the mournful owlhoot of a train or, more disturbingly, by sirens. Those wails hurt my ears; they were harsher and louder than any howls a wolf pack could make. They emanated from vehicles that were usually speeding while sporting a variety of flashing lights.

One day, I was taken to a building that had an aroma quite foreign to me, but this was a scent I would never forget. The humans inside the building were pleasant enough, but I could hear nervous and anxious dogs wailing and moaning, and I had a strong sense of unease. For some unaccountable reason, Pamela had forgotten my breakfast that morning, and I wondered if the suffering dogs were being starved to death. Before I could think about it too much, however, I was poked with something sharp in my leg, and next thing I knew I was waking up very groggily with a strange plastic shield around my neck. My nether parts itched, but the collar prevented me from turning around and licking them. However, I was soon home and recovering, and very quickly forgot about it, although every time I smell those aromas I associate them with fear.

A new word was now entering the humanspeak vocabulary that surrounded me: "Airport." One day, after a ride in the car (which I was pretty used to by this time) we came to a vast windy place full of totally different exhaust smells and the screaming noise of huge lumbering metal birds. They were called Plane. What ear-splitting howls they made! I was astounded that they could travel through the air as I never once saw them flap their short, stubby wings. Instead, they glided ponderously like the swans I had seen on my river walks. Even swans flapped when they wanted to get into the air, though. These birds just hung there, often encased in a shimmer of air and fumes, while they crawled through clouds that were weeping with rain.

This, then, was Airport. What was I going to be introduced to next? It was none other than the doggy-Depends. My tail was grabbed and slipped through a hole conveniently placed in the back of the diaper, and the sticky-sounding tabs were snugged tight. I was then put into a crate. I couldn't move around a lot because the crate was padded with lumpy knitted objects that vaguely resembled humans, although one was mostly head and the other extremely elongated. There were tears mixed with the rain on Pamela's face as I was loaded onto the luggage trolley, and then, to my great apprehension, I was wheeled over to a metal bird. It was not one of the huge ones that lumbered so low overhead and trailed faint aromas of faraway places, but a much smaller one. It looked like a tin can with wings.

I was placed in a cramped, dark room in the belly of the creature. Would there be eggs in here? But no, it seemed as though I would share the space with various suitcases, bags and boxes, all having different aromas, and belonging, I thus surmised, to different humans. The plane motors made a high-pitched whining sound—quite different from that of a car—and suddenly the noise increased and we began to move. I could feel the slight trembling as we ran along the ground—and then the bumping stopped. It seemed as if we were no longer attached to anything. Was this flying? Was this what eggs felt like before they were laid? It was still pretty noisy, but there was nothing I could do, so I dozed off in my crate alongside the stuffed humans.

I was awoken by a change in the motor sound. The floating sensation increased, as if our bodies were not quite joined to the floor; almost at once, there was a bump, and we seemed to be rolling along the ground again. The motors were switched off and the door of the luggage compartment was opened. In poured cold sunshine from a brilliant new world.

Once again, the transition from one place to another was startling. No city noise and smells here; no constant drone of traffic, no gloom of heavy rain—and not a lot of human smells either. My nose told me that the human population density in the area was obviously quite sparse—more spread out even than at my first home. There were quite a few dog scents on the air, but otherwise the most dominant olfactory signal was the cool aroma of pine trees and melting snow. With a small lift of my heart, I realized there was a great deal of space in this country. It gave me an immediate sense of freedom. Who would be waiting for me here? I wondered. The Lady from Paradise Yard? Pamela from Vancouver? Or would it be someone completely new?

I had arrived, it appeared, at another Airport. I had not realized there were more of them in the world. This one, however, could not have been more different than that which I had left behind in Vancouver. The pilot, who was still standing beside the plane, had mentioned "Anahim Lake Airport," which sounded fancy; but fancy,

Anahim Lake was not. Apart from the runway, the whole airport consisted of a battered-looking trailer attached to a large plywood shack that was big enough to hold a plane, but which my nose told me was now stuffed full of all manner of machines: chainsaws, snowmobiles, a couple of trucks, and stacks and boxes of old, oily parts.

My crate was wheeled a short distance to a fence. The man handling the trolley was laughing and smiling at the bulky-looking woman with the big feet standing by the gate. His amusement was apparently due to a note taped to the front of my crate. The big human female read it out loud. *My name is Harry. My mom's name is Chris* (I won't attempt to write her last name) *and her phone is ...*

"*Mom*," I heard Chris mutter in a snorting kind of voice. It would appear she was embarrassed. "Oh my gosh—stuffed toys," she said. "And what's this? A *diaper*? Goodness! I didn't know they made diapers for *dogs*."

That endeared me to her a little. She seemed to realize that I was not a small, furry human. Also, she sported the definite aroma of another canine, whose scent was so strong I knew he could not be very far away. Maybe he would be a friend.

As soon as the business with the snowbank was over (let the local canines read *that* signal and see what they think!) we walked over to a van. In the shadows in the back, tied to the spare wheel, was a large, black, shaggy mutt. He stared at me unsmilingly and with some reservation. He was obviously sizing me up. He was bigger than me, or wider at least, and I did not really know what to make of him. We did not have time to greet properly as Chris tied me into the front of the van and started the motor. I gave a big, mental sigh. Was this still not the end of my journey? Was the rest of my life going to be spent moving from one place to another?

The town of Anahim Lake was tiny—smaller even than the one near Paradise Yard. It comprised two general stores, a gas pump and a school, and was surrounded by a sprawly First Nations village. Total population: maybe a hundred human souls. Probably almost as many dogs, as well. I could smell them in every direction, and three diverse mongrels lounged around the front of one of the stores, yapped at or ignored by other canines in the two pickup trucks that were parked outside. Chris got out of the van and went inside the store. I could smell doggy treats, such as I had now become accustomed to, and a variety of other aromas like meat and smoked hide, every time the door whooshed open. But Chris came out with none of these good things, only a small bag of uninteresting vegetables. The large black dog in the back of the van had said nothing to me while we were waiting. He was still trying to figure me out. Well, two could play at that game.

We drove for a long time—longer even than I had been in the plane, longer than it had taken to go from my first home to Vancouver. At last we slowed and started to bump along a very small road. The highway had been bare of snow, but it still lay in heaps along the side and in an unbroken sheet through the spindly forest beyond. This new, small road was mostly frozen and covered with snow, although at the latter end, where it dropped down and faced the sun, it was coated with slush and the van slithered somewhat alarmingly. There were no human or other dog smells after we left the highway. We passed through an old log fence, lurched along some icy ruts, and then turned sharply into an unfenced yard. It was bounded by forest on three sides and a small cliff on the fourth. Beyond the cliff could be heard the song of a river.

A human cabin faced the river, but it was unlike any I had seen before. First off, it was small. Secondly, it had no lock on the door—it didn't even have a metal handle. The door was fastened by a rough-looking wooden bolt. Thirdly, there were no electrical noises like lights or fridges. It was very, very quiet.

An aroma of woodsmoke permeated the air, and near the door was a shed full of split logs smelling of resin. The snow had been well packed down between the woodshed and the cabin. Chris opened the door of her van and let the other dog out.

"Okay, Badger," she said. "Let's see how you get on with this guy." Chris was not going to let me run loose, though; I hopped out of the van with the lead still snapped to my collar.

"We'll keep you tied up until tomorrow," she said. "In the meantime—Harry, meet Badger, Badger, meet Harry."

Badger lifted his leg pointedly against a fencepost but then came over to meet and greet. He shoved his nose into my rear end as a matter of form, but wasn't particularly interested in making friends. For my part, I pretty much ignored him, too.

I have never liked being tied up. I tolerate it when I have to, but I just can't relax. Chris led me back along the road a little way, trying to make me go to the bathroom, no doubt, but when I can't go, I can't go. I managed one tiny piddle, and Badger immediately marked over the top of it. Then we turned around and Chris led me back to her cabin.

As we came to the top of the bank, we could look down on the river. Only a narrow channel was open, dark and rushing, for most of the riverbed was covered in great slabs of ice. Across the water I could smell other humans but could see neither them nor their houses. There were at least two humans in residence there, plus Cow, Dog and Cat—and (*Yes!*) Chicken. There were other animals as well. They smelled meatish, but also a bit like the heavy sweater Chris was wearing.

There was another aroma, however, that was a lot more interesting. It came from a tangle of leafless trees on our side of the river. The bank below the cabin dropped to a flat bit of ground, and these trees were on the left-paw side. The dominant smell was frozen, slightly rotten meat—*oh, yum!*—and this was accompanied by all kinds of wild animal scents, some of which I had never experienced before. Wolf, yes, Coyote, yes, Chickadee, Eagle and Fox, yes. But what was that? Something very foreign and very powerful. Scary even.

Chris did not give me a lot of time to ponder these things, as she took me inside. The cabin had two rooms; the outer one was not much warmer than the outdoors. It was jammed with tools and other human Stuff, and also held two boxes padded with blankets smelling of dog. The other room, where Chris obviously spent most of her indoor time, was bright with sunlight and quite warm. A big, ugly iron stove stood in the centre; otherwise, the room was crowded with a jumble of human possessions—pots, pans, boxes, books and a computer—all stacked on rough plank shelves. However, there were things missing from this cabin that I'd seen in the other houses I'd lived in. There was no radio or TV, no indoor bathroom, no fridge or washing machine or dryer. No electric hum.

The sun was low by this time and Chris put a fresh fire into the ugly iron stove. The new wood spat and popped as the flames took hold. She put pots of human food on top and soon the aroma of her supper filled the air. Dog kibble was stored in a metal garbage can near the door. She fed me in her room, and Badger outside. (I was to find out later that there was a good reason for this.)

I was tired after my long and eventful day, and soon we were all asleep in the warm room of the home. After breakfast the next morning, Chris finally unclipped my lead. Badger and I looked at each other. I had dismissed him as being too old to prance about, and not very bright, to boot. But all at once there was a twinkle in his eye. He suddenly pounced in front of me, his front paws spread out, his rear end in the air, tail wagging. My goodness! The old guy wanted to play! Well, I needed no second invitation. We tore around in the snow like a pair of lunatics. At last, we were exhausted and flopped down on top of the bank beside the cabin in the sunshine.

"I haven't done that for a very long time," Badger panted, his long red tongue hanging down out of his jaws.

"Why ever not?" I asked. He wasn't all that fit but he had obviously enjoyed it a lot.

"Chris is too old to run much, and my last pack mate was a real bitch," he explained with a curl of his lip. "The one before was okay, but he wasn't with us for very long." There was a pause as he looked at me speculatively. "I suppose it's going to be my job to indoctrinate you into the pack's Wilderness Dog Saga."

"Wilderness Dog Saga! What on earth is that?"

"You've never heard of it? I guess that's because you were abandoned and homeless, and no one bothered to educate you. Few canines can be relied upon to do things properly these days. It's the duty of everyone in a pack to pass its history from one generation to another until the pack either dies out or is dissolved. Without the Saga, we have no roots, and this is why so many young pups go astray.

"Humans used to pass their histories on by telling stories to their children, but most people nowadays have lost the ability to remember words without making marks on paper or feeding them into a computer screen. That's how humans communicate. Some canines have learned this human way of recording stories on paper. Have you heard of Lonesome, the Wilderness Dog?"

"Of course," I said. "She's famous! She wrote a bestselling book. I've never seen it. I've only heard rumours about it." I wasn't going to admit that I wasn't quite sure what a book actually was.

"Well, most of us can't read or write like she could, so we rely on our superior memory to pass the stories on. You must listen carefully to what I tell you. It's a sacred duty for you to repeat the tales word for word to the next dogs you encounter in your life after I have gone."

"Gone? You're going somewhere?"

"We all go somewhere eventually—but I don't expect to go for a long time yet! Now settle down and I'll begin. I'll tell you my story first."

This was a bonus. I absolutely loved hearing stories. I flopped down on top of the sunny bank overlooking the river. The water burbled between its icy banks, Chickadee whizzed about the bird feeder, and Badger wuffled through his whiskers and began to speak.

2

BADGER

HOW I MET CHRIS

I HAVE NOT HAD A PARTICULARLY HAPPY LIFE. CHRIS ISN'T TOO BAD TO be with—she is quite a reasonable human compared with many I have come across, but I have been unlucky with canine pack mates, too. The last one was a really nasty piece of work; if anyone got her just deserts, however, she did. But I'm getting ahead of myself. It's best that I start from the beginning.

I seem to remember that my earliest years were spent on a farm, but when I was quite young I was taken to a city and tied with a chain in a little, bare backyard. I had nothing but a leaky kennel for shelter. I was never let off the chain and I was hardly ever taken for walks. It was a rainy climate and everything was mouldy and damp—I am convinced that this is why I have the aches and pains that trouble me today.

It was a pretty monotonous life most of the time. I could hear vehicles and people and other dogs beyond the confines of the yard. If any dogs walked past, either on-leash or loose, I would always bark to tell them of my plight. If the humans were home in the house behind me, the result was generally a chorus of yells. Sometimes the people would erupt from the house and scream at me: "Shut up!" The dogs who were loose outside the yard would sometimes commiserate with me briefly through the broken slats in the gate, but if there were humans present the dogs were usually yanked away. For the most part, I had only the wild things for company. A couple of skinny cats skulked along the alley, and a few small brown birds hunted for food, or, in the spring, collected tufts of my soft undercoat that had fallen out and were blowing about the yard. They wanted them to build their tiny bird kennels.

I began to assume that the circle defined by my chain was All There Was To Life. As other creatures moved back and forth through the alley, I had some idea that there might be other ways of existing, and occasionally I would have a vague feeling of longing and hope that something might change.

I had rarely seen the younger members of the human pack. They were both male and fairly close in age (although not, I believe, from the same litter). They were quite small—only half grown—but they had suddenly started to sprout up awkwardly. One of the males had a voice that kept changing from a squeak to a bark. They often smelled of cigarettes. (Can you imagine anything more stupid than putting a burning stick in your mouth and sucking it?) Sometimes they would flick a flaming match in my direction, but my coat was thick and the fire never touched my skin. I stared at them soulfully, but that sometimes angered them and they would mouth harsh words and then run off giggling. Once in a while, other boys would join them. They would run around with a stick and ball. I tried to keep out of their way, but one day, while they were at this game, one of them tripped over my chain.

"You stupid dog!" he yelled, and he brought the stick down onto my back.

My thick coat protected me well enough and the blow was inaccurate, so it did not hurt too much. Then another picked up the stick.

"Look at him run!" he screamed and brought the stick down again and again. I crawled into the kennel and the stick was beaten against the rotten wooden sides until they broke. Now there was nowhere for me to go. I did not know what to do. But then some long-forgotten instinct came to my aid. A rumble started in my belly and came out of my mouth like the roar of a lion. I didn't attack the boys, just growled.

"Wow—look at him! He's dangerous, man!" The boys swung the their weapon wildly, but the growl had done its work and the boys had jumped far enough back that the stick could not connect.

"Oh come on, let's go," said one of them.

They dropped the stick and, laughing loudly, ran out of the yard.

The growl, I had discovered, was power. After the beating, every time one of the males came into the yard, I would let loose my beautiful voice just to let them know they shouldn't mess with me. The two females in the family were fine. They were not particularly friendly but they held no animosity, and they were usually the ones who gave me my food. There was an older male in the house, and one day, when he came into the yard, I growled at him, too.

"Okay, that's it," said the man.

He picked up the same stick, which was still lying in the yard, and held it between us. He grabbed my chain and hustled me into his truck, where he locked me into the back. We drove through the city and out of it a little ways. The area where we stopped seemed to be composed of large metal buildings, many of which were enclosed by very big fenced yards. Machinery hums and whines issued from some of the buildings, and odd chemical scents that I could not begin to identify came from others. We pulled to a stop in front of a small concrete structure, from which a solid-looking chain-link fence spread on either side. My nose was instantly assailed by a multitude of aromas—dogs, animal food, wet concrete, and dozens of cats. And what a racket issued from behind that fence! Barks and yelps and howls, whines, screeches, grumblings, meows and purrs. There was a forest of misery in there.

"He growls at men," I heard the human from the house say. "He seems okay with women. I had quite a problem getting him in here. Maybe you'd better get him out. He's called Reno."

A woman's face swam into view as the back of the truck opened. "Welcome, Reno," she said.

"He's a bit of a mess, I'm afraid," said the man. He had the grace to look ashamed. "I just didn't have time for him and my boys were playing with a hockey stick when they accidently hit him. He's been untrustworthy ever since."

The woman approached me somewhat cautiously, but I sensed no danger from her and was quiet while she clipped a lead to my collar and encouraged me to jump out of the truck. I was taken into a small, crowded room. Cats in tiny cages lined one wall and a small desk was pushed against the other. A cacophony of dog sounds and smells came from the back.

"It's thirty-five dollars for the drop-off," the woman said, "and we ask everyone to fill out this form. The questions are things like why you are giving up the animal and what he's like with other dogs, kids, and cats and so on."

The man looked put out. "I thought you only had to pay to get an animal, not drop one off," he muttered. He grudgingly handed over a few of the little bits of paper that humans use to trade for things, and he briefly scanned the form. He scribbled a few marks and dropped the papers on the desk. "All right, then," he said, and he turned on his heels and stomped out to his pickup without a further word.

The woman turned to me and smiled. "This is the Salmon Arm SPCA," she said. "It will be your new home for the time being. We hope it will only be temporary, but we will feed you well and get your coat clean and beautiful again. You're really quite a handsome fellow, aren't you?" And words to that effect.

"We know how accurate his form's going to be," the woman confided to another lady, who had just emerged from the dog area. "That story about Reno being accidently hit by the kids seems a bit far-fetched. Still, the dog doesn't look in too bad of a shape. He has obviously been fed, and a good worming and brushing will probably do wonders. Let's find an empty cage for him tonight and see how he eats and drinks, and tomorrow we'll check him out medically."

The cage I was put in was a lot smaller than my old yard, but I was not tied, it was warm and dry, and large separate bowls of food and water were put in front of me. I gobbled the food with great speed. I was not really starving, but I was never quite sure when I would next get a meal. In the yard, even when food had been brought to me, the food dish was sometimes not placed close enough. I would salivate hopelessly while birds and mice made off with my dinner.

In the morning I was amazed to be given another plate of food. What kind of a place was this? Later that day I was taken into another small room with harsh lights and shiny surfaces. I was poked and prodded in several somewhat intimate places, and lights were shone into my ears. I wasn't too happy with some of this personal invasion, but the humans stayed calm and pleasant, and it was soon over. After that, I was taken into a small outdoor yard where a couple of other dogs were snuffling around in a desultory manner. I looked at them without much interest, and even when I was let off the lead, we did no more than give each other cursory sniffs.

"He seems to be okay with other dogs, initially at least," said the woman to her assistant. "But we will have to monitor that a lot better before we can be sure. Let's see what he thinks of cats."

The lead was put on and I was brought close to the cat cages. This looked like it might be a bit more fun and I gazed intently into one of the cages where a slit-eyed moggie was sneering at me with disdain.

"Uh oh," said the second woman. "Look at the gleam in his eye. I think we may have to state that he will need watching with cats."

Just then, a woman with two small children—both girls—arrived in the office. The children were quite young, walking and talking, but not a lot taller than me. The three people were obviously friends with the SPCA staff and apparently they came in often to take dogs for walks. I was still on the lead, but now a strong hand grabbed me by the collar.

"You got a new one there?" asked the mother human.

"Yes, his name's Reno. We're just evaluating him. He seems pretty good at the moment, except with cats. He was beaten by boys but he doesn't seem to be worried by your kids. It's a bit soon to let them pat him. We'll need to know more about him first."

The door opened again—and in walked a man. "I've got the car parked," he began to say to the mother human, but the moment I saw him I crouched down and began to growl.

"Oh dear," said the woman holding my collar. "Looks like he is man-shy. He was beaten by a bunch of teenage boys," she explained again.

"Let's have you out of here," said the man to his wife and children. He shepherded them through the door and closed it, but he remained in the room. I calmed down a little but continued to growl in the back of my throat. "I've got the usual treats in my pocket," the man continued. "How about we try him with a cookie?"

He approached me slowly, holding a cookie out in front of him. At first I tried to back away, still growling. I looked at the man; he looked at me. The cookie came closer. It smelled very good. I stopped growling and took the cookie from the man's fingers. From then on, that man was my friend, and I soon looked forward to hearing his voice and the sounds of his family, for I knew they would take me for a walk.

Although I was alone in the cage, I was certainly not as lonely as I had been in the yard. Various people apart from the cookie man and his family came to give me a walk. These hikes were not all that interesting, being quick trips around the block where I peed against chain-link fences and pooped on cracked concrete sidewalks. I was always kept on a leash. Usually I led the way, yanking my minder round the circuit as fast as I could. This was not because I did not want to walk, but because I wanted to expend as much energy as possible in the short time I was given away from the cage. Once in a while I was turned out into a small exercise yard, sometimes with other dogs, whom I mostly took no notice of, and when I came back, the floor of my cage would be damp and redolent with a smell of wet concrete. The rest of the time I sat around and tried to ignore the fear, anger, or sickness emanating from the other cages. I was used to being bored, so it was not as great a hardship as it might have been.

I could see into the cages on either side of me, and across the narrow walkway. Most of the cages held other dogs, and the place was rarely quiet: yips, howls, barks, whines were all indications of the dogs' varying distress. Humans would walk between the cages—

not just the people who worked there, but often strangers. Many of these were accompanied by their children. It was then that the noise level in the cages would rise to a crescendo. Some inmates were a lot more charismatic than others, especially the soulful ones and of course the puppies. The strangers would stop and ooh and ah at them, and sometimes these inmates were let out, and either carried or lead-walked away. Occasionally they would be returned, but not very often. Their cages were never empty for long—soon there would be new occupants who would sulk or whine or whimper, depending on their temperament or circumstance.

These stranger-people did not very often stop in front of my cage. If they did, they would stare at the little card attached to my kennel. I knew what was on it as the SPCA person who had put it there had told me it was my bio and explained what the words said.

Reno
2½ years old
Rottweiler cross Labrador cross Shepherd cross Collie

"Oh, I don't know about a Rottweiler," the strangers often said when they had read the card. "I wouldn't want one of those."

Now, I have nothing against Rottweilers—some of my best friends are Rottweilers—but I wanted to tell them that I was not a Rottweiler at all. The colour that gave rise to this misconception was because I have some Bernese Mountain Dog in my genes. My nose is much longer, and more aristocratic, than that of a Rottweiler.

I began to relax into my new life, but I couldn't forget the beatings in a hurry and I had a very hard time accepting new human males. One time a woman stood a long time outside my cage. "I'm going to bring my husband in tomorrow," she said to one of the SPCA carers beside her. "I really like him. He looks so sad."

True to her word, the next day she appeared with a man. He was wearing a baseball cap, just like the kids had worn when they were beating me. The man trailed behind the woman at first, but as soon as he got to my cage, all the bad memories of the yard surfaced and I felt the growl in my throat. I backed into the furthest reaches of the pen.

"Just give him a cookie," said an SPCA worker nearby. "He's got used to all the male members of our staff that way. All it takes is a single cookie and he is your friend for life."

"Try it, dear," urged the woman. "He really is sweet."

The man very hesitantly took the cookie and tentatively pushed it through the wire. But I was not fooled. He was rigid and I could see he was frightened of me. Fear makes people aggressive. I continued to growl.

"Forget it, honey," said the man standing up and turning to the woman. "We can't risk that sort of behaviour around the kids."

As they walked away, the woman gave me a sorrowful glance. They then stopped in front of another cage whose occupant had been there only a few days. He was a Golden Lab teen and about as much trouble as anyone could wish for. He had been incarcerated for chewing up a couch, peeing on a carpet, and knocking over a child—none of those facts were put up on the cards in front of the cages. But he didn't growl, and the humans took him away. Well, I'm not a vindictive dog, and I wished all of them the best.

And so time went by. I was used to my own thoughts, and at that time I had not experienced much excitement in my life, so I was not unduly sad. I assumed that this was all there was to look forward to. I had food, shelter, quite a lot of kind pats, and the entertainment of the goings-on in front of me. I spent a lot of time contemplating my water bowl. I have since learned that some humans pay a great deal of money to go to fancy places just for this kind of meditation. I was able to do it for free.

One day I heard and smelled another stranger in the outer room—the one that people had to walk through before they came to the cages. This was nothing unusual and so I didn't really take much notice. The woman—for the stranger was a female—was saying in a rather loud voice: "I'm looking for a large, strong dog who doesn't bark all the time and who has a thick coat. I have a tourist business so he must be good with people."

"Oh," said the SPCA woman in the outer room. "Have we got a deal for you!"

I lifted my eyes from the water bowl to see a large lady, somewhat wide at the hips, with her head-fur cut short and untidily.

"He's smaller than I really wanted," said the stranger. "How long has he been here?"

"Eight months," replied the SPCA person.

"Eight months! What's wrong with him?" said the woman.

Wrong with me? I thought. *There's nothing wrong with me!*

"He doesn't like men," admitted the SPCA person. "He growls at them. He was beaten by boys wearing baseball caps. All a man has to do, though, is give him a cookie and he's his forever friend. He's really a sweetie. Such a gentle dog. It sounds as if your home would be perfect for him." She opened the cage door and clipped a lead to my collar.

The stranger-lady approached—as far as I was concerned, she was just another in a long line of humans, neither good nor bad, and I accepted her advances with indifference.

She thrust a cookie roughly toward me. "I have to do it that way," she explained to the SPCA person, "as people often don't know how to behave around dogs, young kids especially, and I have to make sure he will not snap at their fingers." I took the cookie calmly and ate it, not because I was hungry but just for something to do.

"Let me see how he gets on with Nahanni," the stranger said.

She took my lead and we went out through the front office. It was spring, and a hot, hazy sun shone on the cracked concrete. Tied to the chain-link fence was a white Husky with a long pink nose. Her coat shone in the sunshine. She wasn't at all interested in me; rather, she was staring fixedly at the cat cages that could be seen behind the wire. I found her equally uninspiring and, thinking I had the lead on to be taken for a walk, started to try and pull the human along the sidewalk. The stranger tugged me back toward the dog.

"This is Nahanni," she said. "Are you going to get along?"

I simply sat down, looking bored.

"He doesn't seem to have issues with other dogs," the SPCA person said encouragingly. "And Nahanni, being female, is less likely to cause problems."

"Okay, I'll take him," said the woman—who, as I'm sure you have guessed by now, was Chris.

I was put back in my cage and given a feed, which I didn't really want. I'd put on such a lot of weight while I had been living at the SPCA, but it was feeding time and I pride myself on never neglecting to clean out a dish. In the meantime, Chris chatted with people in the office, signed some documents, handed over some Money, and I was then taken into a van. The van was stuffed full of boxes that smelled of paper, and sacks that smelled of dog food and grains. The back part had been kept empty and was walled off with a strong mesh barrier, and I was put behind this. Nahanni was allowed in the front.

We drove for a very long time. I couldn't see anything; there were no windows. I began to get dizzy swirling around in the back of the van and soon my recently eaten breakfast retraced its journey back into the big wide world. It was the first thing the woman saw when she opened the door.

"Oh no," she said. "Not another carsick dog! I forgot to ask about that." In fact that was to be the only time I ever threw up in a vehicle. I guess it was just because everything was so confusing.

We were let out at a house with spring-green grass all around. My collar was grabbed and the woman clipped on a chain, but she didn't realize that the buckle on my collar had come undone. I gave a shake—and for the first time in my conscious life, I was free.

What a funny sensation to run over grass and among houses that had trees all around. Chris lumbered in pursuit, yelling "Reno, Reno," but of course I took no notice. She would go round one side of a house, and I would promptly go round another. This was a wonderful game, although I was not too sorry when Chris gave up. I had not had such a lot of exercise since I could remember, and my heavy black coat was making me very hot. I watched while she took Nahanni on a lead over to a bucket under a tap. She turned on the tap and out gushed water. I suddenly realized I was powerfully thirsty. I ran right over and stuffed my head in the bucket. I was not even aware of the collar being refastened around my neck.

Nahanni and I were put in the backyard of the house under the shade of a big fir. We were chained in such a way that we could be friends if we wanted, but could each get away from the other if we preferred. I sensed animosity coming from Nahanni but I had no intention of crowding her, and at present we simply continued to ignore each other. We were fed at the extreme ends of our chains so that we could not reach each other's food dish. The water bucket was placed in between us. I could tell, by the absence of canine smells, that this was not a place where dogs usually lived. Were we going to stay here?

After feeding us, Chris disappeared, and I heard her vehicle start up and drive away. When it returned, a second person came

round into the backyard. This new person was a young man. He was wearing a baseball cap.

At once I backed off and growled.

"Uh-oh," said Chris. "I was warned about this. The lady at the SPCA said all you have to do is give him a cookie and he will be okay. Are you up for it?"

The young man looked at me and then stepped forward confidently with a cookie in his hand. I stared at him for a moment. He smelled of cities and strange places, but he didn't seem nervous or angry. I stopped growling and took the cookie. I never worried about this young man again, and in fact I soon forgot to growl at anyone. Just once in a while a man has come into my life that I have taken an instant disliking to. Then you should hear me perform!

Wwoofer Ben from Australia with Badger and Nahanni.

Chris calls these kinds of people "rednecks." She says I can pick them out unerringly.

The pleasant, grassy yard was indeed not the end of our journey, and the next morning we all piled into the van—the young man included—and drove for several more hours. At long last, we arrived here, at this cabin beside the river. It was a bit later in the year than now; there was no snow on the ground, but it was still spring with the leaves not yet open on the deciduous trees. The river was running full and free of ice, and birds were singing and caterwauling in the bushes.

"I think I'll call you Badger," Chris said. "You tried to dig a big hole under my friend's tree, and you're fat and you waddle when you walk. What kind of a name is Reno for a dog anyway?"

Humans have a thing about names for animals. I didn't care what she called me as long as it was not late for dinner!

I've been with Chris nearly two years now. I have to admit that life with her is really quite good. The only thing to mar it has been Nahanni. She was the white Husky that Chris had with her when we met at the SPCA. She was a very difficult dog to have around. Her lack of compromise was her undoing, however—she came to a very sad end.

Which I will tell you all about—another time!

3

HARRY

LIFE AT THE
RIVER CABIN

CHRIS TOOK BADGER AND ME FOR HIKES SOMETIMES, BUT DURING MOST of the daylight hours she always seemed to be occupied with some kind of work. A lot of this took place about a ten minutes' walk away from our home on top of a small hill. Many trees had been cut down and they now lay all over the place half covered in snow. Chris was cutting the trunks into short lengths and dragging the branches to great piles, where she set them on fire.

"What's she doing that for?" I asked.

"Who knows," Badger replied. "Humans do a lot of incomprehensible things. Some of the stuff I know about. The short bits of wood will be split into pieces and fed into that ugly iron stove. She uses the heat to warm the cabin and cook her food." I started to open my mouth. "Don't ask me why she cooks her food," Badger forestalled me. "It's just another weird thing that humans usually do." But in fact I knew this already, and I had been going to comment about it. The Lady of Paradise Yard and Pamela in Vancouver did the same. They even cooked Chicken before they ate it.

"That flat part with no trees on it at the bottom of the hill below the bonfire place is a pond," Badger explained to me. "It's hiding beneath the snow and ice now, but it's a lot of fun when it thaws. Duck and Goose land on there and squabble, and Muskrat lives among the sedges. Sometimes we even get Beaver."

I wasn't going to admit to Badger that I didn't know what Muskrat or Beaver smelled like. I would no doubt find out soon enough.

Badger and I were soon bored with chainsawing and burning, but we invented our own games and had a wonderful time. One of us would move; the other would think something was happening and jump up, too. The first was stimulated by the other, and soon we were running pell-mell along the open ground. Then we would stop and look at each other, and wonder what we were running after. Chris laughed to see us enjoying ourselves so much.

We had our quieter moments, too, particularly at the end of the day. We would sit at the top of the bank beside the cabin and monitor the scents that came up the slope.

The river channel was widening amid the ice and, because the sun blasted onto it, patches of bare ground began to appear on the cliff below us. Ever-present was the delectable slightly rotten aroma wafting up from the tangle of trees to the left of the flat area.

It was at times like these that I would bug Badger to tell me more of the Saga. He wasn't always forthcoming—it depended what mood he was in—but one day I must have pressed the right buttons.

"Why was Nahanni so difficult?" I asked him. "What kind of a bad end did she come to?"

"All right," said Badger. "It's a story you need to know for your own safety in any case. Some of this was told to me by Raffi, and a bit by Nahanni herself. Chris has also written parts of the tale on the computer, and when she is writing, she often reads the words out loud. So I have been able to put together Nahanni's part of the Saga quite well." Badger stretched a little, and made himself more comfortable. Then he began to speak.

4

BADGER

NAHANNI'S STORY

NAHANNI WAS A VERY PRETTY GIRL—SNOW WHITE WITH A LONG PINK nose that she kept quite firmly in the air. She was a purebred, she immediately had me know—a designer white Husky born in the Arctic. She really could not be expected to associate with anyone of lesser ilk.

However much breeding Nahanni might have had, she was distinctly short in the manners department. The first meal we were given illustrates this very well. As you know, this cabin has two rooms—I was fed in front of my kennel in the outer room, and Nahanni was fed outside. When she finished, she had the gall to sashay up to my dish and stick her precious pink nose in it! I had

long since cleaned out the food (no one can eat as fast as me!) but I soon let her know with a growl that I was not going to allow that. Chris is the only one who can take food or the food dish away from me. Instead of backing off, however, Nahanni snapped back. Immediately, there was a whirlwind fight. Chris rushed out of her room, yelling, and tried to yank us apart. We backed off on our own but not before Nahanni's pretty white coat collected a few bright red bloodspots. She never learned, though. Chris got into the habit of tying us both up during feeding times and removing our dishes before she let us loose. But if I was wandering around and found a treat such as an old bone, Nahanni would fight me for it every time. She never really wanted the bone; she would fight just for the sake of trying to prove she was boss.

Old bones are abundant around here. This place was once a farm, and many animal remains lie around. Most are hidden from human eyes, but of course it's no problem for a dog's nose to discover

Nahanni

them, no matter how long the animals have been dead. I soon found an ancient scapula and gave Nahanni a small warning growl when she got too close. I'm not sure what she thought she was doing—did she really think herself so above everyone else that other dogs' signals didn't matter, or was she merely stupid? Whatever, she came within the red zone and precipitated another fight. This kind of thing happened on quite a few occasions. Chris tried to find the bones before I did, but a human's sense of smell is so pathetic, she never had a clue where they were. Once Nahanni and I even had a furious dust-up right inside Chris's room. She let us in there quite a bit to try and get us to be friends, but because of all the Stuff, there was not a lot of space for us to lie down. That particular fight was over a dead mouse caught in a trap, which Chris had not yet noticed.

"Out!" Chris yelled, grabbing at the trap. And out we went.

Chris did her best, I'll give her that, but, like me, she could not figure how to get through to Nahanni. The dog was basically unhappy. Not at being with Chris, or even because she missed the Great White North. No, I think she was born unhappy.

In fits and starts, I pieced together her story. She first saw the light of day in a cozy kennel near a town called Inuvik, which is as far north as the road goes in Western Canada. It is a land of midnight sun in summer and noontime darkness on the shortest day. When Nahanni was a puppy, a human female fell in love with her precious looks and bought her as a house pet. She did not have the temperament to live indoors like a city dog, though, and when the human female wanted to return to the South, she decided that Nahanni would not be able to go with her. She gave her back to the breeder.

Nahanni

Nahanni's pack mates were used as sled dogs for a tourist business. Every one was as white as snow. They must have looked very pretty in their red harnesses flying along with the tourists in tow. Problem was, Nahanni didn't want to do this. All Huskies love to run, and when they are with a bunch of other dogs they run all the faster. This works only if they don't get in each other's way. Nahanni blundered into the other traces and would not fit in with the pack. She would not pull in the right direction. Whether it was just her temperament, or whether her time with the Southern city person had spoiled her for any meaningful work, I don't know. She was simply on a path of her own.

Dogsled outfitters always have a number of dogs who, for one reason or another, they would prefer to pass on to other homes. Either these dogs are no longer able to breed, or they have an injury that might not be serious for normal life but which prevents them from doing their very active job. Then there are those—like Nahanni—who simply never belong.

A friend of Chris's went to work for the owner of the tourist dogsled business, and that's how Chris found out about Nahanni. When she checked the website, she found the adoption page. Chris lived with a canine called Raffi at the time (now, he was much more of a Rottweiler than I am!) and had lost Raffi's companion a few months previously. She was looking for second dog. Chris knew almost nothing about Nahanni then, only that she was twenty-one dog years old, and, judging by her picture, a real beauty. But Inuvik was thousands of kilometres away. How was Chris going to get Nahanni down here?

Inuvik is so far north that it is impossible to raise vegetable food there so everything has to be brought in from the South. Personally, I've never understood why humans enjoy eating roots and leaves—they might just as well grow hooves and be done with it. As it is, they go to great lengths to import plant foods to where they are living. A lot of the stuff that arrives in Inuvik is airfreighted from a big city in another part of Canada. But to get the food to where the plane takes off means a drive for over a week on big trucks, even before it is put onto the plane, so by the time produce reaches Inuvik, it is definitely no longer fresh. It's also extremely expensive.

A lifetime and a half ago (in dog generations) a human male called Tony decided he would drive South and pick up vegetables in a truck. This was not as easy as it sounds; in good conditions, it took three days each way, and in winter there were all sorts of weather problems. During freeze-up and breakup, he could not drive anywhere at all. Inuvik is situated on the far side of a river. The river is crossed by a ferry in the summer and an ice road in the winter. When the water is not open and the ice is not good, Inuvik has no road at all.

Tony started with a small truck, but over the years his vehicles have got bigger and better, and he agreed to bring Nahanni south on his next trip, which was to be his first crossing of the ice road that winter. He expected the journey to take place between Christmas and New Year. If all went as planned, he would pass through Williams Lake, our nearest big town, on December 29. He and Nahanni would meet Chris at around 6:00 P.M., at—very appropriately—the Husky Gas Station.

Williams Lake is nearly a half-day's drive from us, and usually quite a lot warmer. Chris left early on the twenty-ninth, taking her other dog, Raffi, with her. She did a bunch of shopping and then went to the Husky Station to wait. The roads in town were paw-deep in slushy snow, and it was foggy and raining and sleeting—a thoroughly miserable winter night. Tony had been in touch with Chris via the satellite phone he carried in his truck. He'd had blizzards and drifting snow farther north but had driven long hours and made good time.

Right on the dot of six o'clock, a huge tractor trailer drew into the yard of the Husky Station. Its headlight beams were lanced with rain and its air brakes hissed. Before Tony himself appeared, out of the passenger side stepped a tiny human female dressed all in pink! This was Tony's daughter; she often travelled with her dad, and she had been looking after Nahanni during the journey south. They had not stopped much, but when they did, Nahanni would be given a bit of food and water, and taken for a short walk.

Chris peered inside the back of the huge trailer. It was cavernously empty except for a dog crate sitting exactly in the centre. Inside the crate was a no-longer-quite-so-white Nahanni.

Chris took her around the parking lot—or rather Nahanni took Chris. The dog might not have wanted to pull in her dogsled harness, but she had powerful haunches and could motor along just fine when she wanted to. Poor Nahanni. It must have been confusing and uncomfortable for her. Three days ago she had left her pristine white northern freedom and was now in the dirty slush and rain of a Southern winter night. And for most of the time in between, she had been confined to the crate in the lonely dark of the trailer, assaulted with the roaring, echoing noise of the motor.

Unfortunately, she still had more travelling to do. Chris lives such a long way from most other people that mega-journeys are an integral part of our lives. She was going to stay at a friend's place in town overnight, and this is where she had left Raffi, tied up under a balcony out of the rain. Now she put Nahanni into the van and took her round to introduce her to her new pack mate.

Raffi was a sweet, good-natured dog who loved to please Chris. You'll hear him tell his story later. He was more than happy to make friends with Nahanni—but she was not so approachable. Periodically during the night, Nahanni growled at him. Chris heard it from her nice warm bed, but it never escalated into a fight, and she figured it was caused by a general cantankerousness brought on by the journey. Even after everyone had been back at the River Cabin for a few days, however, Nahanni's temperament was not a lot better. She beat Raffi up a time or two; he was passive in nature and very quickly learned to keep away from her.

"You realize," said Badger (pulling himself out of Nahanni's story for a moment) "that this is not our only home. You didn't know? Well, you'll find out about the other place soon enough. We usually go there about the time the leaves pop out on the trees. The cabin we are staying at now is used only in the winter. In summer we head off into the mountains where Chris has built a tourist resort. Chris guides hikers—and she expects us to carry backpacks to take along the gear. Don't know what a backpack is? Oh, you are in for a treat! That is what you are here for, young pup!"

Dog backpacks (Badger continued) are like saddlebags on a horse: they are fitted so that they hang down on either side of our backs. Chris makes the packs herself, and she decided to try an old pack on Nahanni to see how well it fit. It was empty, but she just wanted Nahanni to get used to the feel of it. Nahanni had been put in harness several times, so Chris figured she should be accustomed to wearing things, but Nahanni had other ideas. She became incensed and took off, the blue bags flapping against her sides. She quickly ran out of sight—and she didn't come back.

The following day Nahanni was still missing and Chris phoned the neighbours, none of whom lived close, and asked them to tell her if a large white Husky turned up. She was such a different animal from the usual farm dogs that she would be easily recognizable. No one, however, had seen her. Chris thought that it would be the end of her.

Two days later, amazingly, she came back on her own. Even more unbelievable, the packs were still on her back.

Chris made a fuss over her, took the packs off, and gave her some food. She tied her up for a while and talked to her a lot, petting her and praising her. But Nahanni hated to be tied, and she was able to put on the most sorrowful expression I have ever seen a dog make. She was a master at it. Her large, pointy ears would droop sideways, her eyes would plead, the corners of her mouth would turn down, and—this was the master stroke—she would lift one paw pathetically. On the one hand, Chris admired this masterful display, knowing it was just a bluff, but on the other, she was always swayed. She would undo Nahanni's chain, and off the dog would go again. (We learned later that she had been in the habit of behaving in just this way in the Great White North.)

Chris's nearest human neighbours (apart from the ones across the river) live four kilometres away. Nahanni would go down to their property sometimes. Once she ate a bunch of cat food, then threw it up all over their deck. The neighbours drove Nahanni home; they were not pleased.

She swam over the river and got among the ranchers' cows. That did not make her popular either. Finally, she crossed the river, crossed the ranch, crossed the highway, and found herself on another farm where she started chasing horses. The owner of the horses was kind enough to phone Chris rather than to shoot Nahanni outright, but I sometimes think that, if he had fired the fatal bullet right then, it would have saved us a lot of grief.

The river, I should mention, was nearly the end of me when I first arrived. It doesn't look all that much now as there is still a lot of ice on it and the water is low. But when the snow melts, the river swells, and it was roaring and brown when Chris and I first walked down there. You see that big logjam right beside the point? All sorts of debris piles up against it when the river floods, and to me on that first hike it looked like solid land. I jumped down onto it—and immediately sunk out of sight. I emerged quite soon, but disoriented. The current was swift, and it was trying to drag me under the logjam. Chris was twittering about on the bank, but she did not dare to go into the river for it was very deep there. By thrashing around I was able to get closer to the bank, and Chris flung herself onto the ground and reached as far as she could. The tips of her fingers hooked into my collar—and she was able to drag me onto the land. So be careful, young pup. That river can be a killer.

But back to Nahanni's story. Last fall, Chris wanted to go away from home for about six weeks. She is an author, which means she writes books, and goes on Book Tours, whatever that means. I have never been on one, but she takes off on these about once a year.

Now I have to tell you about Wwoofers—the human kind! Yes, they really do call them that. The initials WWOOF mean something totally unrelated to dogs in humanspeak, but basically they are people who want a working holiday. They might be from anywhere in the world. I have met a number of them here, and no doubt you will, too. The young man Chris brought home with her when she picked me up from the SPCA was one of them. He was from Australia. Wwoofers are usually a lot of fun.

Before she left for the Book Tour last fall, Chris had another Wwoofer working with her, a young woman called Kelsey. Kelsey was a pretty and good-natured human, and she was happy to stay here and look after us while Chris was gone.

Our place, as I have mentioned, used to be a farm, but as no living animals are kept here anymore (except Dog and Human), the fences have not been maintained and are in need of repair. All around is scrubby forest where Range Cow rustles for food in the summer. Cow is rounded up and taken to a neighbouring ranch for the winter. Most of the mothers and babies are easy to take home, but Bull has a mind of his own. He often strays onto our place through holes in the fences. That year, a Red Angus Bull hung about. He was not aggressive to humans or dogs, but if we tried to move him, he simply wouldn't budge. I would bark, Nahanni would rush at him, Chris would yell and wave her arms, but he just stood there. Chris phoned the rancher a time or two before she started on the Book Tour, but nothing was done about fetching him.

Not long after Chris had left home, we found Bull dead, upside down in a ditch, and frozen solid. Kelsey was horrified and she dragged us away and immediately sat down at the computer to email Chris. The worst thing of all, as far as Kelsey was concerned, was that Nahanni and I had been snacking on it! But Chris replied that she thought it was great.

"Chris says you can chew on it as much as you like—she said you will get some extra protein that way," Kelsey informed us, trying to sound upbeat about it. But her expression said something quite different. You can always tell what humans are thinking by their body language. Kelsey was from the city and a lot less used to having dead animals lying around. Nahanni and I thought it was a fabulous treat to have a frozen beef bar down there.

When Chris got home from her Book Tour, she promptly bewailed the fact that Dead Bull was out of sight.

"I can't see what's going on down there," she said.

It was not far away from the cabin, but the ditch where the animal had come to rest was surrounded by those dense alders to the left of the flat bit at the bottom of the bank. Chris could hear the birds, Eagle and Raven and Chickadee, calling to each other while feasting on the carcass, but her nose was too inefficient to identify the more silent visitors. Sometimes Coyote would boldly run across the frozen river in the middle of the day, but it was only when Chris walked down there after a fresh skiff of snow had fallen, that she realized Wolf and other large animals had been feasting there as well.

Coyote was fun to chase, but, mindful of my dunking, I was leery about going too far across the ice. There were always open bits of water, even in the middle of winter, and you never knew when you were going to fall through. Nahanni also had a modicum of respect for the ice, and Chris had less worry about letting her go free.

Chris had been home several days before Nahanni disappeared again. Because the dog was white, and there was snow on the ground, it was hard for Chris to spot her at first. I, of course, knew exactly where she was, but as she was such a prickly character, I was quite happy to let her stay away. We no longer had many fights, but this was only because we had learned the best methods to keep out of each other's way. The snow cover was thin and hard so did not often hold tracks that Chris could see, and she was totally useless at following a scent. Eventually, however, she discovered Nahanni in a sort of cave under a swooping-branched spruce tree. The ground underneath was frozen but mostly bare of snow. The low winter sun was able to poke in there during the late afternoon, and Nahanni found it quite a congenial spot. It was also close to Dead Red Angus, so she did not have to go too far for a snack. Chris put a lead on Nahanni and she came home willingly enough. Chris fed her and patted her and kept her in the house for a while. Nahanni responded by putting on her one-paw-in-the-air-pathetic look, and soon Chris let her out again. She stayed around for a few days and then took off once more. Chris found Nahanni in the spruce cave, put a lead on her, and brought her back. This happened several times—and finally Chris got fed up. Come suppertime, she stood on top of the bank and rattled the food dish and called. She knew that Nahanni was under the spruce, and knew that Nahanni would have no trouble at all hearing her over such a short distance. Nahanni did not come home.

Next day, Chris went to the spruce and fetched her. The day after that, she failed to come home again.

Chris figured she would eventually get hungry. She continued to call and rattle the food dish, but did not go down to the spruce again. Two nights later, Nahanni still had not come back. There had been a sprinkling of snow overnight, and Chris decided to go down to the tree cave and see if Nahanni was there; if not, the fresh snow might show up her tracks. She put me on the lead so I would not run ahead and destroy the evidence. Sure enough, fresh pawmarks led away from the spruce cave to the frozen carcass. About half of the bull had been eaten by this time, and tracks of birds and mammals abounded around the feast. Chris quite cleverly was able to sort out which tracks were Nahanni's—my nose told me she had been feeding as Chris and I approached, but had run off as soon as we had come close. After that, Nahanni never returned to the spruce cave and Chris had no idea where she spent the nights. Every mealtime, Chris would rattle the food dish at the top of the bank and call Nahanni's name, but to no avail. After a couple more days, she phoned around the neighbourhood and talked to people at all the places where Nahanni had wandered before, but she always hung up disappointed. No one had seen the dog.

I barked at night when animals came to feed on the carcass, and even when Chris yelled at me I wouldn't stop. After all, I had to warn these dangerous creatures that the cabin and its immediate sur-roundings were our territory and out of bounds for them. Eventually Chris got fed up with the noise (which was kind of ungrateful—I was only doing my job!) and she started to keep me shut up in the cabin with her at night.

One morning, when the darkness was just showing the tiniest glimmer of dawn light, I asked to go out. Chris was already up and reading by candlelight—she has always been an early riser—so it was no chore for her to slide the wooden bolt and open the door. I was at once aware that something very important was happening down by the carcass. I stood at the top of the bank and started barking loudly.

"Shut up!" Chris screamed.

I never took much notice of her when she was in that mood. I took a few steps down the bank. Oh my gosh! Something was flying up toward me—a dim, speeding shadow on the snow taking huge, leaping strides! I ran back to the corner of the cabin barking like mad. The foul-smelling Thing kept coming. I tore around the cabin to the door of the outer room, which was partially open, and dived inside. I barked and growled and snarled and made such a racket that Chris rushed out of the main room to join me.

"What on earth's the matter, Badger?" she exclaimed. "I've never seen you behave like this before!"

In two big steps she was jammed beside my vibrating, snarling body and looking through the partially open door into the blue winter dawn. Finally she could see the Thing. It was sitting in the snow between the cabin and the outhouse, hardly more than a dark silhouette against the twilit snow. It was the most terrifying, dangerous predator I had ever encountered. I had never been so petrified in my life.

"Oh, wow!" said Chris, more in awe and excitement than fear. "Cougar!"

With a soundless bound, the interloper fled. Chris seemed quite pleased at the sighting, but I was so frightened, it took several days before I could go out of the cabin without being scared to death.

I have mentioned my predilection for bones. There is something so satisfying about chewing on them: their chalky, gritty texture, their effluvium of ancient flesh, or, if I'm lucky, the fresh scent of a kill.

A few days after the Cougar incident, we were plodding along a trail covered with hard, frozen snow. My nose led me to an enticing scent—and oh joy, here was a new treasure! Most bones that I found were from Cow or Horse, but this one was much smaller. It was stripped clean except for a lump of fur covered in ice at once end. There was barely a trace of marrow left in it, but it was from a fresh kill. I carried it home and chewed on it for quite a while. Then I let Chris take it. She fancied herself a naturalist and always tried to identify the bones I collected and piece together the story of the creature's demise. She took it inside and thawed the lump of ice off the frozen end. Scraps of fur emerged. They were (as I could have told Chris) pure white.

I had known right away that the bone was Nahanni's. Chris went back with me to see if she could find the rest of her, but although the snow was frozen hard and there were no sign of any tracks, she was smart enough to come to the conclusion that Nahanni had not been killed there. The bone had obviously been dropped by something that had found the remains and carried this prize away. A clever human can often reach the same conclusion that we dogs do—it just takes them longer. Chris searched around for blood on the snow, and later, when the ground was bare, for a patch of weather-snaggled white fur. It would have shown up well on the naked ground in the spring before the vegetation started to grow. But there was never any other sign of Nahanni. Even I, with my superior sense of smell, could not find out where she had been killed. The most recent smell on her was Coyote, but that was just the thief who had stolen the bone before I found it. I suspect that Cougar was the executioner.

5

HARRY

COUGAR!

WHEN BADGER HAD FINISHED TELLING ME ABOUT NAHANNI, MY EYES
were as big as tennis balls.

"Wh-what's Cougar?" I breathed.

"It's a kind of Wild Cat. But big." Badger stopped uncertainly. He
had not given me a very good picture, but seemed unable to express
himself in a better way.

Cat! I thought. My only experience of them was as small, snarly
creatures, generally fluffy, with very pointy claws. One or two lived
half-wild where I was born—they were skinny and unfriendly, but
they generally left me alone. The rescue lady of Paradise Yard had a
couple in her house, but they were fat and lazy, and by the airs they

put on it was obvious they thought they were the queens of the world. I tried to pounce on one once, but she hissed and all her hair shot out at angles, making her suddenly twice as big. I got such a fright I stopped dead, and she dived out of my reach through the cat door.

Badger and I were sitting in the warm, spring sun in our usual spot atop the bank beside the cabin, looking down toward the river and beyond, to the thick tangle of alders where Dead Bull lay.

"Is that the strange scent I can smell?" I asked. "The one that's different from Eagle, Chickadee, Wolf and Coyote?" It was faint but nonetheless quite frightening. It didn't smell like the kind of Cat I knew.

"Probably. It's much wilder and gamier than a domestic Cat. You take care, young pup. The snack bar might smell very tantalizing, but Cougar is not an animal to tangle with."

Maybe not. But Badger was not young anymore, and he was also a bit stiff in his back legs. Plus he was overweight! I could run a lot faster than he could—I'm betting I would be able to run faster than any sled dog.

A small breeze wafted the delicious scent of raw, slightly rotten beef up the bank. How I would have loved such a feast when I was starving. The only dead things I got hold of then were small animals like Pack Rat and Cat and Weasel—all of them usually well past their sell-by date. Now I could hear Eagle giving his maniacal giggle in the trees, and Chickadee twittering and wheezing as she snaffled treats. Raven *gonked* as he flew overhead with slow wingbeats. The gamy aroma that I was not familiar with was faint and old. Its owner obviously wasn't around at the moment. I really wanted to go down there and get a few treats of my own. I snuck a glance at Badger. He had curled himself into a snoozeball and seemed to be dozing off. All that storytelling must have tired him out. I eased to my feet and tiptoed quietly down the bank on the trail that was worn into the snow. I crossed the flat stretch alongside the river, entered the alders—and there it was! A Feast for the Dogs.

Bull had died upside down in the ditch, and his legs were pointed up into the air. More than half the carcass had been eaten, but the feasters were having problems getting to the underside as it was hidden by the internal organs and trapped by the frozen sides of the ditch. The exposed bones were fairly clean—only Chickadee could get much of a meal out of them at that stage—but everyone else was trying to get under the big balloon of the stomach. Small tunnels had been excavated into the frozen flesh by Mouse and Weasel.

There did not seem to be anyone around except Birds, and they gave me due respect as I approached the carcass. I stuck my nose into one of the tunnels but could not get much more than a sniff and lick. It was like trying to eat a Popsicle from the inside out. I jammed my nose in farther, trying to get a claw in there to make the hole bigger. The scent of the meat was overpowering, and I was oblivious to every other aroma.

How fortunate I was that a small part of my brain was still receiving signals through my ears! For suddenly there were angry twitters and *frrrrp* noises from Chickadee's wings as she flew away. I lifted my head—and walking slowly and quietly toward me on the snow was...

A monster! She had a Cat face and paws like dinner plates! She was three times as big as I was. Her whiskers were like broom bristles and her long tail swung like a rope. The strange gamy scent hit my olfactory centres full bore. She realized I had spotted her, and I could see her muscles start to tighten, ready to make a run and pounce. I turned tail and fled! I have always prided myself on my speed, but I have never covered ground so fast in my life. I tore through the alders, across the flat stretch, and up the cliff at the speed of light.

If I'd hoped to regain the top of the cliff without Badger knowing, I was out of luck. He was sitting up and watching me, bemused.

"I guess you know who Cougar is now," he said. "You're lucky she didn't follow you up here. Dogs are among her favourite things to eat."

I was unable to speak. I was gasping hard from the wild run. My tongue was hanging so far out of my mouth it practically touched my toes. I could only nod.

THE SAGA WAS NOT TOLD TO ME ALL AT ONCE. IT WAS INTERRUPTED BY many things: eating, hiking, chainsawing and burning, trips to the post office and Badger's occasional grumpiness when he didn't feel like storytelling. One day, when we were lounging near the burn pile after chasing Squirrel near where Chris was working, I sensed that Badger might be in a talkative mood.

"What about Raffi?" I asked. "You said he was the dog that was in our pack before Nahanni came. What happened to him? Was he the only other dog to live with Chris?"

"Not at all," Badger replied. "Quite a number have shared their lives, or at least part of them, with her."

"I really need to know their stories," I said, but cautiously. If pushed too hard, Badger was likely to get cranky.

"You don't *need* anything except food and shelter, and you have plenty of both," Badger grumbled. "However, since you asked respectfully, I suppose now is as good a time as any to tell you more of our pack's Saga."

"Fantastic!" I said, grinning and settling myself to listen.

"It all started," Badger said in his ponderous voice, "with Lonesome."

"Lonesome!" I exclaimed incredulously. "The world-famous canine writer? What does she have to do with Chris?" I caught Badger's smug smile. "No!" I exclaimed. "She was here? With Chris? Chris lived with a celebrity? That is too cool! Is she still alive? What—"

"If you don't calm down, you won't get a peep out of me." Badger fixed me with a fierce glare. With considerable difficulty I sucked my tongue into my mouth and curbed my excitement. Badger stared at me for a moment. Then, seeing that I was quiet and attentive, he began.

"Lonesome didn't actually live in this cabin—Chris has had this place for only a couple of years, but she was the origin of our pack. The matriarch of the Saga, if you like. And no, she's no longer alive— she would be about 140 years old by now if she were!" Badger scratched his ear deliberately, as if by doing so he could marshal his thoughts.

"It was Lonesome who guided Chris through the first stages of her wilderness career. Chris was pretty naive before she met Lonesome. Like a good many humans, she had some weird idea about building a cabin in the woods far from others of her kind. She fancied a life close to nature—she figured she was more skilled than many of her fellow humans to follow this course, but Lonesome soon revealed how inept she really was."

"Chris seems to be pretty comfortable here," I said doubtfully.

"Oh, sure. She has a shelter she built herself, and the wits and experience to survive in the bush—as long as she takes all sorts of *Stuff* with her. She needs extra skins to keep warm, different skins to keep off the rain, and still others to keep

Lonesome

away biting insects. She carries food, pots to cook it in and matches to light the fire to cook it with. She moves through nature with some skill and enjoys observing it in all the details that she notices, but she's never really part of nature. Of course, she is pretty handicapped."

"Um, handicapped? What do you mean?"

"Why—she can't smell anything, of course! She is only aware of what she can see or hear. Her eyes are fairly good, but unless they are actually pointing toward something, she is often oblivious to what is going on around her. She hears some things, but her ears aren't anywhere as good as ours, and her sense of smell is all but useless. She can't even smell Dead Bull from this far away—or Cougar!"

My eyes rounded and my jaw dropped open. I gave a shudder at the thought of that powerful gamy smell and how close I had been to almost missing it myself.

"An aroma," Badger pontificated, "has to be overpowering for her to be able to register it at all. What's more, the scents that she raves about are from things that are totally useless, like the smells of flowers, and balm from cottonwoods. Those won't put a meal in the food dish."

"Hmm," I said thoughtfully. "But she seems to have food, and she gives us food, too."

"That's because she makes Money. These are bits of Stuff made of metal and paper that she hands over to other people and gets things like food in return."

"Well, it looks as though she's managed to find a way around her handicap."

"Not very effectively," Badger replied somewhat huffily. "To hear her talk, it would seem that Money is one of the hardest things to obtain."

"Where does she get it from? Does she grow it? Does she gather it in the woods?"

"No, she has to work for it. In the summer she entertains tourists—those are people who live in the city and actually pay Money to experience something different from their usual existences. Chris also writes Books."

"I thought Lonesome was the writer. Did Chris learn how to do it from her?" I paused for a moment. "But what exactly are Books?" I eventually asked. "And why would people exchange Money for them?"

Badger sighed again, with some exasperation, but then decided that, although he had not looked for it, life had presented him with the task of educating the next generation, and he was going to have to do his best.

"Books are used to store information," he explained. "Our memory is good enough to retain any knowledge we want, but most humans are somewhat pathetic in that regard, so they have to put words into a kind of code that can be written onto a computer screen. When they are printed onto paper, they make Books."

"Chris spends a lot of time looking at these things," I acknowledged. I thought for a moment. "Are the words in Books a true indication of what people are thinking?"

Badger looked at me a bit perplexed. "What do you mean?" he said.

"Well, when they are speaking out loud they often don't say what they're feeling. You can tell, because their body language is saying something else. It's very common among humans. Why do they do that?"

"I'm not sure," Badger replied. "Perhaps it's because they lead such artificial lives that they no longer know what their true feelings are. They have climate-controlled houses and cars, and they wear clothes to further insulate them from nature. These people have Stuff like you wouldn't believe. Houses with multiple rooms—one to sleep in, one to swim in, one to cook in, one to eat in—and each room is filled with sleeping places and dozens of sitting places. They have boxes that make sounds, and even boxes that have moving pictures on the front. Humans sit for hours in front of these."

"I've seen some of these in Vancouver," I said. "I guess if you have no olfactory sense you have to give your brain something else to do."

"You may be right," Badger agreed. We both paused and imagined the awfulness of being unable to smell.

"Their lack of ability to express their feelings might also be a result of having no tail," Badger continued. "Can you imagine what it must be like for animals who have nothing attached to their rear ends to show their emotions? How can they properly tell others whether or not they are happy, sad, frightened or angry? Some animals, like humans, are naturally born tailless and that is bad enough. The worst is when humans cut the tails off the dogs who live with them. These animals often become neurotic because they're no longer able to express their emotions properly."

I spent a moment mentally admiring my own ginger plume. Badger's black tail was also richly furred. "So you think that when they speak, they don't even know what their body language is saying? But what happens to the words in Books?"

"I'm not sure," Badger continued. "I can't read Books, so I have no idea how representational many of the words are, especially if the Book is written by someone else. Chris often reads out loud while she's working on the computer so I know that she's describing our lives in the wilderness. That's why I know so many details of Nahanni's story. I have to agree that some of Chris's word pictures are fairly accurate, although I'm sure I could do a better job myself. Other humans don't want to live the way Chris does, but they certainly enjoy her stories. Even though we can see Chris's life is full of things to protect her from nature, most humans think she is only one step up from being a wild animal."

Badger paused for a moment. His eyelids drooped, and I thought he might be about to fall asleep. But I was bursting with curiosity.

"How does Lonesome fit into all this?" I blurted out.

"Ah, yes. Lonesome." Badger heaved himself to his feet, turned round three times, and flopped down with a grunt on his other side. "For a start," he continued, "Chris would never have managed to live in the bush without her. It was Lonesome who showed her where Bear was hanging out, and Wolf, and Deer. Lonesome never liked the bush, and was often afraid of it..."—*Like you with Cougar*, I thought to myself—"but she was born into it, and Chris was not. Oh, sure, Chris could make things with her hands and tools, and she was fairly observant of the natural world, for a human, but she had to learn. Lonesome was her teacher.

"She was a very smart dog and actually managed to find out how to encode human words and put them into her own Book. It was called *Lonesome: Memoirs of a Wilderness Dog*. That Book made much more Money than any of the Books Chris wrote."

Badger again paused reflectively and I took this opportunity to ask, "What was Lonesome's life with Chris like?"

"Lonesome's story is a long one and, as it has already been told in detail, you will have to be content with a condensed version from me. Who knows? You seem reasonably bright. Maybe you will learn to decipher the human code and read the Book yourself." He sniggered, as if he never believed I would be able to do *that*. My brain immediately started working, however. It was a whole new idea. I mulled it over and listened with secret delight while Badger continued with his tale.

"Lonesome was just a puppy when she and Chris first went into the wilderness. They drove for a while on a very rough road. When it ended, Chris parked the truck she had then and put a big bag full of Stuff on her back. Lonesome didn't have a pack at that stage, so Chris was carrying Lonesome's food as well as her own. They started to walk over a rocky trail through the forest. A raging river roared below. They scrambled over boulders to get around one lake, then found a bit of a trail to get around another. They ran out of daylight and Chris hauled out all the Stuff she had been carrying so that she could cook, eat, sleep and keep off the bugs. Lonesome simply curled up in the previous year's crispy cottonwood leaves. The next day they walked some more, and soon came to a farm, which was somewhat of a relief to Lonesome, as the whole hike had been redolent with the strong smell of active Bear.

"The couple on the farm gave Chris some land to use, across the river from their own house, and on it Chris built a great cabin out of trees. It was her first experience using a chainsaw, an item that she had a very bad relationship with, judging by the uncomplimentary words she called it. While she built the cabin she lived in a canvas house called a tent. The building took nearly two years to finish.

"There was all manner of wildlife around that place. Bear was common, both Grizzly and Black, and also Moose, Deer, Cougar, Wolf, Lynx, and even Wolverine. There was a great variety of smaller animals and birds. Chris found these all fascinating and often ignored the danger, although she learned to have a healthy respect for Bear. Chris wrote her first Book about being in that cabin, and it was very popular among city humans, because those people could not begin to imagine a real person living that way.

"Lonesome was just starting to get used to this isolated life when Chris decided to move to an even less friendly place, high up in the mountains. When she was partway through constructing her first cabin there, a huge windstorm nearly blew it off the face of the earth. As a result, Chris decided to call the place 'Nuk Tessli,' which means 'West Wind' in the Carrier language. She liked to be reminded that nature was boss. Once again, Chris and Lonesome travelled for days on foot through wild country uninhabited by humans to get there, but this time there were no close people at all. Lonesome was very lonely. Chris built two cabins at Nuk Tessli. One was for her and Lonesome to live in; the other was a shelter for tourists. Yes, tourists actually handed Chris Money so they could come to this remote and dangerous spot. They didn't hike overland, however. They were smart enough to arrive by float plane. Like Chris, they paid more attention to the smell and sight of flowers than they did to the scents of the animals that also lived there. I've been to this place, for Chris still goes there in the summer, and you will go there, too.

"Unfortunately, dogs do not live as long as humans, and Lonesome began to get old. The rough life, the long hikes from the road and the severe winters began to take their toll. When the weather was too bad to travel into the mountains, Lonesome and Chris often stayed at a farm with Sheep and Horse, Dog, Cat, Chicken and Duck. Chris would work with the animals and in the garden. The woman who lived there, Tina, loved Lonesome, and agreed to take her for her retirement years."

Badger paused and opened his mouth so that his tongue hung out. "Phew! I am getting too hot so am going to move over to the shade of that pine tree. It's high time for a nap, in any case. I advise you to take one, too. This hot weather will bring out the mosquitos in force. See those Barn Swallows?" He nodded toward a couple of slim-winged birds swooping near the eaves of the house. "The other Swallows have been here for a while but Barn Swallow arrived yesterday. It's a sure bet that when she turns up, the blood-sucking bugs will hatch in a day or two." And with that, he heaved himself to his feet, plodded to the pine tree, and scraped the pine needles away from the cool earth.

"Is that all? Weren't there any other adventures? What about Cougar? And Bear? And blizzards? And what happened after Lonesome? Were there other dogs before Raffi and Nahanni? Do you know their stories?"

Badger decided his napping spot was perfect, and he flopped to the ground. "Of course there were lots of adventures," he said. "But Lonesome has already told her story." He wasn't going to say any more at this point, and he stretched out on his side and blew out a big, relaxing breath.

I sighed, but I had to agree—it was hot. Maybe he would continue Lonesome's story later, maybe not. One could never tell with Badger. He had given me a great deal to think about, however. As I turned around in my own spot ready to have a bit of a doze, I remembered how Badger had called Lonesome "a very smart dog." Well, I was the smartest dog I knew, and I figured that I was at least as clever as she was. I vowed that I would I learn the human code and read her Book. And hard upon the heels of that thought was this one: if I could read her Book, there was no reason why I couldn't also write my own!

THE DAYS WERE NOW LONG AND SUNNY, AND THE SNOW WAS BEGINNING to melt, revealing the winter-drab ground beneath. Life with Badger and Chris had settled into a routine. We would be up early, and if we didn't go for a hike or run errands at the store, we would walk up to the burning place and work. Various birds that heralded the arrival of spring came to Chris's feeder. These gave her a lot of pleasure. She would get out her camera, and twitter almost as loudly as they did; but as she never ate them, I'm not sure why she liked them so much.

I had to admit that, although I sometimes missed Paradise Yard, life wasn't too bad. I had plenty of kibble, a nice kennel, and a really good buddy. I learned early on not to interfere with Badger's food bowl. Chris knew he was possessive of his dish. She would tie Badger up while he ate and wait for me to finish (I was a much slower eater) before picking up both dishes and untying him. I was quite happy to concede his superiority in this, and we never had a fight, but it was a bit irritating for me to find a nice bone and then have Badger give a warning growl or even a snap before taking it away from me. I wasn't that fixated on bones anyway. Sometimes Chris would give us new ones, which were fabulous. But after an hour or so of chewing, I felt I had extracted all the flavour I was going to get from mine and usually left it. Badger, however, would nurse these treats for days. He would find them weeks later and even dig old ones up from under the snow. Somehow he seemed to get even more out of them when they had been buried for years, even if there was no trace of meat or sinew left on them.

The river still had big chunks of ice on its banks, but it was beginning to fill with snowmelt. Soon a new smell came wafting up from the remains of the Bull. Neither Badger nor I needed telling what that was. Bear was out of bed.

It was Bear who finally pulled Bull's remains out of the ditch. There was a new flurry of activity around the carcass now that more food was exposed, and the rotten smell grew stronger. Cougar's aroma was fading. I frequently heard Chris tell her human friends that other dogs in the neighbourhood had been eaten by Cougar during the winter, and a hunter had tracked it and shot it. Badger and I would bark at Bear, but we did not like to get too close to the carcass when she and her cubs were around.

In between all these goings-on, Badger continued with the Wilderness Dog Saga. While Lonesome was still with Chris, a farm dog named Sport came to live with them. According to Lonesome, Sport was not a very engaging animal. The farmer was ready to shoot him because he chased Cow. Chris also found that Sport had an incredible nose for garbage; when they were out of the mountains and staying with other people, Sport would take off and travel for miles to get at it. I don't know why the humans minded so much—they were just throwing all these delectable morsels away anyway—but it meant that he had to be tied. And when he was tied, he whined. Constantly.

In the bush he wasn't much better either. He wasn't good at learning things, and he could never figure anything out. He howled and whined at anything he didn't understand, which was most things apart from his food dish.

Early in Lonesome's career, she was introduced to her backpack. These were saddlebags that rested on her shoulders and upper back. She hated them at first, but she eventually accepted them and became a very good backpacker. She could negotiate any tangled obstacle with skill. However, she was smaller even than me, and Chris felt that having two dogs to carry her stuff in the bush was a lot better than one. Sport was lacking in the brains department, but not lacking in strength. He carried all the heavy Stuff for Chris: tent, cooking gear, dog food, human food, and so on.

When Lonesome went to her retirement home, Chris picked up another canine, whom the humans called Taya. When Badger started Taya's story, he repeated it exactly the way she had told him. That, apparently, is how the Saga is supposed to be passed on. Not all dogs can manage this; Sport, for example, was simply not bright enough. Taya was perfectly capable, though, so here is her story told in her own words. As Badger told me Taya's tale, his voice changed—it became deeper and more hoarse. If I closed my eyes, I could imagine a completely different dog sitting beside me.

Lonesome

6

TAYA

TWO ECCENTRIC LADIES

A LOT OF HUMANS THINK I'M BEAR BECAUSE I'M BIG AND BLACK AND fluffy. I was thirty-five years old when I came to live with Chris. Some people see Chris as eccentric, but let me tell you: Chris can't hold a candle to the first human I knew. Patty was much better looking than Chris, and much more feminine. Yet she lived far more of a wilderness life. She was a hunter and trapper, she bred dogs for sled racing, and trained dogs for movies. She galloped through life with huge energy, smoking cigarettes like they were going out of style and talking nineteen to the dozen. She also seemed to be perpetually in heat, judging by the number of male humans that constantly hung around. If their tongues weren't actually hanging out, they gave the impression that Patty had only to snap her fingers and they would start panting.

Patty had scores of dogs and the downside to her life was finding homes where they could all live. She didn't own property herself. Most humans didn't like the noise we made when we were excited, and were horrified when a great mob of us moved in next door. At mealtimes, we each thought one of the others was getting a better treat, and when the food dishes appeared, we generally made a great racket. At other times, there were wild dogs to communicate with: Wolf and Coyote who sang through the night and encouraged us to sing back to them. Some of my pack could howl almost the same as Wolf. I, for one, could not; I could only bark. However, I have a deep, wholesome voice—a cross between a howl and a growl—that is very distinctive and of which I am particularly proud.

Humans tend to think that the words "sled dogs" describe a particular breed like Husky or Malamute, but in fact most of us are a mixed bunch. We need a good coat with lots of underfur to tolerate being outside in the cold, and, naturally, we love to run. We love to chase things. Wild animals, farm animals, domestic pets, and each other. As soon as something moves, the adrenaline kicks in, our legs extend like pistons, and we are away! Humans want us to do this when we are in harness, but most of them get mad if we try to run down their other animals when we're not working. Our hunting instinct is refined to such an extent, however, that running and chasing are all we live for. Too bad if a creature that a human likes gets in the way.

Most sled dogs don't like to swim, and one time Patty stashed us on an island in the middle of the Fraser River, to which she would row every few days with a sack of kibble, or bits of dead Cow if she could get them. Some of my pack mates soon learned to cross the

water, however, and when they were on the loose they were a danger not only to animals, but also to the heavy traffic that roared along the highway nearby.

Patty didn't live on her trapline, but she had a couple cabins there. Once in a while she would get friends to stay in these cabins and take a bunch of dogs with them. The cabins were a long way from the road and other neighbours, so it was a better place for us to be. One year I went to one with a young German guy called Nick. He had not come from a dog-friendly background, but he was a fast learner and I liked him a lot.

The first time we went up the lake with Nick was in April. Patty was waiting for news that the ice was breaking up, and one day she yelled: "It's open! Let's go."

Nick and Patty threw all manner of equipment into Patty's truck, piled in ten dogs, and we drove to the lake. For the night, Patty and Nick had use of a tiny cabin on the lakeshore; we dogs were tied to various trees outside.

Patty's dogs getting ready for a boat trip. Taya is lying down in front of Tundra, the big dog standing on the left. *Photo by Nick Berwian*

Next morning we all clambered into two boats. Patty and Nick, a large pile of freight, and five dogs climbed into the bigger one, and the rest of the pack was put into the smaller boat.

Only the bigger boat had a motor. Patty fired it up, and we eased away from the shore. The tow rope between the two boats popped out of the water, spraying droplets, and with a small jerk the second boat started to follow. The dogs in there were all tied on very short ropes to keep them as restricted as possible, but they still wriggled and shifted, causing the little craft to dip and sway. The journey took several hours. The boat motor was really too small for the job, but we couldn't have gone much faster because if the leading boat sped up, the following one would plough into the water or veer sideways. Balancing the cargo was the key to a smooth ride, but although the supplies were well secured, it was impossible to prevent the dogs from moving.

This was just the sort of excitement that Patty seemed to love: the crazier and more bizarre a problem, the more energy she came up with to solve it. A smooth trip up the lake, well equipped, prepared and planned for wouldn't have been half the fun! However, the dogs eventually calmed down and no one went overboard.

We finally pulled to the shore in front of a sagging, weathered log cabin that Patty called The Lodge. I had been to it before: life wasn't so bad here, as we could make as much noise as we liked and we had a certain amount of freedom. We still had to be tied up most of the time, but every day one or two dogs would be allowed to run free. We all looked forward to this great treat.

Nick was going to spend the summer in this cabin with us dogs. He was not to be entirely alone, however, for the Lodge was already inhabited by Cat. Patty put Cat in all her cabins, and even though these animals were left to their own devices over the winter, they would usually be around to greet her in the spring. Cat, as far as I am concerned, is a snooty, impolite creature, but Patty loved him, and he did help to keep Mouse from destroying too much. The Lodge was inhabited by a proud old feline called Owl, and when he realized all the dogs were under control, he cautiously came to greet us.

On this particular trip, Patty had brought along Kitten, whom she hoped would eventually be company for Owl. Kitten was not allowed outside until she was used to all the dogs and all the dogs had learned to accept her. A white bitch called Chinook wanted Kitten for a puppy, and when Kitten sat on the windowsill inside, Chinook tried to mother it by pressing her nose against the glass. Yukon, a young Malamute, was the only dog who actually got to play with Kitten.

Three of the dogs in the pack at that time were big, strong males that were not to be entirely trusted. They often had fights, even biting Nick quite badly on occasion. Tundra was the fiercest of the lot. It was his turn to be loose one day. The cabin door, which didn't fit very well, was not properly shut. Kitten ventured out and, in one bite, Tundra caught her and killed her.

The summers were fine enough, but usually somewhat boring, as we weren't allowed to run all that much. The times I loved best while living with Patty were the winters. I loved being in harness and pulling the sled. I was often the lead dog, and I made sure the rest of my team stayed in order. However, being a star in that field is a young canine's prerogative, and when I began to slow down, I was happy to relinquish that status to an up-and-coming young male.

I assumed, when this happened, that I would simply have a gentler life. Dogs came and went from the pack all the time, but I could not imagine that I would ever live in a different way. I had no idea that Patty had started to look for another home for me.

After the summer spent with Nick beside the lake, we moved to a ramshackle house surrounded by farmland. I was one of a dozen

dogs tied to trees. The ground was frozen, although it was not yet covered by much snow. Half-grown pups tumbled about the yard, and in a box on a porch behind a gate was a bitch with a new, blind, squirming litter. I had produced many puppies in my time, but it seemed that part of my life was finished as well. It had been over a year since I'd had any babies.

One day, into the yard drove Chris. I had no idea, of course, that she was about to change my life. She parked her little truck and headed over to the rickety wooden house where Patty, Nick and another young guy were living at the time. All us chained dogs leaped about and barked. The fuzzy-coated puppies dived onto Chris's feet and pounced on her bootlaces when she waded through them to get to the door. Patty emerged, oblivious of the cold, wearing salmon-pink satin pyjamas (it was the middle of the day) with a cigarette perched between two fingers of one hand. A lot of humans rattle off about nothing very important, but I have never heard anyone push out words as fast as Patty. She welcomed Chris, invited her in for coffee,

Taya (at the back) running with the sled dogs. *Photo by Nick Berwian* introduced the young men in the peculiar way that humans do (they *never* sniff each other), apologized for the puppies in the yard and showed her the newborn litter, all in one breath. The human voices faded as they went into the house and the door was closed. We dogs in the yard quieted down.

When Patty and Chris came out, they first stood in front of Fleur, who looked much more like the Husky that most humans associate with sled dogs. She had light fur, a patch of dark about the face, and blue eyes. Fleur was a bit snappy, and when Chris stood in front of her, she put her ears back just a little and lifted one corner of her mouth. Chris looked at her doubtfully, and she and Patty then walked over to me.

"This is Taya," said Patty. I started to jump up and down and bark again at the end of my chain. "She's a bit older and has been a great dog, but she's too slow for racing now. I would keep her for breeding but she hasn't had any puppies for at least a year so I expect she's barren. She's trained for the sled and as a pack dog."

Chris started to smile. "Are those real ears?" she asked Patty. A lot of humans have commented on my ears and they usually laugh, but I am very proud of them. They are bigger and rounder than those of any other dog I know, and are made even larger in winter by the thick rim of fur around them. Chris guffawed. "They look like fuzzy table tennis bats," she said.

"What's her temperament like?" Chris then asked. "She's big and black with a great, heavy head. She looks just like a bear. I have a tourist business and can't afford to have a dog that's not people-friendly."

"Oh, she's a love," said Nick in his strange German accent. He had come up behind us while we were talking. "She doesn't usually bark much. You can't judge her properly in this situation. There's not enough snow to take the dogs in the sled right now, and they are all anxious for a run."

Chris shoved her hand in front of my face. I could smell other dogs on her clothes, but they weren't with her, and weren't of great interest. I did stop barking, though. Chris seemed to be trying to communicate with me in some way, but human signals are often confusing and I could not figure what she wanted.

When she put a rope around my neck and took me into her truck, I was somewhat surprised. But it did not occur to me that I would never see Patty and the rest of her pack again. We rode for a while, then came to another house, this one on a small farm with buildings close to a road. Horse and Sheep grazed in a field below them. Four dogs were in the yard: a huge black shaggy one, with the longest tongue I have ever seen on a canine; a smooth-skinned, bony one, now quite old; a Lab mix with a lugubrious face; and a very shaggy smaller dog who was definitely getting on in years. I could tell by the scents about the yard that only two of the dogs lived there: the Lab mix and the smaller scruffy one seemed to be visiting. They had Chris's aroma more strongly about them, and from that I assumed Chris didn't live there either. However, we all stayed for a few days, and the humans celebrated the feast they usually have to represent the rebirth of the solar year. (The smells of the cooked birds were delectable. We were all given treats—the owner of the house made just as much fuss over us as if we were part of her own pack.)

A day or two later, Chris loaded her pickup and was obviously preparing to leave. The little truck had a canopy on the back, and the Lab, who was called Sport, was put inside. Chris led me to the front. The passenger seat was a bit too small for me but I could perch on it without sliding off if I sat up straight. As for the small shaggy dog, whose name was Lonesome—it seemed as though she was to be left behind. Chris was hurrying to be gone. She kept pulling the muscles of her face in all directions, something humans often do to try to hide emotion.

"Goodbye, Lonesome," she called brokenly as she started away. Lonesome sat in the middle of the driveway, looking bewildered. She knew, I think, that something momentous was happening in her life. She'd been with Chris since she was weaned, and although she had visited the farm and its kind owners many times before, this was the first time she had been left behind. It can't have been easy for her to realize that she would never be part of Chris's pack again.

After driving for most of the day (with me constantly sliding off the seat and having to hitch myself up again), we arrived at a cabin not all that different from the one on Patty's trapline. The ground was rock-hard under the snow now, but Chris often complained that it had been built on a bog; every time the bog froze or thawed, the cabin heaved and shifted. The door frame was skewed and the door no longer fit properly into the gap. The wall logs had big spaces between them where they joined at the corners. I was chained to a tree beside a very rickety kennel which was a bit too small, but I was used to sleeping outside in the snow. In any case, Sport told me that this was still not the end of our journey. What a lot of distance there is in the world. We wouldn't leave right away, however, because we were waiting for good ice. I knew all about this from living with Patty. In winter, you need good ice to travel. In spring, you must wait for the ice to be gone.

Sport was fastened onto the lop-sided porch of the cabin, where he whimpered and muttered complaints most of the time.

Chris was exasperated with this behaviour, but said, "I can't let you off. You'll go straight to the garbage cans or chomp on the chickens."

Lonesome

There were three or four houses not too far away, and Chicken scratched around in the dirty snow all day. Chicken was accompanied by some much bigger birds, the likes of which I had never seen before. They periodically gave forth piercing shrieks. The females were mottled and pretty enough; they stood nearly as high as me but were much longer. The males were spectacular. Their necks glittered with iridescence, and every now and then they would fan out enormous tails as big as half a cartwheel. This movement was accompanied by a rustling noise like walking through dry cottonwood leaves. Each of the long feathers on the tails ended in a great eye, which I found a little disconcerting. Two eyes is enough for anyone; half a wheel full is a bit overpowering. I believe this display was the male birds' way of attracting a female, but they would show it to anything that moved: Chicken, Cat, Sparrow (who snuck in to peck at grains the domestic birds had missed), and even the human that came to feed them.

Chris would tie ropes to our collars and take us for walks a couple of times a day. Sometimes we hiked up the nearby bush road, but often we went out on the frozen lake that stretched in front of the cabins. The lake was a big one, and in the distance we could see the tops of a few low mountains. The ice was still quite new and not many people had ventured onto it yet. Chris seemed to know what she was doing. She walked cautiously, not too close to the edge, and gave every greyish or open spot a wide berth. These weak areas, or spring holes, would take a while to be safe. It was not long before the people who lived in the houses got bolder, and soon the drone of snowmobiles was a common sound on the lake.

A few days after the snowmobiles ventured onto the ice, Chris started to pack Stuff. Some things, like dry food and large bags of dog kibble, had never been taken out of her pickup. Now she added tools and clothes and all manner of things in sacks and boxes. Sport, in his sighing, grumbling way, said that we were going in a plane. He was hungry; he had not been given any breakfast. Chris told him he had to go without as he often threw up in vehicles. He, of course, did not think that this was fair.

Around the middle of the morning, when the sun had warmed the air a little (although it was still well below freezing), a tiny aircraft hardly bigger than a mosquito touched down onto the ice in front of the cabins. I had seen these things before near Patty's trap cabin, but they had arrived when the lake was open and they sat on the water on big canoe-like feet. This plane had runners underneath it like a toboggan.

Chris added a few extra boxes into her truck—fruit and vegetables, by the smell—then loaded us aboard. She drove right onto the ice beside the plane. It was a very tiny aircraft, and I did not see how everything was going to fit in. In fact, it didn't. The pilot said he would have to come back for a second load.

To me, a plane is just like a car. But Chris, I was to learn, has a thing about them. She is terrified of being in them. As various boxes were stuffed into the body of the plane, Chris grew more and more nervous. There was not much room for us dogs, but we were tied with very short ropes to loops of metal on the floor and we had to put up with the cramped space. Looking scared to death, Chris got into the seat beside the pilot. There was not a lot of room for them, either, especially as they both wore bulky winter coats.

"How come I always have to let the seat belt out when I sit in your plane?" said Chris in an attempt to sound relaxed. "All your other passengers must be pretty skinny."

The pilot smiled, but he was a quiet man not given to idle chat. He flipped a key. With a loud, whining clatter, something started to turn round in front of the humans' window—soon it was going so fast it was just a blur. With a little jerk (the toboggan runners had slightly frozen to the ice) we began to move. All of a sudden, the motor noise increased a hundredfold. It was so loud it hurt my ears. Gradually we moved faster, and then suddenly we were floating. Thankfully, the motor noise was then reduced somewhat, but it was still very loud. Chris and the pilot were wearing big round things over their ears to help block out the sound.

We headed toward the low mountains on the horizon and at first, our journey was quite smooth, but as the hills grew closer we began to bump a bit. I couldn't see a lot out the small side window, but as the bumps became stronger, I caught glimpses of rock and ice lurching by. Suddenly, we flipped up, then dropped with a bang into quite a big pocket of air. Chris's face was set and her eyes were closed. But then things calmed down. Another frozen lake stretched in a white sheet below us and I could see much bigger mountains in front of the whirling fan. The lake was surrounded by a solid carpet of dark forest that swooped up toward the treeless mountain summits. The pilot took the plane round in a big circle. He dipped low and touched the ice, then rose into the air again.

"Overflow near the cabin!" he mouthed at Chris. (It was too noisy for the humans to hear each other very well but I could read the words their lips shaped just as easily as I could understand them spoken.) "I'll have to land farther out in the lake."

He made another circle and gently came down again, but this time he stayed down, and soon we slid to a stop. Chris gave a big sigh, as if she had been holding her breath all through the flight.

Sport was let loose right away and he immediately ran around happily. Chris tied me to a float strut while she and the pilot unloaded the possessions onto the ice. There was quite a bit more snow here than at the other lake. Chris had brought a tarp to sit the boxes on, for between the snow and the ice was a thin skin of water. This is common in the early part of winter, especially when there is a lot of snow. The snow's weight pushes the ice down and unfrozen water wells up between the cracks. It doesn't freeze under the snow cover—this is the overflow.

The final items to come out of the plane were a sleeping bag, a pair of snowshoes and a kids' plastic toboggan. The boxes of produce were slid into the sleeping bag and placed onto the toboggan. Next thing, Chris had slipped the toboggan's ropes around my shoulders.

"Grab your other dog," said the pilot.

Chris called Sport.

The pilot added that he did not want him running loose in case he walked into the plane's nose fan. He wasn't particularly worried about hurting Sport, but he sure didn't want to hurt his airplane.

He fired up the motor again, rocked the plane a little to free it from the ice, and started off across the lake. Chris had put up her hood, and she stood with her back to the aircraft, preparing for the furious blizzard of stinging snow that the propeller would throw at us. My thick winter coat was protection enough. As the plane turned, the blizzard veered away. The aircraft gained speed, hit a bump in the ice, and took to the air. Slowly it wheeled in a big circle and swung back the way we had come. A great silence descended upon us, broken only by a thin wind coming from the big mountains.

So far, I had known Chris only when she was travelling, visiting with friends, or staying in the Cabin-in-the-Bog. Once she got out of the plane, she was a different person. Her shoulders relaxed, her mouth smiled, and her eyes danced.

"Taya," she said, "you have no idea how good it is to be home!"

I now became aware of yet another log building crouching at the edge of the lake. It was some distance away, half hidden by a number of small, forested islands. Sport had told me that Chris had built this one with Lonesome. He was running all over the place, but I was still attached to the toboggan.

"Patty told me you were good at this, Taya," Chris said. "Now you can earn your keep."

She put the snowshoes onto her boots, placed a backpack on her shoulders, and started to trudge toward the cabin. She clutched the lead in one hand, and I followed in her broken trail. It was far from easy to walk on it, however. The moment Chris's snowshoes broke through the snow crust they sank into the overflow. Soon the snowshoes were clogged with frozen slush. Chris kept trying to beat it off, but without much success, and it was soon obvious by the way she was walking that the snowshoes had become immensely heavy. That was why the plane had landed so far out in the lake: if its skis had touched the overflow, the slush would have frozen onto them and the plane would not have been able to take off. The slush was starting to jam in between my toes and it became quite painful to walk. The toboggan was increasingly harder to pull. At the edge of the lake, the land sloped up quite steeply to the cabin. Chris knocked the snow off an overhanging branch with her mitts and tied me to it. She began to flounder up the steep bank; without the snowshoes on her feet, she would have sunk to her waist.

She plodded alongside the cabin and rounded the far end. I heard the slide of a wooden bolt, and the faint squeak of metal hinges. Heavy footsteps sounded inside, and then there was the rattle of a stove door. Within moments, smoke started to come out of the chimney. Chris popped out of the cabin holding a large bowl. She packed snow into it and took it back inside. I heard the pop and hiss as it touched the heating metal. Humans don't like to eat snow like we do. They prefer to melt it before they consume it, and they often put flavourings in it.

Chris came back to the toboggan, dragged the vegetable boxes up her new trail and placed them inside. Then we turned back and fetched another load from the lake. The ice and sludge on the trail became worse and worse. We had not got all the Stuff off the ice before we heard the thin drone of the plane coming back, and once again the pilot landed far out on the ice. The remaining freight was piled onto the tarp.

"Okay, that's it," the pilot said, standing for a moment beside his open door. "When do you expect to come out?"

"Late March or early April," Chris replied.

"Don't forget, my lake will go out a month before this one," the pilot admonished. "Early April would be absolutely the latest I would be able to fly you."

"I'll bear that in mind," Chris said, "but if the weather is reasonable I'll snowshoe out. Travelling conditions are usually quite good by then and the days are getting nice and long."

"Okay. I guess we'll see you one way or another in three months." The pilot climbed into his aircraft, fired up the motor, and pulled away. The motor roared its battering crescendo and blew its mighty blizzard while it strove to get the plane going, but soon the metal bird was skimming across the snow and rising into the air. As it flew back overhead, it rocked from side to side; the pilot was waggling the wings to say goodbye. Soon the aircraft was the size of a housefly, and its sound was hardly greater. And then it was gone.

CHRIS AND I WORKED VERY HARD FOR THE REST OF THAT DAY, AND AT the end of it, all those piles of human possessions had been hauled laboriously through the overflow and stored in the cabin. I was a bit put out when Sport was given nothing to do, but he mumbled in his vague way that he did his share of the work when we went hiking. After that, however, life was pretty easy for a while. I was let off the chain and could roam without harness or restraint—a pleasure I had experienced only intermittently until then.

The door of the cabin was sheltered by a porch, and built into the back wall were two boxes with dried slough grass inside. Sport

and I slept in there during bad weather, but most of the time I preferred to curl up in the open, either in a tree well or simply in the
snow itself. Now that Chris's outside stress and plane panic were
behind her, she relaxed into an almost euphoric state. She cheerfully
tramped back and forth along the trails to the outhouse and onto
the lake in her snowshoes until the trails were packed hard enough
to bear her weight and she could walk in just her boots. On our
second morning home, Chris lugged the chainsaw a few paces out
onto the lake and cut a large hole in the ice. As the bar of the saw
broke through, water fountained up and covered her clothes, where
it instantly froze. Her pants creaked as she walked back to the cabin.
From then on, she kept the hole open with an axe, chopping out the
new ice every day so she could carry water to the house.

"I can't just keep melting snow," she said, grinning at us. "You
guys pee everywhere, and when fresh snow falls I won't know where
you've been! I would hate to put that in my tea."

Chris chatted to us a lot when we were alone. Nick and Patty
used to do that, too. People would often ask Chris if she talked to
herself when she was in the bush for so long without human contact,
and she admitted that she did, but she said she sounded less crazy if
she pretended to talk to the dogs. We didn't always bother to listen
to her words, as they were fairly meaningless, but we enjoyed the
sound of her voice. It made us feel like more of a pack.

After a couple of days, we went for our first hike. Chris put on
her snowshoes and began to break trail through the snow-covered
forest behind the cabin. Sport and I plodded behind. In places, we
went over fallen trees, and their branches would snag the gaps in
the bottoms of Chris's snowshoes causing her to mutter words that
I would not want any well-bred puppies to hear. These spots were
minefields for dogs' feet, too: our paws often crashed through into
holes below the branches. On each subsequent trip, the broken trail

became firmer, and we gradually extended our hikes farther away from home. Sometimes more snow would fall and the trails would have to be broken all over again, but with the solid snow underneath, it was never so much hard work as the first time.

During the early part of the winter, we were not able to go onto the lake all that often because the overflow would freeze to the snowshoes or the skis that Chris sometimes used. It also froze to the thick hairs between my toes, and I had to keep stopping and trying to bite it out. The wind was often very strong out on the ice, and if it blew from the mountains, it made going onto the lake extremely unpleasant. For many of our earlier hikes, therefore, we stayed in the forest.

One day, however, it was calm, and the overflow was not too bad, so we crossed the lake to where the water emerged from under the ice and tipped over a rocky sill before tumbling down an ice canyon bedecked with frilly icicles. Just before the river started, there was a deep pool and, because of the movement of water in it, parts of it did not freeze properly. Chris gave the pool a wide berth, but the ice closer to the opening had less snow on it and no overflow at all, therefore it was much easier to walk on. I headed over. Chris was calling to me to try to make me come to her, but I was never particularly good at taking orders from others. Easier was better as far as I was concerned.

I was almost across the river when the ice broke. I went completely under, but soon bobbed up again. I could get my front legs onto the ice, but I have a heavy body. My back legs kicked hard, but there was only water underneath. I was quite frightened and started to whimper. Chris did not dare to go on the thinner ice so she tromped around in a wide circle on snowshoes. She seemed to be going very slowly but it was probably as fast as she could manage. I'm not sure what she planned to do as I was too far from the thicker ice by the other shore for her to reach me, but finally, with a great heave of my shoulders, I managed to scramble out. I shook myself immediately, but as the temperature was far below freezing, my outer coat became an instant mat of ice that rattled and tinkled. I wasn't cold, though. Chris poked her fingers into my under fur and found it to be warm and dry. Still, we went straight back across the lake to the cabin. My outer coat was stiff like armour, and I creaked the way Chris's legs had done after she cut the hole in the ice. Despite my protests, I was brought inside the cabin until I had thawed out and dried.

The days grew longer and the snow became a little firmer. Our trails had expanded so much that now we could hike above the treeline. It was generally pretty cold up top, and there were few smells to interest me, but Chris seemed to find some enjoyment in heading onto these bleak and lonely slopes. She revelled in the great panorama of lumps of ice and rock that surrounded us, stretching as far as the eye could see. There was absolutely no sign of any human endeavour except an occasional contrail where a high plane slipped across the heavens like a tiny silver fish in an endless blue sea. Our lake was a white slash in the pelt of dark forest in the valley below. Our trail wound down through the unmarked snow like a thin thread joining us to that tiny capsule of comfort and warmth. Chris, seemed to get a great kick out of this vast loneliness, but personally, being used to a noisy gang of canines and humans, I would have enjoyed a bit more socializing. Sport, don't forget, was not a very interesting companion.

Where the unbroken snow curved like a wave away from the shelter of the trees, I could sometimes smell Pika. These tiny animals nip off plants and dry them under overhanging rocks, then store them deep between boulders. They don't hibernate like Marmot does, and they eat this hay during winter. On warmer days, they occasionally pop out, and their little feet make tracks on the snow. One such incident excited Chris greatly as she tried to piece together the story from the tracks. My nose told me instantly what had happened, but although she took a while, she seemed inordinately pleased with herself for figuring the story out.

Pika tracks emerged from a hole in the snow near a rock. Within a few of its steps, two large wing beats marked the snow and red blood had soaked into the white. But Pika was not killed. You could see more of his little tracks and blood spots, but now he ran lopsidedly. Again there were imprints of the wings and more blood spots, but still Pika staggered on. It was able to dive into another hole, but was obviously badly wounded. This had happened just before we got there. I could smell the wounded animal below the boulder. I didn't think it was going to survive. If I could have, I would have dug it out and eaten it, but it was too far under the rock. Chris speculated furiously as to which attacker had left the wing marks in the snow, trying to decide if it was Hawk or Owl.

"Pikas," she ruminated out loud to the silent wilderness, "tend to be daylight animals, so the bird must have been a hawk."

Full marks to Chris for that. She really compensates quite well for having such a poor sense of smell.

IT DIDN'T SEEM LONG BEFORE SPRING WAS IN THE AIR. IT WAS HOT IN the sun, and the slope below the cabin that dropped to the lake began to show bare rock and a little needle-littered soil. Chris shovelled the deck off; Sport and I sprawled on the bare wood, and Chris often brought a chair out and sat in it. Very little fresh snow had fallen for a while, and the overflow disappeared from the lake. The surface of the ice was smooth and easy to walk on, although it could be very slippery for Chris's boots. Sometimes she would put her skis onto the toboggan and tow it behind her on the lake, and then venture into new areas in the forest. One of these was a series of treeless swamps, all frozen then, spread out in a long line. Many animals used this forestless expanse as a trail. We often saw fresh Wolf tracks trotting along it. Sport and I could use their prints for our paws, but they didn't help Chris much. She liked to see them, though.

Now that the days were getting longer, we had to start our hikes early, as that was when the snow was frozen. Later in the day it became soft and slushy—not so much a problem for coming downhill, but very hard work if you wanted to go up. One day, we started to break trail up a steep, shady slope. This was quite difficult for Chris as the snow was deep and soft, and she often had to grab on to rocks and branches to heave herself up. After a while, we reached a flattish area, scattered with stunted, high-altitude forest and small frozen lakes. On that occasion, we simply turned around and came home. The next time we hiked up there was on a warm afternoon, which was a bit puzzling, as it made the ascent extremely hard work. Chris, however, seemed satisfied, and the reason became apparent the third time we used the trail. It was early in the morning again and the pressed-down snow had frozen so hard we could walk on it easily. Chris did not even have to use her snowshoes.

This third trip, however, was not attempted without a great deal of preparation. Chris spent days carrying Stuff into the attic and securing it in strong containers. She packed all the paraphernalia that humans need to spend winter nights out in the wilderness, along with that strange tool they point at us sometimes, which they call a camera.

She also did a lot of stitching. One day she put the thing she had been making across my shoulders, and fastened it in front of my chest and behind my belly. "There's your backpack," she said.

Sport already had one. It was very worn and patched, and Chris repaired it in a few places. Finally she loaded the bags with her food, our food, a tarp, a couple of small cooking pots, and one or two extra items of clothing.

There was still a ton of ice on the lake but the surface was beginning to disintegrate, so we left very early, just as the sun crept over the low east ridge. That meant we didn't have to dodge the puddles and slush that would appear later in the day. Our enormously elongated shadows stretched smoke-blue in front of us on the pinkish ice. Our legs were like enormous trees tapering to a vast distance; our heads were no bigger than pieces of dog kibble.

Chris had loaded the toboggan with things she could not fit into our packs, such as the axe. Her sleeping bag and down coat were stuffed into her backpack, and this was tied down into the toboggan so that the shoulder straps were upward. She pulled the toboggan across the lake like that, but when we got to the steep trail that we had tramped over that warm afternoon a few days before, she loaded her gear onto her back and walked up the frozen trail carrying the snowshoes in her arms. The black toboggan curved over her load like the carapace of a giant beetle.

On the lake, Sport and I had no trouble with our packs, but once we were in the forest, we had rocks and sticking-out bits of trees to negotiate. Many of these were buried in snow and we didn't see them until our packs clonked into them. Sport simply forged ahead; if a rock or tree was in the way, he barged through until he broke free. No wonder his saddlebags were so torn and patched.

I was more circumspect. I reckoned it was a lot less effort to twist my body and wriggle past obstacles. I was able to move just as quickly that way, and with a lot less effort.

We climbed in the shade until we reached the top of

Sport and Taya

the steep bit. Now we would have unbroken snow to deal with. As the sun grew higher, the snow became warm and sticky and clogged onto the snowshoes and our feet. Once again, I had to keep stopping to bite at the frozen slush packed between my toes. We were in the flattish area, but moved very slowly because of the difficult snow. After a while, we came to what my nose informed me was a trapper's cabin, although no one had used it for a while. I could smell old traces of other people, as well as Chris—she had obviously been here before, but not for a long time—and strange Dog and Horse. Faint effluvia of Fox and Marten and skinned meat hung at the fringes of my olfactory nerves. I recognized all these scents because of my times at Patty's cabins. This cabin was much smaller than hers, however. It was so tiny that it was almost buried in snow. Very little of it could be seen.

Chris took our packs off and gave us a vigorous rub; immediately Sport and I enjoyed a good roll in the snow. Chris dug down to the door of the cabin with a snowshoe. The door was very crudely made and tied to a rough frame with wire. Chris let herself in. The interior was a dark cave; there were small holes for windows, but these let no light in at all as they were covered in snow. There was no furniture inside apart from a small, thin-walled metal stove propped on a pile of rocks. The floor was a mix of dirt and wood chips. Chris came back outside and squinted at the drifted-over roof.

"I wonder where the chimney is," she said. "Perhaps if I light the stove, smoke will seep out and show me."

The smoke seeped out all right—through the door. The cave became filled with a thick, unbreathable fug. Chris had found an old shovel in the cabin and, donning the snowshoes again, she tramped up onto the roof.

"Hope it's going to hold me," she said. "The trapper told me that a cabin doesn't fall down when it freezes, but when it thaws."

She dug for a while and at last a wisp of smoke appeared beside her feet. She enlarged the hole and shovelled around a bit more before finding the chimney pipe that had fallen over. I'm not sure why she needed to go to all that work. Sport and I were happy enough to sleep on the snow, and she could have brought food that didn't need cooking. But humans, it seems, as the caddisfly larvae that blunder around in the bottom of ponds, have to spend a great deal of energy carrying elaborate households around with them.

"Well, guys," said Chris. "I know there's plenty of daylight left, but it's too warm to travel easily. We're going to camp here for the night and set off very early in the morning. With luck, the snow will be colder and better for us to walk on then."

She meant early, all right. It was the middle of the night when she got up, made a fire, and cooked another meal. It was not all that dark, though, for a full moon poured a silver light from the sky. She had timed our hike for just this event.

It was not as cold as we had hoped, for the snow was still soft, but the temperature was below freezing and the snowshoes and our feet did not get clogged up. For all that, there were problems. Although the moon was bright, the shadows beneath the trees were dark, and Chris's poor vision meant she kept stumbling into holes. Sport kept up a constant muttering and sighing whenever his pack got caught up on a branch. However, after a while the trees grew more sparse, and we could make better progress over the open ground. Eventually we climbed out of the forest altogether. The moon was dropping toward the big mountains behind us by this time. We slowly crested a shallow ridge, and for a while the land in front of us sloped very gently downwards. A wind was blowing from the mountains, and the surface of the snow was swirling along like snakes, the way it often did on the lake. The moon was at just the right angle to light up the swirling snow, but not the ground beneath it. We marvelled at the strange sensation of having our feet glide through impenetrable darkness while we waded through these hissing, silver snakes.

We walked for a long time. At last there was a hint of light in the sky ahead of us. We were back among scattered, twisted, high-altitude trees by now. Chris pulled off our packs and dug below her gear on the toboggan for a small scrap of roofing metal. She placed this on the snow, collected some twigs, and lit a fire on it. She cooked some food and boiled some water, into which she put the strange, foreign leaves that humans seem to like. Chris made "Mmm" noises as she drank it.

"Sure would be nice to sit here for a while," she said. "We must have been travelling for at least six hours already and I'm really tired. But if we stay any longer, I'll never move again. Even though the day is now warming up and the snow on this south-facing slope in front of us will be rotten, I really want to get over the ridge before tonight."

We were now on a bit of an old trail. The branches of the scrubby trees that brushed past us were vaguely aromatic of Horse and the man whose smell had hung around the trap cabin. Going up that ridge, however, was a major slog. As the sun climbed higher, we became extremely hot. Chris stripped down to a thin shirt, but even then she had to rest in the shade, and every few steps she had to knock the sticky snow off her snowshoes. Finally, the trees thinned out again and the snow grew patchy until it disappeared altogether. Above the treeline, the combined forces of sun and wind had swept the snow away altogether, and we sat on rocks and drank tiny puddles of water that lay in stony hollows. They were diamond clear and icy cold, and tasted of lichen. There was not much sign of animal life, but I could smell Caribou. Three or four of them had been this way not too long before.

Once again, we did not stop for long. I had hoped that our walking would be easier now, for we would be going downhill. But as soon as we topped the pass, the conditions changed dramatically. All the snow that had been blown off the sunny side of the ridge had piled up on the shady side, and it was very deep and soft. There was no trail. Down we floundered—down, down. Even in the deep trench that Chris tramped with her snowshoes, our paws could not touch a firm bottom, and we sank to our bellies with every step. At least we were no longer being blasted by the sun, and it was a little cooler. Soon we entered the forest again. These trees, however, were not as scattered and open as they had been before, but quite thick and full of windfalls. Soon, we could no longer see where we were going. The low mountains that surrounded us on this side of the pass and the flat plain we had seen far ahead from the top of the ridge were hidden by trees. We continued to stumble down and down.

It was very slow going. We had had an extremely long day, and we were all exhausted. Even though the sun did not reach this part of the mountain, the air warmed as we lost altitude and the snow became soggy and hard to walk through. It was no longer quite so deep, but it was still over Chris's knees. All of a sudden, we stumbled upon a tiny gully that had a trickle of water running through it.

"The first open creek of the year!" Chris exclaimed. "Spring is on its way!" She looked around. "We're already much lower than Nuk Tessli; we can't be too far from the bottom of this valley, and it's going to be dark soon. If I can find a bit of flat ground big enough for my sleeping bag I think we'll spend the night here."

As soon as our packs were off and we'd had a good roll, Sport and I curled up in the snow. Chris went through her usual ritual of collecting twigs and making a fire, rummaging for her billycan, filling it with seepage from the tiny creek, and then making the Mmm-water with the bitter-smelling leaves. She dredged other dried human food out of my pack and cooked herself a meal. Sport was carrying our kibble. Chris didn't trust him with human food, but she figured that if Sport went into the water and allowed our kibble to get wet, it wouldn't matter, as it wouldn't be ruined. Before Chris ate, she tipped our rations into hollows she packed into the snow. As the fire died down, she spread a tarp and put her sleeping bag on top. Finally, after all this rigmarole, she crawled into the sleeping bag and went to sleep. Sport and I, of course, had gone to bed long before then.

The only real problem we had the next morning was crossing the creek in the bottom of the valley. It was not all that wide, but most of the ice had gone and it was belly deep on me. One of the many strange human conceits is that their feet must be kept dry.

"Oh well," Chris said with a sigh. "There's nothing else for it."

She sat on her pack to take her boots off. She removed the liners and socks, and then replaced the outer covering of the boots onto her feet. "I can't just go barefoot," she said. "My feet will become so numb in that icy water I would not know if I cut them on the rocks. I can't afford to be lame way out here." Carrying her pack and both of ours, she waded across. The outer coverings of her boots were not waterproof and she gasped and groaned as the cold hit her.

Once we were across, she dragged on her socks and footwear as fast as she could and set off at a tremendous pace, stamping her feet hard on the ground so they would warm up again.

We were now on the sunny side of the valley and had reached a rough little trail that was occasionally bare, but was mostly covered in a mix of frozen snow and ice. I could smell that Chris and her canines had been here before, although not for quite a while.

"This is our summer trail," Sport mumbled between his sighing and complaining.

Chris's snowshoes were now superfluous so she lashed them on top of her toboggan. The little sled grated on the bare patches of ground between the snow and bumped over exposed roots. Sport and I were still tired after the previous very long day, but it was so much easier walking on the trail that we made good time.

Suddenly, we encountered some old snowmobile tracks. From then on, it was like hiking on a sidewalk. However, it was still a good while before we arrived at a ploughed logging road. Soon after, a pickup came by. These were the first humans we had seen since the pilot left us in the mountains all those months before.

"We're going out for mail," the driver said. "We can give you a ride to Nimpo."

"Perfect," Chris replied. "I figured if I timed my hike for a mail day I might just be lucky enough to get a ride. I would need to make another overnight camp to get to the highway if I had to go on foot."

"Let's put the dogs in the back," the driver said, getting out to open the tailgate. Sport managed to jump in; I needed a bit of a boost. Strong I might be, but I am quite heavy and my legs aren't as long as Sport's. The back of the pickup smelled of farm animals and oil—piquant aromas when you haven't smelled anything like them for so long. But I was only too pleased to curl into a ball and let the movement of the truck soothe me. It was quite a relief not to have to do any more walking.

7

HARRY

THE HOLE IN THE GROUND

"WHAT AN AMAZING LIFE TAYA HAD," I SAID. "IS THAT THE PLACE WE'RE going to soon? I can't wait until we get there. When will we be leaving?" We were walking up to the usual working place, and I skipped along in front and dodged from side to side as I always did. "I bet I'd be able to walk like that without getting tired and complaining like Sport did. I'm not so sure I want to carry a backpack, though."

"Carrying Chris's camping gear is what you are in our pack for, young pup," Badger said snidely. Then he relented at my crestfallen expression. "But Chris doesn't do those long endurance expeditions anymore. She's too old. She doesn't even spend the winters in the mountains now. Not since she came to live here. We still go on camping trips in the summer, though, and we still carry most of her Stuff in our packs. And we do a lot of hiking without camping. You are going to love it there."

"But when are we going?" I asked again.

"Not sure," Badger replied. "The snow has gone and the leaves have opened on the aspen trees. We're usually getting ready to fly in by the time that happens. I think she must be waiting for something else to happen."

As we came within nose-shot of the building site, it became apparent that another human had arrived, bringing with him a huge machine.

"It's the backhoe!" Chris said excitedly.

"Ah ha!" Badger said, puffing a little because of the climb. (He was getting old, too.) "I do believe that this is what she has been waiting for."

The backhoe clanked across the new clearing on caterpillar tracks, which chewed up the sparse kinnikinnick and grasses and made deep chevron patterns in the dirt. The machine had a long neck that ended in an enormous iron thing shaped like the top half of a mouth. When the machine was fired up, the neck bent and the mouth part bit into the ground. The machine jerked as the jaw scooped up a great gobbet of dirt; then it turned around and spat it out beside the machine. A huge hole appeared in the ground very quickly, and the dry, silvery soil was dumped into two great piles, one on either side of the hole. Badger loves dirt piles. As soon as the operator went away at the end of the day (leaving behind the machine for the night), Badger climbed on top of one of the piles and lay there.

We were still down at the River Cabin the following morning when we heard the machine start up again. We hurried up to the big new hole. The driver of the machine was replacing the iron jaw with a bigger one. Apparently he was going to move some of the piles of dirt. The road he had driven in on had been cut out of the bush by Chris and some Wwoofers last summer, but there was a low, wet spot in it. It was too boggy for Chris to take her van through, and she had asked the man to put down an underground pipe and cover it with the soil taken out of the hole. Chris hoped that the pipe, which she called a culvert, would drain the water from the bog.

Before he climbed back into the cab, the driver pointed to the tracks his machine had made the day before. Superimposed upon them were the large prints of an animal. Badger and I knew, via our noses, who had come by long before Chris's eye-picture reached her brain.

"Grizzly!" she crowed.

"It's a big, old male," the machine operator said. "You can tell by the size of the big toe."

Old Mr. Grizz had come along the new road, climbed over one of the dirt piles, and headed down toward the pond. Our noses told us that he wasn't close anymore, but we would have to keep our olfactory senses on full alert.

By now the pond below the building site had thawed. Duck and Goose honked and quacked and splashed about. Soon I knew all about Muskrat. He is the size of a small cat but he has a naked tail and spends most of the time swimming around in the pond. He eats the roots of the plants that grow at the edge of the water; often he sits on a fallen log like Squirrel, holding the food up to his mouth.

If I saw Muskrat's movement in the water, I was after him like a flash. The bottom of the pond was thick, black sludge that was difficult to

Muskrat

walk through, which prevented me from catching him, but I always had fun. I would trot back to Chris with thick black mud almost to the top of my back. I knew it would soon dry and fall off, but Chris always pulled a "phee-uw" sort of face and never gave me a pat when I came to her like that.

The new hole was so big it could have swallowed the River Cabin. After the big-mouthed machine left, another man arrived with large, white, hollow building blocks. He and Chris and a couple of the man's friends hooked the blocks together (they were very light) and made a sort of room inside the hole. A few days later, along came more machines and more people. Two of the machines were trucks with bodies that slowly turned round and round. The third had all sorts of arms and legs folded up against it. It parked near the edge of the hole and shot out great feet on either side. Then a great long tube came out of its head. One of the other trucks joined itself to it like a mating aphid. A switch was turned, and thick, porridge-like earth started to pour into the hollow block walls. But it didn't smell like the porridge Chris often gave us to eat; it smelled of wet mud.

Harry

Everyone worked hard manoeuvring, smoothing, and banging the walls with two-by-fours to make the porridge settle. By the time the trucks disappeared, you would not have been able to eat it—it had set as hard as stone.

"It looks as though she is building an underground kennel," I said.

Badger was quite concerned that the usual time for going into the mountains had long passed. The leaves were fully out on the aspens and Chris had a lot of Stuff packed, but she still continued to go up to the worksite every day. She was now alone. A pile of logs was stacked near the hole. Chris wanted the big logs to lie from one side to the other on top of the new white walls, but a large ditch, deep enough to swallow Chris completely when she was standing up, surrounded the walls. She had to place shorter tree pieces across the huge ditch so that she could roll the big logs over the gap. After the earlier hot, dry weather, it was now snowing. Chris worked with a face as dark as thunder.

"Is this really what she wants to do?" I muttered to Badger while we sheltered beneath a tree. "She doesn't look at all happy."

Badger shrugged. "That's human beings for you," he said.

I was somewhat chilly, and wanted Badger to run around with me and play, but Badger headed toward a comparatively dry spot under a tree, and lay down with a grunt. "I don't feel like galloping around much in this wet, snowy weather. My bones ache too much. But if you like, I'll tell you more of Taya's story."

"I like!" I exclaimed, grinning. We huddled together and watched Chris toiling and swearing, and the next chapter of Taya's Saga unfolded.

8

TAYA

MY NUK TESSLI ADVENTURES

ONCE OR TWICE A YEAR, CHRIS MAKES A LONG TRIP BY ROAD THAT SHE calls a Book Tour. She goes to many towns, large and small, and, with a tool like a big flashlight, throws pictures on a wall. She then tries to sell the books that she and Lonesome have written.

Chris loves standing in front of an audience and showing off. Sometimes I would go into the showing place with her, and when I arrived the people would forget Chris and lavish praise on me. Chris would pop my pack onto my back—empty, fortunately—and hundreds of photos would be taken. The audience might have come to see and hear Chris initially—but I was easily the star of the show.

After our very long hike out of the mountains in the snow that spring, we went on one of these Book Tours and drove for many days. We visited hippie towns like Nelson, and then crossed a big mountain range to a huge flat area called the prairie. Animals that were quite new to me lived here: Antelope, Badger, and many water birds. On our side of the mountains, little snow had remained, but on the prairie side, it was much colder, and drifts still lingered beside fences and in ditches where they had accumulated.

It would have been very interesting exploring these habitats if Chris had let Sport and me run about like we wanted to, but for most of the time we were kept on chains and walked on leads. Chris didn't enjoy this any more than we did and she was often in a bad temper when we tried to pull away. It wasn't just the wild things that attracted us; items that humans call garbage were often irresistible as well. There was not much wild country in this flat land, and our walks were usually close to human habitation. Old food wrappers and Styrofoam containers lay about everywhere. Even if the food had long gone, the scents were fascinating. The aromas from other dogs both wild and domestic proliferated as well: this was P-mail with a vengeance. I often left my mark to show them I had been there. I wondered what the regulars would make of the message from a stranger who had travelled from such a faraway place.

One of the things that happened while we were kept on a lead surprised me enormously the first time it occurred. We were walking in a small patch of city forest surrounded by a lot of houses. Not far into the excursion, I needed to go to the bathroom. I squatted, left my offering on the ground, and started to walk on. And do you know what Chris did? She actually *picked it up!* I looked at Chris with the utmost astonishment. Then I looked at the poop (it was in a plastic bag), and looked at Chris again. I wondered what on earth she was going to do with it—would you believe it, she actually carried it with us. Eventually, we arrived at a garbage can that, I could smell, was full of other dogs' feces, and she put the bag in there. I thought I was well versed in human idiosyncrasies by then, but I had never seen anything like that in my life!

After a few weeks of this restricted existence, Chris finally turned the pickup back toward the mountain range. We crossed it and dropped down into the moist warm forests again. Finally we arrived at the Cabin-in-the-Bog from which we had flown in the tiny plane during the winter. The ice had gone from the lake now and the water lapped against the shore, driven by a chilly spring wind. Duck quacked. Mosquito had hatched and his whining and biting nearly drove us mad! Sport was particularly affected. He had developed a skin condition—apparently he was allergic to dog kibble. Chris grumbled about having to take him to the vet and spend a lot on medicine. She also bought him special food—which I was never allowed to eat. It didn't seem to help him much. He still itched, and the biting insects made him worse. My coat was so thick that few flies could get to me, but they sometimes nipped at my nose and the skin around my eyes. I soon got used to them. Chris was bothered by the insects almost as much as Sport. Humans are terribly handicapped without a good coat of hair. To prevent the flies biting her face, Chris stuck a special skin over her head. It was made of netting so that she could see through it. Chris always made her Mmm-water using loose herbs, but Patty preferred hers sown into little cloth containers. When Chris wore her fly-skin, she looked just like one of Patty's teabags.

We were, it appeared, waiting again. Then, suddenly, Chris was galvanized into action.

"The pilots have told me that our lake is open," she said to us, grinning delightedly. "Now we can go home."

I well remembered how excited Patty used to be when she heard that the ice had gone out.

"We could have walked in earlier," I heard her tell a human visitor, "but I would need supplies right away. My lake breaks up about a month later than this one."

Once again there was a furious packing and loading of the truck, and again I was reminded of Patty and Nick as they got us all ready to go up the lake to the Lodge. In the morning we set off early, but drove for only a few minutes before we turned into another property that also lay beside the lake. This place boasted several buildings—cabins and a big house that tourists stayed in—all facing out over the water. A long, floating wharf was tied to the shore, and snugged against this were three little planes, all wearing their canoe-shoes.

"I'll put the stuff in the hangar," Chris said to the pilot. "It's labelled from *most urgent* to *least urgent*." She indicated some scribbles on the sacks and boxes. "The most important must come on the first flight. The other stuff can wait until there's plane space. Give me three days to get in. I expect to get there in two, but it's best to be safe. See you then!"

She was enormously happy as she climbed back into the truck and started up the motor again. Soon we turned off the highway once more, this time onto the logging road where we had managed to hitch a ride after our long winter trek from the mountains. Almost immediately we hit some great, muddy bog holes. Chris gunned the motor and we slewed and slithered our way through them. Sport and I were tossed around in the back like leaves in a storm. Then the road became drier and sandier. Finally, we arrived at yet another lake, this one so big it was difficult to see the far shore.

We branched off onto a smaller, rougher road that ended beside a creek. I recognized where we were—we had hiked out this way during the winter. Then, however, the creek had been frozen and easy to cross. Now it was roaring with spring runoff. Someone had once built a bridge across it, but very little of this structure remained.

One log and some rotten wood still clung to both banks, however, and with great care Chris picked her way across. She was carrying her own pack. She came back for ours, and then let us find our own way over the water. As soon as our paws hit land, she grabbed us and loaded our packs on our backs. She kept a lead on me—she knew I wouldn't listen to her if I wanted to go after something. I didn't like being on a lead, but there was nothing I could do about it.

At first we plodded up a trail that was well used, although I could tell by the smells that Chris was the only human who had walked along it this year. There was no snow now, of course, and parts of it were very wet and boggy. The good trail did not last long; then we were faced with a rough path that was so narrow Chris and I could not walk abreast, and I had to stay behind. I remembered coming down here in the winter. Sport usually walked after me. I hardly hit anything with my pack, but it was amazing how many roots and rocks Sport managed to bang against. As usual, he was sighing and moaning about his lot.

Our route took us beside a series of small lakes. We had walked down the middle of them in winter but now we had to scramble around the edge fighting windfalls, and crossing great swamps full of water. No wind penetrated this part of the forest; it was dull and humid, and Mosquito buzzed and whined. Blackfly was plentiful, too, but he is silent and sneaky. He bites you without your noticing. Soon we all had blood running down the exposed parts of our bodies. With us dogs, it was our eyes and nose that were bothered; Chris got bitten on her hands, and the bugs sometimes got inside her teabag head-skin. Tree branches brushed against us, and Chris's teabag often got tangled up. Sweat dropped off her nose and steam fogged up the glass windows she wore in front of her eyes.

At first the ground was bare, but as we climbed, we began to hit a few patches of old snow. It was soft and rotten, but when we could not find a route around, we had to plough through. I found this particularly hard work. Sometimes Chris grabbed my collar and hauled me and my pack up bodily. Sport had longer legs and managed a little better, although not without a lot of whimpering.

We walked for a good part of the day, and at last came to a more open space. We were now on new territory as far as I was concerned, for at one point in our hike, we had passed the place where our winter route had brought us down to the trail.

We were almost at the edge of the forest. A treeless mountain-side covered in snow climbed above us. Upstream lay a small lake half covered with drifts that had turned a pale turquoise where they had sunk into the water. Near the place where the creek ran out, there floated Duck—a small, dark bird that Chris called a Barrow's goldeneye.

"They live in this high-altitude country," Chris informed us. "They're a sign we are getting into our home environment. Oh, look! She has babies!" Tiny black and white fluffballs followed the mother duck. Chris's expression took on something of the look that a bitch has for her puppies when they are very small, but my first thought was that Baby Duck might be easy to catch and eat. Chris gave me a sharp look and tied me to a tree. Sport, as always, was unobservant of his surroundings, and when his backpack was removed, he simply flopped down, rolled around and scratched at his itchy skin. I don't know if it was the disease or the drugs he was fed, but an unpleasant smell emanated from him.

Chris had said that we were in our home environment, but I could smell nothing of the cabin we had flown into for the winter. We did indeed still have a long way to go, but first, we were going to camp for the night.

Chris gathered twigs and branches and lit a fire. Soon sweet woodsmoke drifted across the little clearing, deterring the biting insects somewhat. We were all tired and content to rest. Chris boiled water and made herself some of the foreign leafy drink. Before long, however, she rummaged in the dog backpacks. In the winter, Chris had slept on the snow in her sleeping bag on a tarp, but now she unearthed fabric and a bundle of very thin poles. Sport and I had been carrying these in our packs as well as the usual food and cooking gear. We were already in rocky, mountainous country, and Chris had to look for a space flat enough to lie down on. She unfolded the fabric and laced together the poles—and she had a little cloth tent.

"I never need this in the winter," she explained. "I carry it in summer because of the bugs."

"Actually, you don't carry it at all," Sport whined. "We do."

Remembering our heavy slog through the snow on our hike out of the mountains, I was a bit alarmed at the solid white slope in front of us. However, when we started walking on it the following morning, we found that it was quite firm.

"It's just the snow in the forest that's so difficult at this time of year," Chris chatted. "Anything above the treeline is usually pretty good."

And once we started walking on the snow, Mosquito disappeared.

We climbed steadily, Chris kicking her feet in at every step, and at last reached the top of a sloping ridge. Patches of snow and bare rock stretched before us.

"There it is," said Chris, grinning.

Far, far ahead, backed by the big mountains I had come to recognize during the winter, was a slab of water, silver in the dull light. It was surrounded by its dark blanket of trees. The mountains were part of a huge panorama of peaks that stretched across the horizon. A wind blew steadily into our faces. And now I could smell it—very far away, but a faint and unmistakable aroma of home.

We walked for some time through the high country, and eventually we passed the spot where we had breakfasted on our winter

hike. We plodded up the long slope we had slithered down through the moonlit, shifting surface snow. We did not go to the little cabin we had spent the night in, but I caught the aroma of where it was. Next, we had to cross a river. We had been able to use the ice to travel over it in winter, but now it was open and too wild and roaring to wade. It came out of a lake that was still partly frozen, and Chris had to take us a long way round to find good ice to walk on. Even so, I could see she was very apprehensive when she crept over the weaker spaces. She would yell at us to stay away from her so that our combined weights were not all together in the same place.

Then we began to descend more steeply toward our lake. It was the trail where Chris had carried her toboggan on her back. The trees were bigger here and the snow was rotten again. Bare ground predominated now, however, and soon we were at the lakeshore. Before we had left in the winter, Chris had dragged a canoe across the ice. With a sigh of relief, she dumped her load. She took the packs off me and Sport, too—and, joy of joys, she also unclipped the lead and I was free! I shook and rolled and waded into the lake to lap the water.

The canoe had been placed upside down, and now Chris heaved it over and slid it into the water. She placed our gear aboard, climbed in herself, and pushed away from the shore.

"Come on Sport, come on Taya," she sang.

"W-w-w-water," I barked. "I can't swim!"

Taya, Chris and Sport hiking home with Nuk Tessli Lake in the distance.

"Wowowowo! The water is cowowowold!" Sport wailed. But he plunged right in.

"Oh come on, Sport. Stop making such a fuss! You know where to go. Look, Taya, I'm staying right by the edge. Just follow me along the shore."

Sure enough, Chris did not go far into the lake, but paddled close to the rocky edge. Sport scrambled out onto dry land and started to run. I followed him, and soon picked up the ancient trail, invisible to humans but obvious to any canine, of the dogs that had run along there before. There were old traces of Sport, of course, and was that just a hint of Lonesome?

Chris paddled, and we ran for quite a while, but now I knew what Chris expected me to do and I was quite happy to travel this way. We came to a point where we could see the cabin across the lake, but there was a big stretch of water in between us. Chris stuck close to the shore; it appeared she was going to travel all the way round the back of the lake. All of a sudden we came to the river. I recognized the place where I had fallen through the ice. Sport gave his usual piercing howl and plunged in to swim across, but what was I going to do? I barked at Chris again, and began to run up and down the shore.

"Come on, Taya, you can do it."

Chris took the canoe across the river and waited by the far shore. I put a foot into the water, then took it out. It seemed not too deep there—maybe I could walk. I waded in deeper. It didn't look too far. One more step—and suddenly I was floating! A strong current was pushing me toward the rocky teeth at the beginning of the rapids. I opened my mouth to bark and water slopped into it. I waved my legs as fast as I could, and within moments hit a boulder under the water. The next foot hit another boulder. I scrambled through the branches of a fallen tree—and I was across! With a great shake I rid my coat of the excess water. How proudly I ran the rest of the way home.

THE PLANE WITH THE PROMISED FREIGHT ARRIVED THE DAY AFTER WE did. As there was no ice or overflow, it could come right up to the rickety logs of the wharf. Once again a ton of Stuff was unloaded—I was, however, pleased to smell that several bags of kibble were part of the package. What's more, I didn't have to do any work this time. Chris carried all the Stuff herself up the short, steep trail, and then lugged it up the steps into the attic.

Chris was now a lot busier than she had been during the winter. She scrubbed walls and windows and floors much more than I thought necessary, and, using a variety of tools, she kept banging nails into bits of wood here and there. I couldn't see that all this work made a lot of difference to everyone's comfort, but it seemed important to her.

About a month after we arrived, the plane came in again. This time, four human passengers were inside. They seemed glad to be at our cabins, but you could tell that they were out of their normal element. They smelled of perfumes and the city. Their clothes had a washing-machine aroma; the fabrics were brightly coloured and did not have patches or frayed edges as Chris's clothes did. Two of the people got out of the plane with bare legs, but that didn't last long once Mosquito introduced herself. For all their awkwardness, the people seemed very friendly. They gave me a lot of ear scratches and some of them even plucked up courage to pat stinky old Sport.

"They are tourists," he whispered importantly—as if I couldn't figure it out for myself. "Sometimes they have treats. If we play our cards right, we might get some."

However, poor Sport did not have much charisma as far as most humans were concerned. Despite being given his special food and the medicine that Chris had bought from the vets, his coat was patchy and he itched and scratched all the time. His unpleasant aroma was noticeable even to the humans.

We took the tourists out in the canoes and on hikes into the mountains. They stayed only a few days, and when the plane came to pick them up, it brought the rest of Chris's freight. Soon more visitors arrived, and this was how the summer went. Some visitors couldn't walk too far, but others were great hikers. Sometimes we went out camping with them, and the tourists loved to see Sport and me carrying our packs.

In between groups of visitors, we would go on our own expeditions. Sometimes Chris took an axe along and marked new trails by putting axe cuts on the trunks of trees. The sap would congeal into these cuts, and on the pines it would turn yellow. These marks were known as blazes. Often, however, there were no trails at all, and many times we would travel for days way above the treeline visiting places even Chris had never been to before. And you'll never guess what Chris was looking for. Flowers! Tiny bits of plants stuck in rock cracks would send her into paroxysms of delight. She never ate them. She never even picked them. She just raved about them and took photos.

When the snow disappeared from the high country, we could find Marmot and Ptarmigan and other interesting things. Ptarmigan and Grouse are related and in an effort to protect their babies, both species will flop around as if they have a broken wing. The idea is that they pretend to be injured so that a predator is led away from the chicks. Sport was fooled every time and he would run after the grown birds, but of course, just as he was about to catch them, the birds would fly a bit further.

I was never taken in by these antics. I had long ago learned that this behaviour meant food. At the first adult squawk I would drop my head close to the ground and listen for movement in the tundra. The babies, like many small animals, have no scent when they are very young. I generally managed to chomp two or three before Chris got to me. Once this happened when we were hiking with tourists. I shall never forget their look of horror as they watched me chewing on a blissful mouthful while the chick's legs stuck out through the gaps between my teeth.

And so the summer passed. It began to freeze at night and the underbrush began to change colour. Many of these shrubs had berries on them and Chris gobbled them with glee. (I nibbled them a bit but, let me tell you, they were not half as good as baby Ptarmigan.)

Sport's illness was growing worse. He was very uncomfortable most of the time. Whenever Chris looked at him, she sighed. We were soon going to have to go on another Book Tour. Sport would be very difficult to transport round in his state. One day, she tied me up, put a treat in her pocket, and went for a walk with Sport. She was carrying a shotgun. I had smelled this weapon in a cupboard in the cabin but I had never seen Chris pull it out before. Patty used firearms all the time so I knew very well what their purpose was.

She and Sport were gone a long time. Then, faintly on the wind, I heard a shot. Chris returned with her face pulled down and water dripping from her eyes. Sport did not come back with her; I never saw him again. Chris and I hiked over the mountains to the road alone.

THE BOOK TOUR THAT FALL TOOK US TO THE BIG CITIES IN SOUTHERN BC. Once again, Chris showed off to her audiences, but of course it was me who was the main attraction. Usually Chris let me loose in the room to visit with the audience and I got lots of great pats. One time, however, in a school, as soon as she let me off I ignored the people and made a beeline for the back of the room. In a cage by the door was a hamster. I would have got it, given time, but there were all kinds of yells, and hands grabbed me quickly. What was the hamster there for if not to eat?

We did not go straight home after the Book Tour, but turned off the highway and arrived at the place where Chris had left Lonesome just about a year before. And there was the old girl herself, looking pretty doddery by now. Her hair had become very long and shaggy, and most of it had turned white. She seemed to be completely deaf, but it was amazing how she could hear Chicken cackling when she laid eggs away from the chicken coop. Lonesome would disappear, and then emerge with bits of shell and egg yolk entangled into her moustache.

We stayed there for several days. Our host and her co-worker were artists—they busied themselves in a tiny cabin making sculptures out of a kind of earth. These they baked in a very hot oven. Strange chemical smells accompanied this procedure. Lonesome lived in this cabin where it was nice and warm. The old smooth-haired dog who had been there last year was gone, but the other hound, the one with the very long tongue, was still lively and happy. He lived in the house with the humans. Chris slept in another little cabin and, although it was cold, I was tied in the woodshed. Well, being tied in the cold was nothing new and I didn't find it at all uncomfortable. At least we often went for nice long walks while we stayed there.

One day Chris left me in the woodshed and drove away in her truck. When she returned some hours later, I at once caught the aroma of a strange dog. This one still smelled of puppy, but when I saw him in Chris's arms, I could not believe my eyes. He was huge. He was covered with a thick coat like mine, but his fur was almost white. Chris walked over to the little art studio and opened the door. I could hear the two people inside turn to look, and then, as if synchronized, they both dropped their tools and said

Lonesome

nothing but ooh and ah for at least five minutes. For goodness' sake. What was so special about him? He was only a puppy!

Chris had found him a little coat. I would not have thought she was the kind of person who dressed dogs in human clothes, but Chris had told me that the cabin she was using had a poor stove in which the fire never lasted the night so it was no warmer than my woodshed in the morning. She herself used two sleeping bags and extra blankets. The puppy slept in a box on the floor beside her bed. She called him Max.

That pup was the biggest brat I have ever had the pleasure of meeting. He wasn't so bad while we were all tied up, but after we finally flew into the mountains, he was a holy terror. He never quit bugging me for one instant—chewing at my ears, yanking at my tail. I would snap and snarl at him, and sometimes get so mad I would put my jaws around his neck and push his head into the snow. He would yelp and scream his apology, as all pups soon know how to do, but he never learned! The minute I let him go, he was at it again. There was barely a minute of our waking hours when he wasn't chewing on one or another of my extremities. On our hikes up the mountain that winter, he must have hung onto my tail every step of the way.

I'd had plenty of puppies of my own, but had never encountered one that was so ill mannered.

Spring came, and Max grew. He was an Akita-Malamute cross, and soon he was bigger than I was. He was still not old enough to do the long spring snowshoe trip to the road, so Chris arranged to be flown out at the beginning of April. And it turned out that Max was even more afraid of flying than Chris was. Moreover, he was also petrified of

Max as a puppy

being in the truck. Whenever she had to get him into any kind of vehicle, she would tie him up long before he heard the motor.

Once again we were in travelling mode as we went on another Book Tour. Our first show was in an upstairs room that was reached by a ramp. Although it was April, it was pretty cold that night, with temperatures far below freezing. Although Max was almost full size, he was a bit nervous about meeting people, and when strangers patted him, he would often piddle. This was why he could not be taken into the room. I always had to stay outside with him, so I missed a lot of the adulation that was my due. When Chris finished the slideshow and came out of the room, she could not believe her eyes. Max had peed every time he had been patted, and the liquid had frozen on the sloping ramp into a wide sheet of ice.

"Oh my gosh, Max," she said. "You look like a drunk in an alley!"

We flew into the mountains again when the ice went out in early June, but once we were home, Chris started to groom Max for his duties. Every time we went on a hike, he had to wear a pack.

At first the pack was empty. He didn't like the feel of it all that much and wriggled and squirmed, and of course he didn't like being kept on the lead. He got used to it, however, and soon Chris padded the pack with empty dog food bags to give it some bulk. He began to learn that he was a lot wider with the pack on and had to make some allowances for rocks and trees.

Max and Taya

He was still growing, and now he was becoming somewhat obstreperous. My admonishing growls would not always subdue him—occasionally he snapped back. Around the middle of summer, Chris began to make plans to trek back out to the road as she had some business she felt she needed to attend to. We would carry gear for an overnight camp. This would be Max's first real backpacking expedition.

A few days before we were due to leave, Max and I had a big fight. Chris had fed us on the deck as usual, side by side, and all of a sudden Max turned on me. I had been in, and witnessed, plenty of dog fights before, and this was quite a nasty one. Chewed food and blood was plastered all over my head. Chris flew out the door but already we had parted. To be fair, Max seemed almost as startled as I was by his behaviour, but I never again quite trusted him. After that, Chris always tied us up in different places at feeding time. When we went to the road, Max was taken to the vet. I could smell the chemicals on him when he returned to the car. He was wearing one of those big collars that look like buckets. It took a while, but his aggression began to ease away.

THE SUMMER CAME TO AN END AND WE WERE ON THE ROAD AGAIN THE following fall. As soon as the ice was good, we flew home for yet another winter. It was a good time for us all. Max was now calm and friendly and he no longer chewed my tail when we went on our hikes. The days grew longer and a hint of spring came round again. Snow still lay on the ground and the lake was frozen, but the days were warm and sunny. One morning the first of the migrating birds arrived. It was a tiny thing, brown with a black head, and it perched on high branches giving monotonous little trills. Chris was ecstatic.

"A junco! Not much of a songster, is it?" she said, beaming at us. "But the first birdsong of the year after so much silence is magic."

This trilling fuzzball didn't do much to elevate my feelings. It always perched too high for me to reach and it wouldn't have been much of a mouthful if I could have snagged it anyway.

It was at this time of year that Chris usually planned to go out for her spring Book Tour, but this year, no packing or preparation of Stuff was happening. However, a plane did come in and land on the ice. It was a small one, belonging to a resident of Nimpo Lake. The pilot had flown in once or twice during the winter just for fun, bringing Chris letters from the post office. This time, however, he was carrying three passengers. Imagine my utter astonishment when, after they had climbed out onto the ice, one of them proved to be my old friend Nick who had looked after me at Patty's Lodge. With him were another young human male and a young human female, who turned out to be Nick's girlfriend.

"Taya, my lovely friend," exclaimed Nick in his odd German accent, giving me a great hug and a cuddle. "How wonderful to see you again. And this must be Max. He's huge!"

The pilot was grinning, but he wasn't going to hang around. "Gotta go!" he said. "This is my last winter flight! Nimpo is already beginning to break up around the edges and I'll be taking the skis off the plane soon as I get home."

"The ice will be good for a while here," said Chris. "It won't go out for at least six weeks, maybe more. I guess I'll see you when the lake's open."

"Grab the tail rope for me, will you? The skis are a little bit stuck. If you hold onto the rope, I can gun the motor and rock the plane back and forth to break it free."

Chris pulled a face because this task meant standing in the propellor's blizzard, but she pulled her jacket's hood over her head and did as she was asked. The motor roared, the blizzard flew, the plane bucked—and off it went, skimming over the ice and into the cloudless sky.

Everything was chaos for a bit while the visitors' Stuff was being organized. These visitors were not going to be treated like tourists. They were going to stay quite a while. They were going to help Chris build another cabin!

She already had two in the mountains—did I tell you that? She lived in the one by the waterfront and used the other for tourists. Lonesome told me that Chris had built both these cabins completely by herself. She had felled the trees, peeled the logs, dragged them home, shaped them, lifted them on to the buildings with ropes and eventually put a metal roof on top. The metal parts and the other things she could not make from the forest, like windows, were brought in on airplanes. I'd heard Chris talking about wanting a third cabin: the tourist season was very short and, it seemed, everyone wanted to come at the same time. Chris had often mentioned that she felt more accommodation would be justified, but she was too lazy to build it herself. The young Germans, however, were full of energy; Nick had been building log houses in Germany, so he was skilled.

The site chosen for the new structure was up on a little hill, facing the big mountains. There was still a lot of snow on the ground. The first job was to fall some of the trees, and soon there was a terrible mess of branches and chopped-up tree trunks, all accompanied by a strong scent of resin. Most of these trees were too twisted or rotten for building. During our numerous hikes, Chris had noted a bunch of pines at the bottom end of the lake. They had been killed by pine bark beetles and most were straight and strong. They were, however, a long way from home. First they had to be rolled and skidded down a snowy hillside onto the ice; then both ends of the logs were put onto little toboggans so they could be dragged home. It wasn't easy! When the sun warmed the day, the surface snow on the ice became slushy. The three visiting humans harnessed themselves to ropes and pulled like carthorses. I kept out of the way. I hoped they wouldn't remember that I had been a star sled-puller in my time. I was getting too old for that sort of thing.

The building site faced the hot spring sun and slowly the snow melted. The ground beneath revealed its true bumps and hollows. Nick said it would be necessary to dig in places to get a good base for the foundations. Very often, however, when the surface soil was pushed away, the layer underneath would still be frozen.

The ice on the lake began to disintegrate, too. Where the sun warmed the rocks around the edge, bits of open water appeared. Most of the lake was still solid, but getting on to it began to be a bit tricky. Nick and his friends loved the open holes, though. They stripped, jumped in and had a bath, balancing their bars of soap and bottles of shampoo on the ice. Chris said they were crazy.

Eventually, four logs were arranged in a rectangle where the cabin was going to be, and all the others had been pulled up off the ice and stacked nearby. It was time for the young people to go. They were going to snowshoe out over the mountains, and if they left it any later, much of the snow below the treeline would be too soft to travel on. Chris and us dogs were going to accompany them across the lake; to do this, we had to leave very early while the surface was still frozen. The humans' packs were loaded onto Chris's toboggan and dragged across the ice to where the trail to the road started. Chris and her friends made goodbye noises, and the hikers started climbing into the forest. We trotted back across the lake. Despite the thin grating of the empty toboggan as it skittered behind Chris, without the visitors it suddenly seemed very quiet.

Although it was still early, the sun was already gaining heat, and we broke through the surface crust into puddles of water. There was plenty of good ice underneath so there was no risk of falling through, but it was a bit scary crashing into water all the time. The gap between the ice and the shore had widened, and Chris had to search up and down for a place where she could jump across. It was the last time we walked on the ice that year.

We were about to experience breakup. Chris had never been at Nuk Tessli during this time of year before as she had always gone out to work. Before she started giving spring slideshows she used to plant trees. She was quite excited about this new experience. No one would be able to visit until the lake was open. Planes could not land until then, and very soon the snow in the forest would become too rotten for any hikers to attempt to come overland. We would be completely alone for quite a while. Chris seemed to enjoy this kind of solitude, but Max and I would have preferred a bit more company. Visitors always made more of a fuss over us than Chris did.

We were able to walk on the snow in the bush for a few more days, as long as we left very early when it was still frosty. Inevitably, by the time we wanted to come down from our hikes, we sank and slithered into slush. Snowshoes would not have been much help because too many fallen trees and rocks were now exposed.

Chris got a little frustrated with her inability to hike and she had to be content with sunbathing on the deck and listening to the bird orchestra that was now tuning up with all manner of peeps and whistles and croaks.

Gradually, the gap between the shore and the ice stretched wider. One day Chris was galvanized into action. She dug out the canoe shelter, which was still buried in snow, and hauled her biggest boat into view. She grabbed paddles and life jackets and squeezed the canoe into the narrow gap of water. Before she jumped in, however, she turned back to get the axe.

"I can hear all these great duck noises by the outlet," she said. "I'd love to see what is making them. That ice joining the main pack to the shore looks like tissue paper—maybe I can get through it." I prepared to pop into the boat with her but—"Stay!" she bellowed. "You guys can run around."

She had a silly, happy expression on her face as she eased into the canoe and began to paddle. We dogs immediately started to slither and scramble over the rocks and snow patches around the edge of the lake. Chris was sitting right up at the back end of the canoe so that the front rode high out of the water. When she encountered a frozen patch, she paddled as fast as she could until half the boat had slid onto the ice, and then she hopped forward. With a crack, if she was lucky, the ice broke. Sometimes, she whacked away at it with the axe. But that fragile-looking ice was a lot tougher than she had thought, and soon she had to give up. We were nowhere near the duck noises. Chris had enjoyed the novelty, however. She said that she would give it a day or two, then try again. But then

Taya, Chris and Max sitting on the deck at Nuk Tessli.

the wind got up and drove the ice against the shore, so that plan was foiled.

We could now walk in very sunny places where most of the ground was bare. We couldn't climb very far up the mountain, but we would often go to a lookout not far from where we had cut down the cabin logs. Chris was never content with what she had. She had wanted to stay through breakup, but now she was anxious for the ice to be gone. From the lookout we could see if there was any open water at the head of the lake. The ice was full of cracks and puddles, but it was still amazingly solid.

"What we need is a wind," said Chris. A strong spring breeze was gusting a great deal of the time, but the ice did not seem to be budging. Then, all of a sudden, we could see open water from the lookout. The next day it was visible from the cabins. The wind continued to blow, and the edge of the ice heaved up and down as the waves of the open water relentlessly weakened it. It started to break into candle-shaped crystals that tinkled as they fell. Suddenly, a streak of open water sped like an arrow into the lake beyond the islands, where planes landed in the summer before taxiing to the wharf. Ice still hung about the cabins, though. The next day, the wind blew and the ice heaved. Chris was writing, which meant she was concentrating on her computer. When she looked up from the screen she exclaimed out loud.

"Look at that!" she said. "There was a solid mass an hour ago—now the ice has completely gone. This means I can go see if there are any ducks by the outlet. I haven't heard them for a few days so perhaps they've moved on. It's too windy right now, but mornings are generally calm. With luck, we can go tomorrow."

She launched the canoe very early the next day and we were able to go right around the lake to the outlet. But the pool by the rapids was empty.

A COUPLE WEEKS LATER, CHRIS FIGURED WE WOULD BE ABLE TO HIKE to the road. Max was able to pack a good load by this time, which pleased me, as I seemed to be getting tired more easily than I used to.

We stayed for a day or two at the Cabin-in-the-Bog with its big gaps between the logs—this time they let in thick clouds of Mosquito. Chris stuffed newspaper into them as best she could but she knew it would fall out again the next time the building flexed its muscles. We didn't need to be there long, however: we were going into town to shop for summer supplies. It took half a day to drive there, and we stayed overnight with one of Chris's friends. We bought food and dog kibble and nails and tools and other building supplies. Most of this was dropped off at the float plane base on our way home, and a day or two later, Chris loaded our packs and we drove to the end of the road to begin our summer hike.

There was one thing of note on that trip. It happened on our second day, while we were crossing the section of alpine. The sky was overcast, and a stiff wind blew against the left side of our faces. Mostly we walked over sodden tundra, but drifts of snow still lay in places. We slogged up a long rise, at the top of which we should have seen the big panorama of mountains, but they were totally hidden by a grey wall of cloud.

We dogs were carrying our packs, of course, but otherwise were walking free. A couple of Ravens cruised on the wind behind us. They did this sometimes. They thought we were Wolf, who would kill something and give them the leftovers. Suddenly Chris grabbed first my collar, then Max's. She had seen something ahead. Because the wind had been blowing crosswise, we had not smelled the animals before she had seen them. The wind veered, and now the smell was plain. Caribou! Max and I wriggled and tried to get free. These animals were aching to be chased! But Chris hung on tight—she could be pretty tough when she wanted. She snagged leads on us and,

because there were no trees, tied the other ends to her legs. Then she excitedly took out that machine she uses to take pictures of flowers.

Ahead were fourteen Bull Caribou trotting from left to right in a single line. They were of all ages; three already had quite big antlers. Caribou have a measured, bouncy trot, a lot prancier than Deer's. Trot, trot, trot, they went, then suddenly the lead one grew faint and sort of dissolved. Like a ghost, vanishing into the ether. Trot, trot, trot, they went, and the second grew faint and disappeared. One by one, all fourteen animals trotted into ghostly oblivion.

"What on earth's happening?" Chris asked—and then the oblivion reached us.

It was a violent snowstorm. Instantly we were in a total whiteout. Chris has no sense of direction whatsoever and didn't know where to go. Max and I could have found our way without trouble, but she was not going to let us off the leads and we had to follow where she went. It wasn't long before we crossed a snowpatch laced with the great, round Caribou footprints. The aroma was intoxicating. Immediately Max and I writhed and whined—these animals were *really* asking to be chased. But Chris hung on and said words I would not like to repeat. The snowstorm blew over, we dropped into the trees, and eventually we arrived home.

Not too long after that, Nick came back! He was alone this time and he continued to work on the cabin. He was a much better builder than Chris. He was faster, stronger and more accurate. Chris helped quite a bit, but she now had more tourists than before to deal with, and she was busy guiding and feeding them. More of Nick's friends

arrived for a while, and, with the increase in tourists, summer was very busy.

The leaves were turning on the bushes when Nick's last log, the ridgepole, was heaved into place. He and Chris then planned some hikes. First Nick wanted to go off on his own for a few days, taking us dogs with him. He figured it would be easier to canoe across the lake instead of going around the edge as Chris always did, but Max had never been in a canoe before. I was put in the boat first as I was calm and used to boats. Then Max was encouraged in and tied so he couldn't move too much. His body language and the expression on his face were quite comical!

Of course he soon realized that nothing was going to hurt him and he settled down. Nick took us away with him and we camped out for a couple of days, just the three of us. It was very peaceful.

Our last hike was during one of those late summer spells where the sky is blue but there's a coolness to the air, presaging autumn. Chris joined us on this trip. We started with loaded packs and headed up one of the trails that Chris had made to the north, where we had often gone before for a day hike. This time, however, we continued into new territory where there were no trails at all. Chris and Nick had talked about trying to cross a mountain and drop down into the valley where Chris used to live when Lonesome first came into her life.

Chris could not keep up with Nick. He was getting quite frustrated and she was getting more and more exhausted. We had to dip into a valley full of forest that had once been burned. The country

was littered with branchy windfalls all tangled up with bushes, and we dogs had terrible trouble trying to get our packs through it all. Chris was not managing much better.

We slowly climbed up the far side of the valley into more open ground and found a little alpine lake not far below the summit of the mountain we were hoping to cross. It was almost sundown so we made camp there, but we were away early the next morning. Once again, Chris lagged pitifully behind. Max forged ahead with Nick, but I have to admit I preferred Chris's much slower pace. Finally we reached the top of the mountain. Chris exclaimed over the panoramic view—and, you've guessed it—went absolutely gaga over some silly little plants she found there.

The plan was to drop over the far side of the mountain, but although the route had looked quite easy on the map, we were confronted by a cliff that was easily the height of four human houses.

"I don't think we can get the dogs down there," said Nick carefully.

Max and Chris near where they saw the fourteen bull caribou.

Actually Max and I probably could have managed it with no trouble if our packs had been taken off and lowered by ropes, as Chris had done on occasion in other places. Nick really meant that he didn't think Chris would be able to manage it; he was just being diplomatic. So we had to abandon our plans and turn back home.

Chris stayed at Nuk Tessli alone after Nick left, and she managed to dodge the wild fall winds and put most of the roof on the new cabin. There was a great deal of work to do inside—floors and wall insulation and so on, but now that the roof was on, some of these tasks could be done during the winter. Snow already lay on the ground when we hiked back over the mountains to go out for our fall Book Tour.

Nick, Taya and Max backpacking with the mountain they were trying to cross over in the background.

9

HARRY

WE PREPARE FOR THE MOUNTAINS

BADGER SEEMED ON THE VERGE OF SNOOZING AGAIN, BUT TAYA'S STORY was so interesting, I didn't want him to stop.

"Is that it?" I asked. "Isn't there any more to Taya's story? What about Max?"

Badger opened a bleary eye. "Hold your horses, young pup," he grumbled.

I backed off and thought about those words for a minute.

"I don't have any horses," I said.

"It's just an expression," said Badger irritably. "It's what humans say when they want you to have patience."

I thought for another moment. Badger seemed to be the one who was impatient. "What's that got to do with horses?" I finally ventured.

Badger sighed and curled up into his favourite snoozeball. "I don't really know," he replied. "If I had a cookie for every weird thing that humans say or do, I would be wallowing in treats. Now it's time for a nap."

"When will you tell me the next part of the story?"

"Probably not until we get into the mountains," Badger muttered sleepily.

"Into the mountains?" I said excitedly. "You mean we are actually going to the place that Taya talked about soon? When?"

"Any day now, I expect," Badger said with a yawn. "I keep telling you we are going to go there. Haven't you noticed all the piles of Stuff that have been accumulating?"

"Well, I have, but Chris spends half her life messing with Stuff. It always seems to make her so cranky."

"You're right, there." Badger's voice was muffled by his fur. "The more Stuff she gets, the crankier she becomes."

"If she hates it so much," I said, voicing something that had been bothering me for quite a while, "why on earth does she have it?"

"Who knows," Badger muttered. "Now let me have my nap or I'll be the one getting cranky."

Chris spent most of the next day loading all the boxes, sacks, tools and her chainsaw into the van. It was jammed to the roof.

"Is there going to be room for us?" I whispered to Badger. I didn't want to get in Chris's way when she was in such a bad mood.

"We'll have to squeeze into a very small space," Badger explained, "But it won't be for long. And when we get into the mountains, Chris's bad temper will evaporate like mist off the river, and life will be fantastic once again. Just ho—"

"Hold my horses," I chuckled delightedly, pleased that I had learned a bit more humanspeak.

"Maybe before we go you could tell me a bit more of the Wilderness Dog Saga? Please, please?"

Badger sighed. "Okay," he said. "But after I've had my nap. Max is the next canine to continue the story."

"Why? Did something happen to Taya? What...?" The words were tumbling out of my mouth faster than I could think. But Badger ignored me—he was already snoring, or at least pretending to, and I knew I would get nothing more out of him until he was ready. That evening, however, when Chris was already in her bed, Badger and I remained on top of the bank as the spring scents wafted up the slope in the mild evening air. And Badger continued the Wilderness Dog Saga in the words Max had repeated to his successors, who had in turn passed the stories down to Badger who was now telling these tales to me.

10

MAX

MY LIFE AS A WILDERNESS DOG

I WAS STILL QUITE YOUNG WHEN I HURT MY LEG. IT WAS DURING THE year after Nick started to build Chris's third cabin. I would have been about eighteen dog years old. We had spent the winter at Nuk Tessli and snowshoed out at the end of March for a spring Book Tour and shopping trip. We started to hike back into the mountains, but it had been a heavy snow year and we ran into difficulties with rotten snow well below the treeline, and had to turn back. Chris and I might have managed—Chris floundered around on snowshoes—but Taya was having a terrible time. Even when Chris put Taya's pack on top of her own, once we reached the steeper climb, Taya's heavy body and short legs were getting her nowhere. She was only sixty-three, but she seemed to have a lot less energy than she should. So we had to regroup at the Cabin-in-the-Bog. Chris's lake and Nimpo Lake were both open; rather than wait a couple of weeks before we could hike in for sure, Chris decided that we would fly.

While we were travelling and staying in the Cabin-in-the-Bog, we dogs were always kept tied and taken for walks on leads; we were let off only on rare occasions. This was mightily frustrating for all three of us; it must drive city dogs and their humans nuts to have restrictions like that full-time. At the Cabin-in-the-Bog, we were chained at night and anytime Chris was inside, but when we went for a hike up the logging road and away from Chicken, Chris often let one of us roam free. It was my turn to be off the leash, and I was so thankful I was tearing about like a spring bunny. Beside the logging road were a number of slash piles; I was hopping about over the branches when suddenly there was a sharp pain at the top joint in my back leg, right where it joined the body. Chris turned back at my yelp—she had never heard a noise like that from me before. I held the back leg up and hopped along on three paws, but soon I was able to put the leg down again. In the couple more days that we spent at the Cabin-in-the-Bog, the pain diminished, and I was soon walking more or less normally.

I absolutely hate flying! So does Chris. The pilot would always look disgusted when he had to help Chris force me into the plane. His temper was not improved when I cried all the time that we were in the air. He was almost as disgusted with Chris. He was impatient with anyone who didn't enjoy being disconnected from the world while being crammed into a little metal box with hardly enough room to breathe. But once we were on solid ground again, how happy we all were. We could look forward to a long and enjoyable summer in the mountains before we had to go back into the noise and stink and tied-up hassles of the world beyond the wilderness.

Although Chris had finished putting the roof on the new cabin at the end of winter, she still had to install the floor, window frames and a door, and insulate the walls. She had a bit of help from various Wwoofers who came throughout the summer, but mostly she picked away at the work alone. Thanks to her Book Tours, she now had quite a few more tourists than when she started at Nuk Tessli, and these visitors cut into her cabin-building time.

Then there were the trips we took for ourselves. One time we hiked to a very high lake underneath a glacier. Even though it was the middle of summer, this lake was still mostly frozen. As we climbed over the moraine and looked down on the lake, we saw movement on the ice. Once again Chris grabbed Taya and me before we could start chasing the animal, so we could do nothing but watch. Across the far side of the lake was Wolf. She had heard us coming and was staring at us. By her feet was something she had dropped. Deciding we were not an immediate threat, she picked up her prize—a lump of Caribou, according to the scent that came on the wind—and trotted off across the frozen lake. Once in a while she would drop the meat and turn to look at us, and then pick it up and continue. We watched her for quite a while as she grew smaller and smaller, climbing the big icefield next to the glacier. When she reached the rockslide above it, she blended in and disappeared. The wind was not in our favour by this time and, when we could no longer see or smell Wolf, we dogs lost interest and Chris let us off the leads again.

During the summer, although I could walk well most of the time, the pain in my leg kept flaring up. It was particularly bad after I had been swimming. When we went out in the fall, Chris very reluctantly took me to the vet. A lot of humans think authors are rich, but although Chris was getting quite famous (thanks to Lonesome's bestselling book, I might add), she complained about Money constantly. We all lived without luxuries. There was no fancy food or toys, no carpets or commercially made dog beds or leads for us—just wooden boxes stuffed with rags and slough grass for our sleeping places, and old ropes slipped through our collars for when we had to be tied. Chris's various skins were generally obtained from thrift stores, and she was sometimes given other people's castoffs. The tourist business brought some income, but she always complained that it was barely enough to cover the cost of planes and the fees she had to pay to the government. Living in the mountains was definitely not a way to make Money. So a trip to the vet meant a big expense that Chris could ill afford. Especially when the vet told her I would have to have something called a cruciate ligament operation, which was going to be pricey.

She decided to arrange for me to have the surgery done at the end of that fall's Book Tour. Afterward she was going to have to keep me on a lead for a long time. No jumping in and out of vehicles during that period either, so it wouldn't have been very practical for me to convalesce while travelling, particularly as I hated being in the truck almost as much as being in the plane. She reckoned the whole process could be better managed when we were home.

The nearest vet to our wilderness cabin was in Williams Lake. Most dogs hated going to the vet, but although I am frightened of many things, I like being there. People there have always been friendly, and I walk in with great pride and confidence. Chris had to leave me at the vet's overnight while I had the operation, and her eyes widened when she picked me up the next day. My whole leg had been shaved and bandaged. I could walk perfectly well on three legs as I had done it for several weeks, but in fact I often touched my bad foot onto the ground.

While we were at the vet's, Chris also took Taya in to be looked at. Taya had been moving more slowly, and she often licked her stomach when she lay down. When he examined her, the vet's face fell.

"She has cancer," he said. "She either needs a big operation, or she should be put to sleep."

"An operation is out," Chris said. "I can't afford it, and Taya must be at least ten years old by now. It wouldn't be worth it."

She and the vet left the other thought hanging between them.

"Trouble is," Chris continued, "Max is such a wimp in my truck or a plane that I really need Taya with him to help keep him calm after his operation. Is she in a lot of pain? Perhaps I can get some painkillers to make her a bit more comfortable for a while."

So it was a somewhat ragged crew that arrived back at the Cabin-in-the-Bog. I was pretty dopey with drugs for the first day, but then I started perking up. Chris told me she was not allowed to take me for long walks but Taya needed to get out.

"As a special treat," she said, "I am not going to leave you tied outside, but will shut you up in the cabin while we are gone. We won't be long."

As soon as she and Taya were out of sight, I panicked. I jumped onto the bed and off again, I clawed at the walls and ripped out the newspaper that had been stuffed into the gaps, and I chewed the cord of a lamp. Chris found me panting and wild eyed and in a terrible state.

"So much for keeping you calm," she said. "Let's hope you haven't done any damage to your leg."

My leg was fine. I couldn't understand what all the fuss was about. Chris spent some hours stuffing the newspapers back in the cracks—winters on the Chilcotin are generally pretty cold.

Obviously we couldn't hike home, so once again we were waiting for a suitable plane—one fitted with skis. In a few days, Chris brightened and told us that a pilot had sent her a message that he was ready to go. The ice was good early that year—it wasn't even time for the humans' midwinter celebrations. I moaned and groaned in the plane, but looked forward to being off the lead as soon as we got home. However, that was not to be.

"I've got to keep you on the lead for a month," Chris told me. "You're not allowed to run."

I couldn't believe this! I had been kept tied up for far too long already, in my opinion. Chris was not to be persuaded otherwise, however. Three times a day she and I struggled at either end of a rope while she exercised me. Both our tempers escalated. Then one day, I gave a big yank, Chris's feet slid on the ice, and over she crashed, dropping the lead in the process. I galloped away.

"Oh well," she said. "It's three weeks since your operation—whatever damage is going to happen has been done. We just won't go for long walks for a while. Taya is quite content to sit around in any case."

She let me run free after that, and I never had any more trouble with that leg.

Chris didn't have time to take us on long walks anyway. As soon as she had broken the trail to the outhouse and cut the waterhole in the lake, she busied herself by putting a rough sleeping platform of planks into the new cabin, along with a kitchen counter. There was no other furniture in there apart from the stove, but she lugged over a foam mattress and pillow, a few pots and pans and a bit of food, and moved in.

"It's a pain living in a cabin while you are building it," she said to us. "I've done it with every house that I have made so far, but I don't want to waste wood by putting a fire in two stoves. Finishing the interior is going to be my winter project."

She always told people how much she hated building and carpentry work, and indeed she was usually grumpy while she was doing it. But for someone who hates it, she has sure spent a lot of her life occupied with it.

"It's the only way I can afford what I want," she would always tell people when they asked. If she had been as efficient as Nick, she might have felt differently about the work, but she struggled with the slightest project and everything seemed to take her so long.

ONE OTHER MAJOR EVENT HAPPENED IN OUR LIVES THAT WINTER. IT'S something I will never forget as long as I live.

Apart from the fur that was shorter on one leg than the rest of me, you would never know I had gone through an operation. Taya, however, was not getting any better. She was listless and her ears drooped. Despite the medicine that Chris gave her, she was obviously in pain. Chris had been looking at her sadly for some time and one day she whispered, "Sorry, Taya, but it's time."

She dug the shotgun out of the cupboard, tied me up, put a treat into her pocket and took Taya out on the ice, out of sight of the cabin. I heard a shot and Chris came running back, bawling her eyes out. She couldn't bury Taya, as the ground was frozen solid. She knew she could not leave the carcass on the ice either and would have to take it well into the bush. If Wolf did not eat it, Bear would find the remains in spring. He likes the taste best when it is well rotted. When Bear has a cache of meat, he will defend it from everyone including humans even though the last thing most humans would want to do is take it from him. Bear doesn't know that, though. So Taya had to be taken to a place where no human would ever walk. Chris was too upset to do anything that day, however. I tried to console her and she gave me lots of cuddles. I would miss Taya, too.

That night the Nuk Tessli wind started with a vengeance. It screamed along the lake and hit the new cabin in great, shuddering gusts. It sounded scary but Nick had made the walls strong. Chris had tied the roof tightly to the main structure, and the cabin would withstand many storms like this. It was, however, impossible to go out onto the lake.

The wind kept up for three days and nights, mixing blowing snow from the lake with snow that fell from the sky. All this time, Taya lay out on the ice. Struggling to the outhouse and back was all the hiking Chris could manage.

It's always a relief when the wind drops after one of these storms. In the new, wind-blasted world, we stepped on to the achingly silent lake with a toboggan, ropes, and an axe. Chris was wearing snow-shoes. The snow on the ice had been blown into bumps and ridges like frozen waves. Taya's carcass was almost buried and as rigid as the ice on which she lay. Chris chopped her out and loaded her onto the toboggan. Tourists liked to walk on a trail that Chris had built around the lake, so she had to drag the toboggan for a very long way before we reached a point of land that the trail bypassed. She then struggled through the bush a short distance with Taya's remains. Taya would have a natural funeral. She would feed a number of grateful creatures before she finally dissolved into components that nourished the earth. Chris was very quiet as we returned home.

When we went out that spring, Chris started looking for another dog. Taya had been such a great pack mate, the first person Chris contacted was Patty to see if she had any other canines that she wanted to pass on. To Chris's amazement, Patty was now in a senior citizens' home. Given Patty's liveliness and attitude to life, this was very hard to believe. But it was true. And she had parted with all her dogs.

Patty knew of one of Taya's descendants, however, who had been taken by a truck driver. The truck driver found the dog too much trouble. His excuse was that he was away a lot and did not want to leave her tied. When loose she would always run onto the busy highway in front of his house. Chris should have read between the lines a bit, but she was so thrilled to think she might have another Taya, she accepted at once, sight unseen.

We had been told that Ginger was a red Husky and a very pretty animal, but she was far from attractive the first time we saw her. She had been delivered to the house where Chris usually stayed when she went to Williams Lake. Ginger was chained to a pillar that supported the roof of an open-sided shed; behind her were a large boat and a car. She was a Husky shape, more or less, but was an unusual colour, being as orange as a red fox. She had a pointed nose, pricked-up ears, and a tail that curled tightly over her back. This might sound as though she was as attractive as promised, but her tail seemed to have been put on crooked, and it flopped to one side. She was also shedding great gobs of fur, and was, moreover, very vocal about her tied status. She didn't bark—she screamed. She gave me a cursory sniff but mostly howled and jumped about. Chris tried to make friends, and there was certainly nothing aggressive in Ginger's demeanor, but I could see that Chris at once had misgivings about this dog. However, she felt she needed another pack animal, and she had promised to take her, so when we arrived at the Cabin-in-the-Bog, Ginger was with us. Because she had not been trained to pack, Chris thought it wiser to fly back to Nuk Tessli that summer.

In fact, Ginger settled down quite well. When she got excited about something, she would give this screaming yodel, but that didn't happen very often. As her coat grew back she proved indeed to be a handsome bitch. We were never very close friends, but we tolerated each other and never had any fights.

The tourists loved her. She was a lot more demonstrative about her affections to them than I was—I would wait to be called and then go over for a pat. Ginger, however, was immediately in everyone's face. Literally. Her first greeting was to lick the tourists' mouths. She was so pretty that strangers went gaga over her, and they thought this behaviour very cute.

"Don't let her do that!" Chris always exclaimed in horror. She and I knew what the tourists didn't—that Ginger's favourite snack was human poop. Most tourists never figured this out. We would be on a hike and someone would need to go to the bathroom. They would work their way into the bushes and come back delightedly praising Ginger for "guarding" them while they went alone into the forest. They never saw what Ginger did after they pulled up their pants. Even when Chris told them what Ginger had been up to they never really believed that such a pretty dog could be so disgusting. They still let Ginger lick them in the face.

Ginger hated water. I hadn't liked it at first but was by now a proficient swimmer, and when I plunged into the lake to cross the occasional inlet, Ginger would run the long way round along the shore. She tried this with the river, but of course ran down the first bank and found nowhere to cross. She came back to the lake and screamed. Chris simply kept paddling along in the canoe and calling, knowing Ginger would have to figure it out sooner or later. Ginger eventually plunged in. But even after that day she never swam voluntarily and did everything she could to avoid going into the water.

Except on one memorable occasion.

Not far from where Taya and I had seen Wolf crossing the glacier was another lake, a little bit lower, where some people were building a cabin. Chris loved to hike in this area, and she had

Ginger

spent a long time trying to figure out the best route to get there. This was not an easy task for her. She now knew quite a bit about getting around in trackless bush, but her sense of direction was even worse than her sense of smell. Part of the country between our cabin and theirs was a flattish area full of shallow lakes and bogs. Chris would get glimpses of a certain mountain, or the sun, and try to hike in a straight line, but soon she would encounter one of the lakes with no idea as to which would be the best way round. Sometimes she would fight through the short scrubby trees that grew along the edge for quite some time to find that a much larger stretch of water was going to make her go back the way she came. Then she would have to retrace her steps and fight around the lake's other side. While she was figuring out the best way to go, she would mark her routes with coloured plastic tape that fluttered in the wind; if she chose wrongly she would have to pick up all the bits of tape again. This all took a lot of time. If she'd followed Ginger and myself, we could have found the route very quickly by using our noses, but it took several different hikes, many of them packing a camp, before Chris finally put together a route that she liked. Then we would carry tools—an axe, bow saw and clippers, and clear out and mark the route permanently. When we climbed higher and the country became more open, the route had to be marked with piles of rocks.

Between work at Chris's own cabins and work with tourists, there wasn't time to make the trail all at once. In fact, it took years, and would not have been finished so quickly even then if it hadn't been for the help of a lot of Wwoofers.

A Wwoofer called Naomi was with us when we camped on the beach, near to where the cabin was going to be erected. There were no trees taller than ourselves beside this lake—it was too high and windblown; instead, Chris explained, the cabin had been built in a log builder's yard and was to be flown in. The shorter logs would be strapped to the outside of small planes, and the longer ones would be slung from a helicopter. We had barely arrived at the site before the first plane arrived. After that, the morning was bedlam with noisy aircraft and people coming and going. At one time there were twenty-five humans on site and it took only a few days to put the building together.

"What a difference to the way I built my cabins!" Chris said. "And what a contrast to this lake's history. Up to now hardly any humans have been here at all. This place is never going to be wild anymore."

A few weeks later, Chris decided we should visit the lake again. We would have it to ourselves this time. She would do more work on the trail on the way up, stay a night or two, and work on the trail coming down again. One part of the route still had not been sorted out, so on our way up she took off all our packs and went back and forth with her ribbons to determine the best way to go. We were still in the forest, and in a swampy area we came upon a great, stinky mud hole. Even Chris could smell it.

"Phee-uw!" she said. "That's powerful. It must be a bear wallow."

But Ginger was thrilled and she rolled and rolled in it until she was black with aromatic mud.

We arrived at the cabin after sundown, when the light was fading fast. Chris quickly found some wood and put a fire in a pit that sat in front of the deck, collected some water, and started to cook her supper. She pulled the dog food out of our packs and prepared to give us our evening meal. Both of us were looking at her expectantly.

Suddenly, not far along the lakeshore, there was a clink of loose rock: something was walking toward us. Instantly, we dogs spun around and charged. We could smell it now—Big Bull Caribou. It was too dark for Chris to see him, and she would never have been able to negotiate that terrain in the dark, so she could do nothing but wait

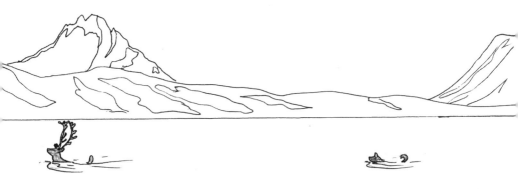

at the cabin. Ginger and I ran for quite a while and eventually Bull Caribou plunged into the water. Although the land was dark, the lake still reflected the paler sky. According to her story, which we heard repeated to a number of different humans, Chris was apparently able to watch the drama through her binoculars.

I dove right in after Caribou and swam strongly after him. Caribou are excellent swimmers and I could not gain any ground. Imagine my surprise to hear a splash behind me. Ginger had also plunged into the lake. I turned my head toward her, but despite the excitement of the chase, she really didn't like water and she turned back to the shore. I hesitated and almost followed her, but Caribou was too tempting. He was paddling steadily across the lake. He had really big horns, and at the other end of his body, his short, stubby tail stuck up out of the water like a little flag. I paddled steadily behind. I was neither gaining on him nor losing ground.

About three-quarters of the way across the lake, I decided that maybe Ginger had the right idea, and I turned for home. And, would you believe it, but Caribou turned back as well. So there we were, both swimming at about the same speed, slowly crossing over the lake again. Once I got to the shore, he veered off up the lake, still paddling strongly. Chris could not stop me from chasing things, but she knew by this time that I would always come back to her. When she heard my feet rattle the rocks along the shore, she called my name. It was quite dark by this time and she could not see me. She was relieved when I climbed into the small circle of firelight.

Ginger had been back for a while but Chris had been so busy watching the drama on the lake that she hadn't taken the time to pull the dog chains out of our packs. When Ginger had returned, Chris had simply tossed the wet dog into the cabin and shut the door. When I arrived, she tied me up and then went to retrieve Ginger.

"Wow," she said, reeling back as she opened the door, "Ginger, you stink! Not only do you smell of wet dog—you also reek of wet bear!"

Needless to say, we dogs were chained outside for the rest of our stay there.

TOWARD THE END OF SUMMER, A TOURIST BROUGHT HER OWN HUSKY to Nuk Tessli. This was a designer Husky, a purebred, pampered pet with brushed fur and different coloured eyes. She lived inside her owner's house and had never done a scrap of work in her life. Chris allowed her to go into the visitor's cabin with them. She asked the tourists to keep the dog off the bed, but every time we looked in the window, that's where the Husky was sitting.

Chris took them all for a walk. Ginger and I were not carrying packs and we were running free. The tourists kept their bitch on a lead.

"You can let her off," said Chris. "My dogs are pretty friendly."

"I am not so sure," the tourist said. "Ginger has a look in her eye. I've seen it before."

Chris shrugged. She couldn't see any problem, but later on, it was proved that the tourist was right.

Ginger's first canine victim was a little old female pooch at a friend's place near the float plane base. It was winter, and dark, and all us canines were outside. Suddenly there was a huge fight. Ginger had the little pooch in her jaws and was shaking her furiously. The humans rushed out of the house and rescued the little dog, but there was a lot of blood and she had to be taken to the vet. When

Chris mentioned this to Patty the next time she saw her, she said that Ginger might have some Wolf in her. In any case, she was an alpha female, and they often attacked other bitches. Chris was a little more careful after that, but there was another incident, with another friend's dog, also a female. Ginger was always perfectly friendly with male dogs and with human beings, but Chris decided she didn't want to deal with that kind of behaviour, so she advertised in the little store that stood near the float plane base. *Pretty red Husky, loves people, but not good with other animals. Attacks female dogs. Needs a home away from town.*

She received a reply from a lady who lived not far away from Nimpo, on the First Nations reserve. When Chris delivered Ginger to her, the woman's face lit up with awe.

"She's so beautiful," she said. Ginger would obviously be loved.

A few weeks later, Chris was in the store again. Hidden by a wall of groceries, she overheard two people having a conversation. They were from the reserve, and they were talking about a new dog that was living there.

"She's killing all the other dogs," one woman said.

There was no proof that this was Ginger, but it seemed very likely. Chris slunk out of the store without saying a word.

CHRIS AND I SPENT THE WINTER ALONE. WE HIKED FOR MANY HOURS, climbing high into the mountains behind the cabins. Chris mostly travelled on skis or snowshoes while I bounded around through the snow.

We had a lot of fun together. When I was a puppy, Chris would sometimes give me an old fuzzy bit of cloth to chew and pull. (It was actually the little coat that she'd got from the thrift store for me, which of course I very soon grew out of.) I never lost my love of fuzzy things, though, and when we were skiing, I would filch Chris's hat or gloves from her pocket and run off into the unbroken snow with them. She could not travel fast through that deep, loose stuff, and when she struggled close, I would grab the nice fuzzy thing and run with it again. Chris would get mad, but it was so much fun for me I couldn't resist.

In the spring we went on another Book Tour. We had a number of friends in the towns where Chris gave her slideshows, and we usually stayed with them when we passed through.

One family lived on the far side of the Vancouver mega-tropolis in a city called Burnaby. Miriam and Len enjoyed animals but the only ones they normally kept in their house were cats.

"These two are part of our family," Miriam explained. "But this mother and her kittens are being fostered from the SPCA. When the kittens are old enough, the whole family will all be offered up for adoption."

The animals were always drastically put out when we dogs arrived. We would be tied by the back door under an upper deck, the only place in the yard that was out of the rain—and it rains a lot in winter down there. The deck was the usual way the cats used to go in and out of the house but they were too frightened to go past us (with good reason, I might add). There was a convenient pillar that supported the steps up to the deck, which made a handy spot for fastening our chains. Chris would sleep on the pullout couch in the room just inside the door, so she could yell at us if we barked.

Taya had a great story about the time she and Sport stayed there. One morning Chris woke to find Taya lying on the mat in the porch as usual, her chain still fastened to the pillar. The pillar, however, was no longer supporting the steps. A raccoon had come into the yard during the night, and Taya had lunged for it, ripping the pillar away from the steps and taking it with her. The white paint on it had hidden the rot at the top and at the bottom. The raccoon climbed a tree to get out of the way and Taya went back to her mat, dragging the chain and the post with her. The funny thing was—Chris never heard a thing!

When Miriam found out that Chris was looking for another dog, she suggested we go to their local SPCA. We drove the short distance to the rescue facility. What a cacophony of barking issued from the kennels! There must have been a hundred dogs in there, most of them jammed three to a cage. They were all fit and well fed and full of beans. They all wanted to be noticed more than the next guy, and so they had to make the most noise.

Chris left me tied to the fence outside for the time being but the door to the office was open and I could hear her explain to the staff member the kind of dog she wanted.

"It has to be a good size to be able to carry a pack," she said. "It should not be an excessive barker." (This would be hard to determine in an SPCA yard where most dogs had nothing much to do but bark.) "It should be friendly with people, and ideally it should have a good winter coat." Her voice was cut off as she went farther into the building, and after a while, she came out leading a brownish speckled bitch with long droopy ears that hung like slabs of sliced liver. She was friendly and didn't bark much, but she had very short fur.

"Max," said Chris. "Meet Tessa."

"I was actually quite taken with a Rottweiller-Chow cross," she explained later to Len and Miriam. "He's a stocky, boisterous animal with a very appealing face. But while I was thinking about trying him out, a woman and two children were already putting him on a lead and taking him away."

Chris looked at Tessa a little doubtfully. "The big problem as far as I am concerned will be her short fur. But she seems a lovely dog otherwise; I guess I could always put a coat on her if I had to."

Our next destination on the Book Tour was Vancouver Island. One of the people Chris stayed with lived near a very long beach not far from Tofino. Chris was not only thrilled to visit this beach, she was also ecstatic to find that she had gloriously sunny weather, a rare occurrence in this place by all accounts. Moreover, Chris had the beach to herself for several hours, something that she revelled in. She always maintained how hard it was to get alone time while on a Book Tour.

We walked for miles. I had the best fun running down to the sea (with its horrible-tasting water!) and up to the edge of the trees where all manner of debris was washed up—some human discards, but also some nice rotten bits of shellfish and the like. Tessa had a great time to begin with, but it was not long before she started to lag behind, and it soon became obvious that she was in quite a lot of pain. Chris was surprised at this—Tessa was supposed to be fairly young still. The vets at the SPCA had told Chris she was fine, and the dog exercisers had complained how hard she pulled when taken for a walk. When we got back to the truck, however, Tessa could no longer jump in, and Chris had to lift her into the back.

She wondered if it would be a temporary thing. She took her to a vet on the Island, who examined her thoroughly but could not find much wrong with her. However, she found some stiffening in the shoulders and figured she might have been hit by a car at some point. Chris had already become attached to the dog, for she had a lovely nature, but she could not keep a dog who was unable to walk long distances and carry a pack. Very reluctantly, she took Tessa back to the Burnaby SPCA. Tessa would make a great house pet for someone, but she was not tough enough for us.

And whom should Chris see when she looked in the pens again but the Rottweiler-Chow mix.

"The family with children had decided he is too much dog for them, so he is still available," explained the SPCA person. "No one knows much of his background. He was found wandering the city streets. We think he's about three years old."

Behind the pens was a small exercise yard. Chris turned me and the Rottweiller-Chow into it to see how we got on. I was not particularly taken with him, and he largely ignored me. He sniffed and peed on a few things—and then he peed on me! Anyway, Chris decided to take him. He had not yet been neutered, which the SPCA wanted to do, so Chris was told she would be able to pick him up in a few days.

Chris and I had a few more slideshows to give, and then we went back to stay with Len and Miriam. When we picked up the new dog, he was wearing the same kind of bucket collar I had worn after my first operation. He didn't care—very few things seemed to bother him. He didn't like being injected with his little tracker, though. He whimpered while the SPCA person tried to get it under his skin.

We had gone to the SPCA in Len's van and when we arrived at his house, the new dog and I were tied under the porch in the backyard. We were chained far enough apart so that we could not reach each other. In a short while, Bucket Head started to bark. He was announcing his presence to a couple of dogs in the yard next door. They were barking back. Most humans dislike that kind of racket, and Chris was doing her best to stop it, but without much luck. Bucket Head looked as if he was going to be a handful.

We were leaving to head back north the following day. Bucket Head had not yet ridden in Chris's truck. She took me for a pee walk first and tied me to the back of the truck. Then she fetched Bucket Head.

Now I hated that truck, but when I saw Bucket Head coming toward it, I let him know in no uncertain terms that this was my vehicle. Bucket Head was a street dog, and his first reaction to my bid for supremacy was to fight. We had a tremendous blowup that resulted in me breaking a weak link in my chain and getting away.

Wow! I had not been allowed to run free for some time and it was a lot of fun. I ran up into other people's yards and Chris, having hastily tied Bucket Head, was running after me. I let her catch me after a while, even though I knew I was going to have to go in the truck. I was put in the back, and Bucket Head was tied to the passenger door handle and allowed to sit on the front seat. At last we set off—and Bucket Head finally made Chris laugh. He would sit with his bucket jammed against the windshield, fascinated by the movement on the road.

"Well," Chris chuckled. "I think you've got a name. You wear that Bucket with such panache! Bucket Head is a bit too long, so I'll call you Bucky."

We had more slideshows to give on the way home, and at one place our host drove us high up on a logging road and took us for a lovely long hike up into the hills. The snow had long gone from the lower areas, but high up a few patches still lay among the trees. Chris at once turned me loose. She knew I couldn't get into much trouble up there.

She turned to Bucky. "You've been with us for over a week, now," she said.

Bucky

"We're a long way from any houses here. I think I can let you run free as well."

Bucky's medical collar had long ago been destroyed by his habit of barging into everything in his way, so he was no longer wearing it. He accepted his freedom, as he did most things, with indifference, but he was soon enjoying sticking his head down and examining all the smells. Mouse lived among the roots in the thawing ground, and Squirrel and Marten scampered about in the trees.

We reached a high point where our host proposed that she and Chris have lunch. I was never given any food in the middle of the day and was quite used to lying quietly while humans ate. But Bucky went insane. As soon as he saw a piece of food, he jumped all over whoever was holding it and tried to grab it. He would have taken food out of the humans' mouths if he could.

Chris of course tied him up at once. I tried to tell him that he was going to be well fed, that he wasn't on the street anymore. (I didn't mention that, after his time at the SPCA, his figure was quite rotund and he was definitely not starving now.) But I guess he still remembered being hungry and stealing any food that he could find as fast as he possibly could.

On the way down, he pulled and yanked and was not very comfortable for Chris to walk with so she let him off the lead again. Eventually, we arrived at our host's car. A grassy area stretched below us. It had been empty when we had arrived, but now a group of horses grazed in the middle. Bucky took one look and was off.

He barked and barked at the horses' heels. They pranced and tried to kick him, but then they did the worst thing possible, at least as far as Chris was concerned: they suddenly wheeled round and ran. Bucky thought it was fantastic. They galloped across the field and into the forest. And tubby little Bucky ran after them.

I would have gone, too, but I was just a bit too slow on the uptake and Chris had grabbed my collar. I was put into the car.

"A new dog like that, in a strange place," Chris wailed. "How ever will I get him back?"

Our host knew the country fairly well and decided to drive lower down and see if she could find where they would come to the road. She took me with her.

"I'll try to follow the horses," Chris said.

When they met up again, she told her host the story. The horses had galloped into the trees at the edge of the field. Their hard feet had made plenty of marks on the soft forest floor, so their progress was easy to follow. But then they split up and Chris did not know which way to go. She could not find dog tracks anywhere. She walked for some time—then, to her great surprise, there was a chubby, wheezing Bucky coming up through the forest toward her. She was amazed that he made the attempt on his own to come back to where he had last seen her. She grabbed him and put the lead on and went back to the grassy area to wait for her friend. Bucky was never again let off the lead until we arrived back into our mountains.

As usual, we spent a couple of days at the Cabin-in-the-Bog while we organized freight and flights. Chris first tied Bucky to the tree beside the kennel where Taya, and later Ginger, had stayed. Bucky, however, proceeded to bark nonstop, so Chris brought him up to the porch. He quieted down there, and after a while she felt we both could be left while she went to the post office to pick up her mail. As soon as she had gone, Bucky fretted and pushed around. The warped door of the cabin never did close properly, and he managed to get inside. As he moved about, he inadvertently nudged the door shut, and he couldn't get out again. When Chris came back she was horrified to see that he was no longer in the porch—at first she thought he'd escaped. Then she heard banging inside the cabin, and she wrenched the door open. Out tumbled Bucky, a small bit of silver foil stuck to his lip. Chris had left a pound of butter on the counter and, although it was quite high and his chain must have held him back somewhat, he had just been able to reach it. He had eaten the lot, silver foil and all. Within minutes of being let out, he threw it all up again.

11

HARRY

THE MOUNTAINS AT LAST

THERE WAS NO MORE TIME FOR BADGER TO CONTINUE WITH MAX AND Bucky's story that night, for early the following morning we went to the place I'd heard so much about, the fabled Nuk Tessli mountains. It was barely past first light when Chris stuffed a few more things in the van and pulled the River Cabin's wooden door closed. She slipped a stick into the catch, something she didn't normally do, but Badger explained that once in a while, the door was opened by wind and the stick would prevent that. We would be away, apparently, for a very long time.

As Badger had warned me, we were jammed into a very tiny space in the back of the van. The journey was not far, however, and soon Chris let us out. I was longing to explore this new place, but we were not allowed to run loose. We were beside a big lake, and in front of us was a wharf. Sitting atop their own reflections beside the wharf were three small airplanes wearing watershoes.

"Just as Taya described," I said, grinning excitedly.

Chris lugged a pile of Stuff along the wharf to the plane. A cheerful man was chatting with her and stowing the objects inside the plane's body. It was nothing like the aircraft I had flown in from Vancouver to Anahim—it was much tinier and looked light as Chickadee and not a lot bigger, either. Its spindly legs ended in the great boat-like feet that Badger called "floats."

The van was only half-emptied when Chris untied our ropes.

"I'll let you park it," Chris said to the pilot. "That way you'll know where it is when you bring in the next load."

She led us along the wharf, which bounced a little as we walked. It gave me a funny feeling to think we were actually floating on the water.

I was now going to take part in the great adventure that I had heard so much about. However, we still had to get into the body of the plane and now that we were closer, it looked very high. The only way to climb in was via three steps made of thin tubes, widely spaced. Even Chris had a problem climbing up them. They seemed to be impossible for dogs to manage. Chris boosted me up, and by scrambling onto the pipes, I was able to get inside. (In fact, I learned to climb ladders all by myself before long.) Badger was much heavier and less nimble, so it took the combined effort of Chris and the pilot to get him in.

If I had thought our space in the van was small, I was not prepared for our allotted section in the plane! Even Badger by himself could not have sat comfortably on the small square of metal floor that was all that was left for us between the piled boxes, but the pilot gave us a shove and slammed the door, and we were in.

Chris looked very unhappy. Badger had told me she did not like to fly, and yet she had a lot more space than we did. She sat next to the pilot. In front of them was a wall of dials and switches, far more than I had ever seen in a car. At the top was a big plastic sign that said (Badger informed me): *Don't press my buttons—I am well-adjusted.*

The pilot was the last to climb aboard. He and Chris put noise protectors on their ears (just as Chris did when she was using her chainsaw) and the plane's motor started. Badger and I had no ear protection, of course, and it was so loud I thought the top of my head was going to lift off. Once we broke free from the water, however, the motor throttled back somewhat.

I expected the air to be smooth, but it was surprisingly bumpy. There were constant little trembles and shakes, and each one seemed to bother Chris a lot. Her face became set and rigid.

"It's just a different kind of car," Badger said. "I can't figure out why Chris has such a problem with it."

I was also quite happy in the plane—a bit uncomfortable because of the lack of room and the noise, but warm enough. Badger stared steadfastly out of the window. I couldn't figure out what was so interesting. All you could see was air and a bit of the plane's wing. Out front, past Chris and the pilot, was a blur of propellor turning so fast it was almost invisible, just like a hummingbird's wing. Nothing to see but sky out that way either. I managed to wriggle around enough so that I could curl up and go to sleep.

I was awoken by a change in the motor noise. The floor of the plane was tilting sideways—we seemed to be going round in a big circle. Then we swooped lower, and suddenly there was a juddering roar. At the same time the plane vibrated briefly, then quite quickly slowed right down. Now the motor was given a little nudge, and it burbled like a boat. There was movement again, but now we swayed to the softer motion of the water. It took a while, but eventually the motor was turned off altogether, and there was a small bump as we drew to a halt.

The first impression was of a huge silence. Then I could hear a bit of a wind and small waves slapping against a rocky shore. The pilot got out and came round to our side of the plane, stood on a float, and opened our door. My nose at once registered pines, lichen-covered rocks still damp from winter, small birds, several unfamiliar plants, a few chunks of needle-covered snow, Mouse, a chimney that hadn't had a fire in it for a while, split firewood, Squirrel, and a big lake full of fresh water. My eyes registered a rough-looking cabin and piles of rocks half-smothered in a straggle of trees and bushes. Then I looked down. There was a long drop down to a tiny, lopsided wharf. Chris had twisted in her seat and was fumbling at our collars to release our ropes. She climbed out and down the ladder. When she stood on the wharf, it whooshed and sank a little under her weight. Water slopped over the lower end—I'd wondered why she had put rubber boots on this morning instead of her usual hiking boots. I found out later that this happened only when the lake was high, as it always was at the beginning of summer.

"Come on, Harry," she cajoled.

I figured I would try and manage the ladder, but I missed all the steps and found myself in the water swimming on top of the sunken dock. I wasn't too worried about that, for I'd been in the river in front of the other cabin many times. I barely bothered to shake myself before I was running on the ground, nose to the earth, mapping out what creatures had been where and when. I expected Badger to follow me, but when I turned around to look for him, I saw he was still in the plane. He was too chicken to jump down. Chris and the pilot had to heave him out. Once on the ground, however, he immediately took charge and showed me around.

It was as Taya had told us. There were three cabins altogether. Chris lived in the new one that Nick had helped her build. It was a little bit away from the wharf, up a steep, rocky trail. Our nice big insulated kennels sat on the porch. Another cabin was closest to the wharf and the third stood farther back in the trees; these, Badger explained, were for the tourists, the people who paid Chris Money to come here. I could smell that Mouse was enjoying the tourists' cabins and certainly not paying anything for the privilege. A tiny building without a door stood back from the two cabins. It smelled of a kind of compost. I recognized the smell, but this one didn't seem to have been used for a while.

"That's just like the little building we have near the River Cabin," I said.

"Yes," Badger explained. "Humans don't usually poop in the woods unless they are a long way from home. They prefer to store it in a hole in the ground." He shrugged but did not give me time to phrase the inevitable question. "No point in asking me why. It's just another weirdo thing that they do," he said.

"In the city they store dog poop, too," I said, glad that I could show Badger that I was paying attention to the Saga. "Remember what Taya told us?"

Badger and I exchanged little sniggers at the thought of human strangeness. Badger was starting to accept me as an equal.

Chris and the pilot unloaded all the Stuff onto dry ground, and the man got back into the plane, chugged his aircraft into the middle of the lake, and flew away. And Badger had been right. Chris was now all smiles. She was a totally different person. Even hauling all the Stuff up the steep little trail and into the cabin could not dispel her good mood. It was amazing, but I felt lighter, too. I wasn't just responding to Chris's mood. The sense of space and freedom here was enormous.

"I don't smell any other fresh human scents at all," I said to Badger. "No Cow or Dog or cars either."

"That's right. There isn't another human being for a whole day's walk in any direction. And apart from the plane, the only way out of here *is* to walk. We will have visitors later, both Wwoofers and tourists, but they almost always fly in like we did."

Chris started to fiddle around with Stuff; then we heard her rattle the stove door and feed wood and kindling into its belly. She popped outside with a bucket, tramped down to the lake and filled it with water, and hauled it into the cabin. Soon the kettle started to sing.

"Sounds like she's going to make her foreign-leaf water," I said to Badger. "She's obviously not going to do anything very active for a while."

I looked at him and tried to judge his mood. Should I ask for more of the story? Would he prefer to have a nap? I decided to risk it.

"Tell me more about Bucky. Is he going to take over the Saga now?"

Badger tried to look cross but he couldn't help but give a little smile. "I thought it wouldn't be long before you asked for the next instalment. No, Max is still the storyteller. Bucky was a canine who had very little thought about anything that didn't concern him directly, and he was not reliable enough to be entrusted with the Saga. I guess he had fun in his own way, but as you will soon hear, not long after he arrived at Nuk Tessli, he had an adventure that nearly cost him his life."

"And are you going to tell it in Max's own words, just like last time?" I asked.

Badger nodded. Goggle-eyed, I settled down to listen.

12

MAX

AND NOW WE'LL RELAX—WITH MAX

ONE OF THE JOBS CHRIS FEELS SHE OUGHT TO DO AT THE BEGINNING OF every season is to check out the trails, especially the bridges she has built to cross various rivers. (If humans could smell properly, she wouldn't need to fix trails because they could find their way no matter how poorly the routes were marked.)

Most of the bridges were easily accessible from the lake, and Chris would travel to them by canoe while we dogs ran along the shore. Some of them needed a bit of repair or adjustment, but as she could carry all the tools in the boat, Chris did not find this work too onerous. Bucky, I should add here, hated water at first more than any other dog I have ever met. None of us liked it to begin with, but we soon learned to enjoy swimming. Bucky was with Chris for two years before he would willingly get wet—and after that you could hardly keep him out of the water. He would chase every last dot of a duck for miles.

One bridge was an hour's hike away, at the top of a steep climb. First we had to cross our lake; it was quicker for Chris to put us all into the canoe and paddle over rather than have us run around the edge. I was perfectly used to being in the canoe by now, and Bucky must have been in boats in his past life as he was quite happy to jump in and sit still.

The first time we hiked up to the bridge, no one was carrying anything—Chris didn't see the point of taking heavy tools unless she was going to need them. The bridge, which was simply a couple of rickety logs propped side by side, had shifted in the spring flood.

"We are going to need rope, a come-along, and various other tools to repair it," she said. "We'll have to make another trip up here."

Before we hiked up to the bridge the second time, Bucky's pack training began. As Chris had initially done with me, Bucky was first given an empty pack. He pretty much ignored it, and after a couple of hikes, Chris padded it with empty dog food bags to give it some bulk so he would get used to being wider.

A few days later, Chris put the tools into her pack— they were too bulky to go in ours—and off we went to fix the bridge. This time, Bucky's

Max and Chris on the bridge before it was washed away.

pack contained a couple of rocks as well as the dog food bags so he could get used to carrying some weight. We dogs were free all day while Chris worked, but Bucky's pack was replaced when we started off for home.

It was quite late when we arrived back beside our lake where the canoe was parked. Just as we reached it, we stumbled upon Moose. Both Bucky and I took off after it. Chris yelled a time or two but you could tell that her heart wasn't in it, as she knew it wouldn't do any good, and her voice soon faded as we gave delicious chase. She had begun to learn that, if she went after us while we were chasing something, it just meant we would get even more excited and be spurred on to run faster. She figured her best policy was to give a token yell or two but then turn and go away in the opposite direction. Usually, we would soon give up the chase and follow her.

And this was what I did. Bucky, however, kept going, his tubby body crashing through the brush. As I headed back home, the noise of his passage faded away. When I got back to where the canoe had been, I saw that Chris had already left. I knew the way home round the lake and arrived not long after Chris. We figured Bucky would soon make it home, too.

But he didn't come.

It had been calm when we had set off in the morning, as it often is at Nuk Tessli, but now the afternoon wind was blowing stiffly down the lake.

"That wind was a bonus to get me home," Chris said. "But I'll never be able to paddle back up the lake against it to the trailhead." She looked up the lake and took a deep breath. "BUUUCK-EEEY!" she yelled. (And she has a good yell, let me tell you!) "BUUUUCK-EEEY!" She turned to me. "He'll never hear me in this wind."

It grew dark. We were due to start hiking to the road the following day—it was to have been Bucky's first real backpacking trip.

"I'll see if he's turned up in the morning," Chris said worriedly. "If not, I'll have to stay here an extra day to look for him and try and order a plane on the radiophone. Otherwise we'll never be out on time for my dentist appointment."

The following morning the wind had died again, and Chris stood on the wharf and called, knowing that her voice would carry well across the water in the calm air. If Bucky were anywhere close to the lake, he would hear it. After a quick breakfast, we jumped into the canoe and paddled to the trailhead, calling and calling, constantly checking the shore around the lake for any movement, but there was no sign of Bucky.

"Perhaps he tried to cross the bridge at the outlet and fell in, and got swept down the river," she said. "If he is still wearing his backpacks they might fill up with water and pull him in and drown him."

The river tumbled wild and furious between large boulders after it left the lake. We tied the canoe to the shore nearby, and forced our way down through the thick willows and brush along the rocky bank, examining every fall and pool of the raging water. After a while the river widened into a calm space where, if Bucky had been drowned, he would probably have washed up. I, of course, could have told her that Bucky had not been anywhere near the river, but Chris's poor sense of smell has ever been her undoing.

Still no sign of Bucky the following morning, and when the plane came, we flew to the road without him. What with the dentist, car repairs, shopping, and one thing or another, we were away for ten days. At last we were piled into a plane with a load of Stuff and we took off back to Nuk Tessli.

Whenever we flew into the lake, it was Chris's habit to fling a quick glance at the cabins to make sure the roofs and chimneys were still in place. This time I saw her squint mightily as we fled past the gap between the islands.

"It can't be!" I heard her mutter.

The plane slowed and turned, and we taxied slowly between the islands to the wharf. Standing there to greet us was a small black shape wearing a piece of red and blue plastic. Bucky had found his way home. Unless he'd found a smidgeon of carcass somewhere in the bush, he had not eaten anything for nearly two weeks. Incredibly, he was still wearing his pack.

"Bucky!" Chris exclaimed. She gave him a big pat. "You look like the 'before' in a dog cruelty poster."

His eyes were sunken, his nose was cracked, and his coat was dull. His build was too stocky and fur too thick for his ribs to show, but he was in a very poor state. At least he'd had unlimited water to drink.

Chris immediately tried to unbuckle his pack, but Bucky growled at her. It was then that she found the reason for his difficulty in getting home. His left front leg had somehow got over the strap that went round the front of his chest. This had not only slowed him down considerably; it had also worn a huge open wound under his arm. It still didn't explain why he had not attempted to reach the lakeshore after he heard Chris calling. He can't have chased Moose that far. He was probably just being ornery. Interestingly, he must have crossed the river somewhere, either over the bridge at the outlet or where it ran into the lake at the upper end. Maybe enough rocks were poking through the water there for him to jump without swimming. I never figured him for a particularly brainy animal, but even though he had not been in the country all that long, he had found his way home.

The pilot was anxious to get going. He had other customers to fly and it had started to spit with rain. Vapour was beginning to swirl around the tops of the mountains. These little planes cannot travel if the cloud is too low and the pilot can't see. So Chris had to unload the freight before she could attend to Bucky. He sat there looking just about as miserable as a dog could be.

As soon as the pilot had left, she took me to the cabin and tied me up, and brought a handful of food down to Bucky.

"It was amazing," she told people afterward. "His ears pricked up, his eyes widened, and with every bite he looked happier."

While he was distracted by a second handful of food, Chris quickly flipped some buckles and whipped the pack off his back.

Within two days, apart from the injury in his armpit, you would never have known he had starved. His energy was back up, his coat was shining, and his eyes were alert again.

Chris kept the pack off him for a while, but it wasn't long before she wanted him to carry a load. She always gave us treats after the pack had been strapped on, and greedy Bucky's little brain could not think past the cookie. The pack was on him before he knew it. Chris thought he might be pack-shy after his ordeal, but he treated it like most of his life—he ignored it. However, after that day, he was always kept on a lead when he was carrying anything on his back.

BUCKY HAD MANY IDIOSYNCRASIES, BUT IN ONE RESPECT HE WAS THE oddest dog I have ever come across. He liked fruit and vegetables. Even the easygoing Lonesome would leave bits of carrot on her plate if they happened to arrive there with leftover stew, but Bucky seemed to enjoy everything. Once, in the winter, a plane landed on the ice to bring produce. A bag of apples split open and the fruit rolled all over the frozen lake. Bucky tore after them, trying to bite each one and eat it before Chris could pack them up. Chris wasn't going to waste these apples—she simply cut the bitten pieces away and ate the rest herself. This fruit habit was handy for Chris when she was out hiking. She was very strict about never throwing any kind of food on the ground, not even apple cores.

"That," she patiently explained to her clients over and over, "is how bears learn to associate food smells with humans. This is why they break into cabins. Then they get shot."

She would always carry an empty plastic bag with her on hikes and carry home the bits of food that people did not want to eat. When Bucky was around, however, she had a perfect solution for apple cores: he gobbled them up.

At the end of summer, when the leaves on the bushes in the forest started to turn colour, Chris usually went berry picking. Her favourites were the black huckleberries—they were not always common, but Chris generally managed to collect enough for a feed or two. Once in a while there was a huge crop and Chris picked for days. She would amass several buckets' worth, which she cooked in jars and stored for the winter.

Berry picking was, like flower hunting, not particularly interesting for me. I nosed around in a few Mouse holes and chased Squirrel when he got too close, but mostly I flopped about and waited for Chris to move to the next picking patch.

Not Bucky. With a slurp and a slobber, he started gobbling the berries off the bushes, snuffling them up like Bear. After a while, Chris realized he was always homing in on the biggest, juiciest berries. As soon as she heard him, she would head straight over and claim his bush. She didn't care that the leaves were wet with slobber; she was delighted that she could fill her bucket much faster.

It was during berry-picking time that Bucky disappeared for several days again. Hikers had been staying in one of the guest cabins overnight. They had planned a ten-day expedition on foot to another lake. They were not expecting to return to Nuk Tessli; the plane would pick them up from their destination.

They were all grouped on the waterfront about to start their trek when a float plane hopped over Bumpy Ridge, kissed the water, then chugged back at taxiing speed to the wharf. It disgorged four more people and a lot of large metal boxes. Also put onto the dock were several black metal sticks covered at one end with long, raggedy black fuzzy stuff. While introductions were happening, I heard Chris say something like "You'd better watch the mics. Max likes fluffy things," but no one took any notice of me. I managed to filch one and almost got away with it, but someone roared and pounced on it and took it from me. Once the excitement of the introductions was over, the hikers set off on their journey. Chris did not expect to see them again.

The visitors who had flown in that morning were going to film an episode of *Great Canadian Rivers*, which would be broadcast on television. The film people deemed Chris an eccentric enough person to add to the show. Chris didn't have a TV, but they promised to send her a video. She still doesn't have a TV, and very few people have equipment to play videos anymore, so the tape has been seen only once. It sits in a box in Chris's attic.

One of the items the visitors had brought was a complicated machine as big as a dog, which they called a camera. It didn't look much like the little hand-held camera Chris used. It was carried in a kind of harness on the filmer's shoulder. First the cameraman took shots of Chris paddling up the lake toward the mountains. It was a beautiful sunny day with a small breeze: perfect weather for the job. Then the cameraman wanted to get into the boat. Chris was a bit leery of this. Most of her canoes were pretty beat-up, because they were used to carry firewood. It was never very easy to get wood in and out of the boats without hitting the edges, and the gunwales were trashed. The smallest canoe was unsuitable for firewood work, so it looked reasonably presentable, and this was the one Chris was using. The reason it was not used for firewood was that it was easy to tip over.

"What happens if we go over and you're holding that megabucks camera?" she said. "Is it waterproof?"

"No, it's not," said the cameraman, "but don't worry, we won't go over." And sure enough, he hopped in like a pro. He sat facing Chris and taking more video.

Film directors seem to think it's okay to be impatient. Another movie man had stayed at Nuk Tessli when Nick was helping Chris build the third cabin. That filmmaker had arrived in his own plane, unannounced, and completely disrupted Chris and Nick's work for most of two days. He had driven both of them crazy.

The current movie crew's tight schedule meant that we could not hike to the really beautiful places around Nuk Tessli, but Chris put a backpack on me and another on herself, and we took off for a nearby meadow. She would have loaded up Bucky, too, but he seemed to have disappeared. This was puzzling as there had been nothing to chase, but Chris was concentrating so hard on the requirements of the movie people, she shoved Bucky's absence to the back of her mind.

A small pond lay in a meadow near the cabin. The cameraman squatted down in the grass on one side and asked Chris to walk along the other so that he could catch her reflection in the water. She was to call me and with luck I would follow her into the frame.

"Don't look at the camera," said the producer. She had emphasized this point several times.

Chris walked to the edge of the pond, made sure I was following, and hiked as if she were all alone in the wild. I, however, was so surprised to see the man squatting in the grass with this great machine on his shoulder, that I couldn't help but stare at him to see what he was doing.

"Do it again!" the cameraman said. He was quite annoyed. I was pretty puzzled as this was obviously not a proper walk, and I didn't know what I was supposed to do. We went back to where we had started the first time.

"Don't look at the camera," Chris was told, and she didn't, but once again I found the man's behaviour so odd that I stopped in exactly the same place and stared at him.

"Again!" the man bellowed.

And again we did it. As I got level, I looked intently at the man once more. One of the women laughed.

"Max just wants to be a star!" she said.

The movie crew left in the afternoon as planned, and now Chris could concentrate on looking for Bucky. There was a stiff breeze out on the lake by now, but she went to the wharf and called, hoping her voice would travel over the water. There was no sign or sound of him. She had a sneaking feeling that he must have followed the hikers, but if he had done so, surely they would have found him and brought him home, or at least yelled across the lake so that Chris would be able to canoe across and pick him up. At least he was not wearing a pack this time. Apart from calling a time or two across the lake, we never went to look for him.

"He'll either turn up or he won't," Chris said grumpily.

Ten days later an unscheduled plane droned into the air space above the lake, and swooped down onto the water. Chris had a strong suspicion as to who was in it and why it was landing. Sure enough, inside were the hikers, and with them was Bucky, looking very pleased with himself.

"By the time we realized he was following us, we had gone too far to want to turn back," one of the hikers said. "We loved having him. We've made him this wooden tag to wear." It was a small, round disc with *Bucky* printed on it.

Chris was annoyed that she had been made to worry, and I could see that she half hoped she would never see Bucky again. He was getting to be a lot more trouble than he was worth. She told the city visitors they could keep him if they liked him so much, but

having him with them in the bush was not the same as the weary-
ing responsibility of keeping a difficult dog in a city, and they all
politely declined.

UNFORTUNATELY, BUCKY WASN'T THE ONLY ONE TO RUN INTO TROUBLE
on occasion. The next time, I was the one to suffer. It was midsum-
mer, and we were on our way out to the road. All of us were carrying
packs, for Chris expected to spend at least one night out en route.
Bucky was attached to Chris with a rope, but, as usual, I was allowed
to run free.

Suddenly I picked up a very fresh and very different scent. I dived
after it. Bucky immediately howled and lunged as he had smelled it
too, but Chris hung onto him. She had, of course, no idea what had
excited us. I soon caught up with the animal; it was the size of a small
bear cub. Its fur was very coarse and shiny—it looked as though the
animal was covered in nails. It didn't run away, but curled into a ball.
I bit it—and was immediately in agony. My mouth and face were full
of fiery needles. I bit the animal again. Bucky was going crazy.

"Let me at it!" he was screaming.

Chris flung his rope around a tree and ran toward me. She
grabbed me and tried to push the animal out of my jaws with her
foot. Froth and blood were pouring out of my mouth, but I still kept
biting. My tongue and my legs and chest were full of needles. So
was my pack, and as Chris hauled me off, the needles stabbed her
through her pant legs. The animal stayed curled in a ball. It looked
totally unhurt. I was in a frenzy. Chris had another rope and she
tied me up beside Bucky.

"I can't believe this," Chris said. "I've seen only one other porcupine in all my years here. This one is quite small—it must be half-
grown. But look at you! What a mess! You must have a hundred
quills in you!"

"I would have killed it," Bucky boasted loudly in his yapping bark. "Chris should have let me loose!"

"Thank goodness Bucky wasn't running free as well," Chris groaned. "Otherwise I would have had two idiot dogs to deal with."

I was starting to calm down, but was now feeling very uncomfortable. Most of the needles were in my mouth and throat; I was gasping for breath.

"Well, we can't hike out now," Chris said. "We'll have to go back home and I'll radio for a plane. I hope they have one available soon."

The descent to the cabin was slow and painful. Chris had both of us tied to ropes. Chris fastened my pack on top of her own, which made a very heavy load for her, as she was not as strong as me. As I stumbled down, I kept bumping into the backs of her legs and poking her with yet more quills.

Back at the cabin, Chris was able to get through on the radio-phone right away, but it was to be quite some time before a plane arrived. By now I was able to close my mouth, but I was unable to drink, and I was in a lot of pain. When we eventually flew out to Nimpo, Chris grabbed town clothes and her wallet from the Cabin-in-the-Bog, and she called the vet from the landlady's phone. We had left Nuk Tessli very early that morning as we always did when backpacking, but because of the slow descent and the wait for the plane, it was doubtful that we would arrive at the vet before closing time.

"They're going to charge me extra because of having to work after hours," Chris complained to the landlady as she climbed into her truck. I had been too miserable to resist Chris loading me aboard.

It takes half a day to drive to town. Usually the vet is quite a busy place, but because it was late, there was no one else in the parking lot when we arrived. At least we didn't have to wait. Chris told the vet I was probably dehydrated as I had drunk nothing since the morning's encounter. The woman took one look at me and gave me a shot of something.

"It's not a full anaesthetic," I heard her say. "It will just make him sleepy. These other injections are simply saline solution placed under the skin to rehydrate him."

It was a funny sensation, because I didn't have the energy to move, and yet I heard and felt things in a sort of fuzzy way. The vet gave Chris some pliers and told her to work on my legs and chest while she propped my mouth wide open with a metal frame and looked inside. Chris had heard that you were supposed to take quills out carefully, but there was no finesse here. Just yank, yank, yank. All the quills were placed into a flat dish and later counted.

"A hundred and twenty-one," said the vet. "I think we've got them all."

"There were a lot more," Chris explained. "They were in his pack and my legs. It was just a small porcupine. You'd think with all that quill loss it would have looked bald, but you couldn't see where they had come from."

The reason we had been heading to the road in the first place was to visit friends for a party or some such special occasion, and we were able to continue to that destination. Bucky and I were tied up most of the time so it was fairly boring for us, but Chris seemed to be having fun and, as I had recovered rapidly from my ordeal and the Porcupine Adventure was told to various humans over and over, I was able to enjoy the extra pats given as commiseration.

It was therefore a few days later when we once again hiked back over the mountains to the cabin. You can imagine that, when we passed that fateful spot, Chris had both of us on leads and she kept a wary eye out for Porcupine. But I never smelled it or any other Porcupine again during my lifetime.

ONE WINTER WE HAD AN ENCOUNTER WITH A DIFFERENT ANIMAL THAT turned out to be even scarier for me. Chris was sleeping in the cabin and Bucky and I were in our warm kennels on the porch. We heard and smelled visitors on the ice. We ran onto the lake, and there was Wolf. There were three of them. We sniffed our greetings, and Wolf started to play. We danced around, not making a lot of noise, but Bucky's occasional yap woke Chris up. The sky was cloudy and the moon wasn't full but a pale light shone on the snow. She squinted hard. It seemed she could not quite make out who was dancing with us—a dog of some sort, she surmised. (This was yet another story she told to people over and over so I know what she was thinking.) Bucky was the only animal she could identify clearly because of his black coat. I was almost white and the wild dogs were also light coloured. She knew we virtually never saw Coyote here, and the animal was too big for Fox, so she figured it must be Wolf. She leapt out of bed and grabbed the flashlight. She stuffed her bare feet into her winter boots and ran onto the deck. Immediately, Wolf melted away into the darkness. Chris was wearing nothing else but her underwear so was ill equipped to follow our visitors further. Bucky and I came running to her, having enjoyed ourselves immensely.

We thought that was the end of it, but Wolf came back a couple of hours later. Bucky and I ran onto the ice again. Chris had gone back to sleep but woke up once more, and this time she was fully dressed when she came out of the cabin. She trotted out onto the ice, but all of us were now out of flashlight range and she couldn't see where we were.

All at once, there was a huge pain at the root of my tail. I had thought we were having a game, but Wolf was suddenly not playing anymore. He hung on for a moment, but although she could not see him, Chris was walking toward him, and he let go of me and ran off.

Chris still had no idea I was hurt. Bucky was running back to her and she was examining the tracks in the snow. Then I emerged from the darkness. I could barely walk.

"Oh my gosh, Max. What have they done to you?" she gasped.

I stumbled up the trail to the cabin. Chris immediately brought me inside and tried to see the extent of my injuries. There wasn't a lot of blood and the thick fur on my body made it very hard for her to see what was wrong. My eyes were staring and I was gasping so hard I could hardly breathe. Chris made a bed for me with old blankets and coats, but I was too uncomfortable to lie down and just kept staggering about. It was far too hot for me inside and I kept standing by the door until she let me out. She knew I would not be able to duck into the kennel so she pulled the blanket and coat bed into the porch. I really needed to go to the vet, but of course I couldn't walk out and it was the middle of the night when no plane could fly. No one would have been listening to the radiophone at this hour, either.

I don't think Chris slept much that night but in the morning she was at least relieved to see that I was calmer. I was lying down by this stage. I didn't want anything to eat, but I was pleased that she kept putting bowls of warm water in front of me. Normally, Bucky and I would eat snow for our winter water; if she put a bucket outside it would simply freeze before either of us had tasted it. Soon I needed to go to the bathroom. Slowly I got up and shuffled along the trail into the forest. It was such agony to go, though, that I came back in great distress. Chris tried the radiophone but was unable to reach anyone, so we simply hoped and waited.

Two days later I was no better. My little nose was hot and dry. I didn't want any food. I kept looking hopefully at Chris, expecting her to make me better, but she didn't seem to know how.

That evening, she came to me with some human food—a can of sardines. She opened it up under my nose. It smelled delicious.

It was only a mouthful or two, but I licked it all up. It was the first thing I'd eaten for three days.

The next morning, Chris found my bed empty. She told me later that she thought I'd gone off into the bush to die. But I had felt so much better, I had gone out onto the ice with Bucky. When we saw Chris, we ran back to her. I even managed to wag my poor, sore tail.

I WAS NOW BECOMING QUITE FAMOUS. WITHIN A VERY SHORT TIME AFTER the first movie was made, a writer and photographer came to Nuk Tessli to do a magazine article. And soon after that, I was on TV again. The famous Lonesome had been on the radio quite a bit, but she never made it onto national television.

The writer and photographer were freelancing for *Beautiful BC Magazine*. They were scheduled to arrive at the beginning of August.

"That's right when the flower meadows are at their prime!" Chris told us excitedly. "At last I will be able to show the world what beauty lies in my backyard. Let's go up there and check them out before they come."

Bucky and I looked at each other.

"Flower meadows," Bucky muttered. "Boooor-ingggg!"

"Usually pretty buggy, too," I agreed.

But it was always fun to set off on a hike, and with luck we'd find Marmot or Ptarmigan to chase. The trail to the meadows was now fairly well-defined underfoot as it was the most used hiking route in the area. We made good time climbing the creek to Otter Lake, then up through the rocky forest to the long, boggy meadows, and finally to the treeline. It was hot and sunny without much wind.

Chris was soon raving about the flowers, but the bugs were the worst I'd ever known! Chris later said she'd never been so badly bitten in her life. She wore her usual teabag skin over her head, and

she fashioned two smaller ones for her hands. She wore her leg-skins tucked into socks and arm-skins right down to her hands. At the end of the day, though, her arms, legs and face were covered in huckleberry-sized lumps from blackfly bites.

It didn't stop her from ecstatically wallowing in flowers hour after hour, however. She took hundreds of pictures—she had a digital camera by then—and sometimes we were included in the shots. Bucky and I were too hot to do much chasing, and we kept flopping down among the flowers. When we arrived home, Chris was able to look at the photos on her computer. One was of an angelic-looking Bucky surrounded by lupins and paintbrush—with about a hundred blackflies buzzing around his head.

Fortunately, when we hiked up with the photographer a few days later, there was a wind and the bugs were not such a bother. The writer was not much of a hiker. He came a short way, but then

Bucky surrounded by blackflies

returned to the cabins on his own. The photographer had an amazing amount of energy. He carried two huge backpacks, one on his back and another on his front, both full of camera equipment. He would run ahead, set up a tripod and camera, and film Chris and us dogs trudging up the mountain toward him. (We all wore packs for the camera, but in fact there was not much in them; they were just for show.) Then he would film us from behind as we climbed higher. Next thing, he would toss his gear into his bags, shoulder his two packs, and run as fast as he could until he had passed us by quite a way. He would set up his tripod and camera and film us coming toward him again. This process was repeated several times. Chris said it made her exhausted just looking at him. The flowers, however, were disappointing. It had been such a hot, dry summer that within the three days since we had last been there, the meadows were shrivelled and shabby. When the magazine article was eventually published, I was in three of the seven accompanying photos. Bucky was in one of them also, but he was half hidden by some other people who had hiked up the mountain with us.

The second TV appearance was very different from the first, mainly because this time the camera crew did not come to us—we went to them.

Chris's fourth Book, *Snowshoes and Spotted Dick*, was published that spring, and as usual, Chris could not wait to go out into the wide world and show off about it. (Actually I had quite a lot of showing off to do myself as I featured in the book quite a bit.) The publisher had drummed up the usual publicity via radio and newspaper articles in the towns that Chris was scheduled to visit. Chris did some of the interviews by phone, but for others, she was able to go to the studio. Most of these interviews were on the radio but there were a couple of TV appearances as well. One was somewhat mundane, but the other was quite different.

We had been staying on Vancouver Island with Tina, the same person who used to take care of Lonesome. After Lonesome had died, Tina had moved to the Island and taken her art studio with her. The dog with the enormous tongue, Oscar, was still around, but he had a number of health issues; the last time I saw him he was obviously not long for this world. A new addition to the household was a pug with a very deformed jaw. She was a happy soul, though. She had been rescued from a puppy mill: for the first five years of her life she had never been out of a small pen. Despite her crooked jaw she'd had several litters of puppies that the puppy mill owner had sold as healthy purebreds. People buy these animals online or from the pet store without having any idea of the poor conditions in which they are raised. The overcrowding and lack of handling mean the puppies will often develop behaviour problems or disease. The websites and pet stores naturally tell prospective buyers that the breeder is reputable, but many of them are lying. People should either go directly to the breeder themselves, or adopt from a rescue organization. That way they would at least be assured of a healthy animal.

Pugs are very popular with humans who don't have the great outdoors to play in, but they wouldn't be able to handle the kind of life Bucky and I were used to. Crooked Jaw had not had a very good start to her life but was now destined for a long and happy retirement with her new humans. They had named her Petunia.

We had been told to arrive at the TV studio about fifteen minutes before 6:00 A.M. Petunia and Oscar lived about an hour and a half north,

Petunia

so we had to get up very early to drive there. Bucky was too unreliable for this kind of performance, so he had to stay in the van. I went into the studio with Chris.

Most TV studios are dark, scruffy, warehouse-like places with tangled cables all over the floor; only the little bit that is shown on the screen is decorated like a civilized place and lit up. The one we went to this time, however, was light and airy, and it had big glass windows. An open door led onto a patio. Chris was given an uncomfortable stool beside a small round table, upon which were displayed a few of the new books. She opened one so that it showed a picture of me. Nearby was a couch, which was normally used for visiting dogs, but it was too small for me, so I lay on the floor beside it. Also in the room was a man behind a counter from which came the tantalizing smells of raw hamburgers. Beside him was a chainsaw rigged up to an Alaskan sawmill, exactly the same kind of setup that Chris used for making lumber up at Nuk Tessli. This saw was much bigger than Chris's, however, and also brand new. I have never seen an Alaskan sawmill or a chainsaw that clean!

A few minutes before the show was due to start, a happy, stocky man, well dressed in a casual way, walked into the room. He was trailed by another human wearing a loose plaid shirt and jeans. The second man carried an enormous camera on his shoulders. It was even bigger than the one used by the crew that had come to Nuk Tessli: I swear it was longer than me! The cameraman wore sneakers so that his feet would make no sound on the floor. He followed the interviewer as precisely as a shadow, trying to behave as if he was the interviewer's third eye.

The stocky man explained to us that the show would start with news and weather, and that we would be interviewed immediately afterward. We could watch the progress of the show via a series of TV screens set high up on the wall. When the last ad had finished, the man turned to Chris and asked her a couple questions about the book. She was nervous with the camera pointed at her, but handled it quite well, animatedly talking about her life in the mountains. Briefly, that great camera was turned toward me.

In a very short time, the interview was over and the man and his camera-shadow were focused on the hamburger stand. Then they gave the Alaskan sawmill and the representative from the chainsaw shop a bit of airtime. To my surprise, the interviewer and camera-man then went out onto the patio and talked to some people out there. A search and rescue truck was parked on the patio, but the most odd thing of all was a large block of ice. It was shady on the patio, but nonetheless it was a hot spring day in a place that rarely saw snow, even in winter, and I wondered how long the ice would last. Beside the block stood another person with a very small chainsaw. He started cutting into the ice.

All the interviews took about ten minutes. The interviewer said something to the effect of "We'll be right back after this message." Everyone relaxed while an ad came on, and Chris thought it was time for us to leave the studio. But not a bit of it. After the ad, the news and weather were updated, and then the interviews started again. Different questions were asked, the hamburgers started cooking and the man on the patio made a few more cuts into his ice block. By this time I was getting very hot in the studio and had sprawled at full length on the floor. The interviewer loved this: as he announced the next advertisement break, he gestured for the cameraman to point his lens at me and said, "And now we'll relax—with Max!"

Toward the end, the show was like a party. Everyone was chatting with everyone else and the hamburgers were being cooked and eaten. The same routine happened for the whole three hours. First the news and weather, then a round of interviews, and, just before the ads came on, the slogan that had become the signature of the show, "And now we'll relax—with Max!"

We've never had so much fun in a TV interview before or since.

AFTER ALL THESE SHENANIGANS, WE ARRIVED BACK AT THE CABIN-IN-the-Bog and prepared to go into the mountains for the summer. Chris was feeling very pleased with herself. It had been a few years since she had had a Book published, and the Money boost with this one was a great relief to her. There had been a lot of bookings for the tourist business as well. She was looking forward to a happy and productive summer.

Local pilots had flown over our lake and told Chris it was not yet open, so we prepared to wait at the Cabin-in-the-Bog for a few days. Bucky and I had been permanently on the lead for several weeks while we had travelled to promote the book, and we were getting pretty antsy. Chris wasn't going to risk letting Bucky go, but as we hiked up the logging road, she at last let me loose. How wonderful it was to gallop free and smell the newly emerged earth and flooded Mouse homes. I jumped over the brush and rummaged around with glee. All of a sudden I gave a yelp. My leg had caught on a branch and twisted. I knew at once that it was the same kind of injury I'd had before. Only this time it was the other leg.

Chris heard the noise I'd made. She came back to me with great concern. I was holding up the injured leg and hopping along with three.

"Oh no!" Chris said. "You haven't made that kind of yelp since you pulled the cruciate ligament on your other leg six or seven years ago at least. I bet you've done it again."

Chris went up to the landlady's house to call the vet. The landlady said it was a holiday weekend (Chris often forgot to look at a human calendar) and no one would be at work, but Chris phoned anyway. She spoke to an emergency person who said that because my injury was not life threatening, nothing could be arranged until the following Tuesday. Chris knew I would recover fairly well on my own if I was not given a lot of heavy work, but she couldn't keep a dog that was unable to hike.

She was devastated. "You're nine years old already. Another operation at your age is not likely to be all that reliable. What are we going to do?"

She kept saying things like if she couldn't find a home for me, I would have to be put to sleep. Chris tried to phone the person she got me from, to see if she would take me, but the woman's business was closed for the weekend and she had an unlisted home number.

"I won't be able to make any decisions until I get to Williams Lake on Tuesday," she said to our landlady. "If we're going to be in town as soon as the businesses open we need to leave at five o'clock in the morning, which means we won't be able to phone anyone before we start." I knew that cellphones did not work in this part of the world.

I wasn't exactly sure what "putting to sleep" meant, but my leg improved a little over the next couple of days. Sleeping didn't sound all that uncomfortable. Chris went through the usual process of packing for the mountains, and I assumed she'd had word that the ice had gone and we could go home. When we threw things into the truck very early on the Tuesday morning, however, we didn't drive the short distance to the float plane base, but headed all the way back into town.

As we drove through the rain, Chris's face was wet. The truck wasn't leaking; it was Chris's eyes that were pouring water. She could hardly see enough to drive some of the time.

"If I can't find anyone to take you," she said again, "you are going to have to be put down."

First we stopped by a place that had an aroma I instantly recognized, even though I had not smelled it for a very long time. It was a bit like the vet's, but this was a place for people. They came here to have their teeth fixed. Humans have pathetic teeth, but I guess they're useful enough for grinding up vegetables. I recognized the aroma, because it was always present in the house where I had been born. And wasn't another underlying scent also familiar? Well, for goodness' sake! Out came the very woman in whose home I had started my life.

"I can't take him home," she said sadly. "My other Akitas would turn on him and kill him."

"That's so hard to believe," Chris said. "Max is so gentle with both people and dogs. Even when physically forced into a plane he has never attempted to bite anyone."

The other woman sighed. "I can't take him home—but leave him with me, and I'll see what I can do."

"That is so kind of you," Chris said. "I'm going to miss him—he's been such a good dog—but I couldn't bear to have him put down."

Chris took me round the side of the building to a concrete patio. There was a tiny place that was sheltered from the rain. She tied me to the railings of a fence. She was still crying. I looked at her, puzzled. I could not begin to imagine what was going to happen.

"Goodbye, Max," she said, hugging me. She sadly disappeared round the house and soon I heard the truck start up and drive away.

"Goodbye?" I thought. "What does she mean by that? Isn't she coming back?" The rain hissed down.

We never saw each other again.

13

HARRY

I LEARN TO BACKPACK

"AND?" I SAID.

"And what?" said Badger.

"Max. What happened to him? You can't just let the story end like that. Anyway, how did you know he never saw Chris again?"

"I've been talking for quite a while without a break," Badger said. "I need a drink." He heaved himself to his feet, but before he left he conceded to say, "I pieced together the story from what Bucky told me and conversations Chris had with other humans. That's what all good storytellers do. Plus, I imagined how he must have been feeling. I know how I'd feel in a situation like that."

Badger plodded down the trail to the lake. I thought he'd come back and tell me more, but he didn't reappear right away. I went down after him and found him dozing on the wharf beside the water.

"I'm waiting," I said.

Badger gave a theatrical sigh. "I should really test you first, to make sure how much you've remembered the other stories."

"Oh, I know everything. I'm smart, remember? Now, tell me what happened to Max. Please, please, please."

"Well..." began Badger with apparent reluctance. But you could tell that the old boy really enjoyed telling these stories. He just put on a show of being annoyed to make sure I knew what a privilege it was for me to hear them.

"Max," Badger continued slowly, "found another home."

"Really? How? Was it at the Tooth Lady's?"

"Well, it was actually quite an odd story," Badger finally said. "A man came to visit the Tooth Lady so he could get his molars looked at. People apparently do that even when there's nothing wrong with their teeth. If they had more bones to chew on, their mouths would be much healthier. But then I suppose people who look after other humans' teeth wouldn't have any Money and couldn't afford to have a house full of dogs..."

"But *Max*! What happened to *Max*?"

And this is what Badger related.

MAX HADN'T BEEN SITTING LONG IN THE RAIN WHEN ANOTHER HUMAN came along.

"Oh what a beautiful dog!" said the man. "Who does he belong to?"

At which the Tooth Lady told him a bit of the story. And he said, "Well, I'm looking for a dog. I have two, and one is very old and not long for this world. If Max is as gentle as you say, he would be a lovely companion for the younger animal. Let me take him home and see if it works. I have a fenced yard, so he won't be tied all the time."

"And that's what happened," Badger said. Max lived for two more years in the man's house and was well loved and cared for."

I digested this for a moment. I supposed it was a good ending in its way. But nobody likes the thought of getting old and sick.

"So I guess Chris had only Bucky, then," I said. "Did she get another dog for the summer?"

"As a matter of fact, yes," Badger said. "She picked him up before she even left town. His early years were shrouded in mystery. He was another dog that had gone through quite a lot of trauma in his early life."

I was just about to stretch out in anticipation of the next chapter of our Wilderness Dog Saga, when we heard Chris calling us.

"Hey you guys! You wanna go for a hike?"

There is nothing—absolutely nothing—better than the whole pack going for a hike together. Even though Badger and I were not tied very often at Nuk Tessli, and had a huge world to explore by ourselves, somehow it was never the same as going with Chris.

We did not need to be asked twice.

WE STRODE BETWEEN THE ROCKS AND TREES BEHIND THE CABINS, AND Chris breathed in deeply the pine-scented air (it seems to be one of the smells that humans can register).

"I love these first walks of the year after the snow goes," she said. "The trails are so littered with needles that they're hard to find. It's as if we are once again the first people to ever set foot here."

"Didn't Taya tell us she would say something like this?" I whispered to Badger.

"Chris says it every year," he muttered knowingly.

The leaves had already opened near the River Cabin, but here we were much higher in the mountains and bare twigs bore locked-tight buds. Even the soon-to-be silvery pussy willows in the swampy areas were still firmly shut. But Chris found some white flowers half swimming in water that pleased her greatly, and she pointed her camera at them.

"Mountain marsh marigold," Chris murmured happily. "They are amazing. They are in such a hurry to bloom they sometimes open underneath the snow."

"Told you," said Badger, giving me a nudge. "She'll go crazy over these things."

Birds squeaked and flitted, and Chris stopped and tried to spot them in the branches. Squirrel chattered. Soon Badger and I were exploring Mouse tunnels and getting whiffs of Moose and Rabbit.

We came to a roaring creek and started up alongside it. The creek was swollen with snowmelt and had flooded over the land in many places. That's when I observed for myself the extraordinary lengths humans will go to in order to keep their feet dry. Chris hung on to branches and wriggled around rocks to avoid places where the water was higher than the tops of her boots. Badger and I, of course, just waded through. We sloshed through a lot of wet places and bogs. Badger told me that the water was always highest just after the ice and snow had gone. These flooded areas would all dry up before long.

Soon we came to a small lake. Some of it was still frozen, but where the creek tumbled out of it, there was a pool of open water. Four black and white ducks rattled off it with great haste when our mob tramped into view.

"She calls this hike 'The Block,'" Badger explained, "and this is Otter Lake. If we were going up the mountain, we would have crossed the creek over that log bridge we just passed. It might be difficult to hike much higher right now as there is still quite a lot of snow in the bush."

Chris sat on a rock and looked at the lake for a while. The rotten ice was grey, and where it still covered the water it was possible to see whitish marks where Chris's winter ski trails had been made. Across a small inlet, loud cheepings came from a hole in a tree. Soon a small black and white bird flew to the hole and stuffed insects into the noisy babies' beaks.

"Hairy woodpecker," said Chris with satisfaction.

Past the lake our trail was very rocky, and we picked a way between the boulders. Then we sloshed through more open wet areas. We visited three ponds—Badger explained that one of them had been used for the filming of Max's television debut. Chris hunted around in a corner, then suddenly bent down with her camera. You've guessed it—she'd found more flowers. These were different ones: they were smaller and the colour of the sun.

"Yellow anemones," Chris crowed. Her face was one big grin.

Not long after we had hiked around the Block, Chris took Badger and me for our first canoe trip—or, rather, she rode in the canoe and expected Badger and us to follow along the shore. When Chris first launched the boat, however, it was too rocky for her to stay close to land and she had to swing out into the lake past an island. Instead of staying along the shore, Badger ran onto the island and, as Chris turned back, he jumped in and swam. Naturally, I followed his lead. I had learned to love water at the River Cabin, so I had no fear of the lake. I was able to swim much faster than Badger and quickly pulled ahead. As soon as that happened, Badger tried to bark. When he opened his mouth, water flooded in, and it sounded as though he was choking. Still he barked and panted and choked and wailed until he got to dry land.

"You dummy," Chris said. "You've never behaved that way before. You're starting to sound just like Sport."

But this was how Badger now performed every time we went into the water. He was fine as long as either Chris or I was behind him. As soon as both of us drew ahead, however, he would go through this barking and choking routine. He really could not bear the humiliation of suddenly being the weakest member of the pack.

A week or so after we had arrived at Nuk Tessli, Chris pulled out an item she had been stitching together over the last few days. It smelled of a strong, plastic chemical. I was somewhat disconcerted when she plopped this thing on my back and started to fasten straps around my chest and belly. It had big floppy pockets on the side, but these were empty. This, then, was the dreaded Dog Pack. I didn't like the feel of it all that much, and I started to wriggle.

"You'll get used to it," Chris said.

Harry

Badger smirked in the background. He was not wearing anything. He was allowing himself a modicum of superiority in this situation.

"Okay, let's go," Chris added, swinging her own pack onto her back. I could smell that she had cold-weather skins in there, and a bit of human food. "The snow has melted a lot in the high country this last week, and I think we'll be able to make it to the top of the North Ridge."

The water levels in the streams and swamps close to the cabin had certainly dropped considerably, so Chris was able to travel more quickly. We hiked up the creek, which was still roaring boisterously even though it was now mostly contained within its banks, and eventually crossed it on the bridge that Chris had made from a fallen tree. We walked along the edge of the small lake that had been partially frozen on our first hike. It was now open, and two little brown ducks eased away from the shore. I tried to go after them, but was hampered by the pack, which caught on branches, and the ducks easily swam out of reach.

The trail wound higher and higher. Soon the forest was more open. Suddenly, Badger and I smelled Rabbit! We were off! I had long learned that Chris's yelling was meaningless, and we took no notice of her. It was a short but glorious chase before Rabbit plunged into a hole beneath a rotten log. Triumphantly, we trotted back to Chris.

Chris wasn't just mad—she was horrified. "Harry!" she shouted. "Where's your pack?"

In the heat of the chase I had never noticed, but I must have wriggled out of it somewhere. I gave myself a shake. I felt much nicer without it. Chris was quite cross and went in the general direction of Rabbit, but of course with such a useless nose, she had no real idea of where we had been. I could have retraced my route exactly, but there was no way I was going to find that miserable pack for her. She hunted back and forth. Then, with a relieved yell, she saw it hanging on a low branch. Apparently human eyes can pick out the colours red and blue much better than we can. She stuffed my pack into her own.

"I am going to have to make these straps tighter," she said. "Then you won't be able to get yourself out of it."

We climbed higher and higher, and soon the forest dropped away altogether. Large patches of snow still lay around up here, and sometimes we had to slog through them. They were sodden and the bare ground between them was running with snowmelt. Mouse had made extensive villages under the snow. Their houses had been made from balls of grass. Another area was a communal bathroom. These places were linked by tunnels that wriggled everywhere. The homes and tunnels were exposed now that the snow had melted and they were totally flooded out. Mouse had gone underground into holes between the rocks, but there were still nice smells associated with their tunnels, and Badger and I had fun snuffling along them. As we climbed even higher, there was a piercing whistle. I leapt up, startled. Badger was already streaking up a rockslide. There was another sharp whistle, then a sort of chuckling sound as the animal dived underground.

"Marmot," Badger panted as I galloped up to him.

Once again we ignored Chris's yells. An enticing scent came from a rock crack, but the boulders were too big for us to move.

"There's another one whistling," I said. The sound was from a long way away and was wavering on the wind. It was difficult to pinpoint.

"They're all over these mountains," Badger said. "They warn each other with their whistles and it makes it very hard for us to catch them. Grizzly is strong enough to move some of these boulders, and he sometimes digs up whole mountainsides to get at them."

I looked around nervously. I'd never met Grizzly, but I had smelled him and his cousin, Black Bear, by the River Cabin. If I concentrated I could catch the same aroma here, but the scent was old and I calmed down.

Higher still we went. Chris had long ago left the trail behind and now, between the snow patches, we crunched over rock and gravel scattered with coarse little plants—a landscape that Chris called tundra. Very little was flowering, but occasionally she found some tiny scrap of a bloom, and she twisted into all sorts of contortions to point the camera at it, to try to obtain what she figured was the most exciting composition.

At last we could not go up any farther. We had reached the top of one of the many small peaks in the area. On the north side was a sharp drop-off and a big slab of snow. All around was a waste of space backed by hundreds of icy peaks. We could see several high lakes that were still white and frozen. It was cold, but Chris was in seventh heaven. Badger and I were tired after our Mouse and Marmot adventures—we had, after all, run at least five times the distance that Chris had plodded—and we found a sunny patch out of the wind to snooze in. Half asleep, I heard Chris call my name. I looked up—and she was pointing that camera at me. *Click!* And she grinned.

"That's a good one!" she said. "If you ever write a Book, that will go on the cover!"

"Lunchtime!" Chris added happily a moment later, sitting down beside us and dragging the human food out of her pack.

I lifted an eyelid lazily and thought it might be nice to have a bite of sandwich, but I had quickly learned that Chris would never share, and there wasn't any point in begging from her. It seemed as though we would be here for a while. I wondered if Badger would be interested in continuing with the Saga, but I didn't have to look at him to know that he was snoring. I shrugged mentally and decided to follow his example. I would have to wait for the next chapter of the story until after we were back at home.

14

BADGER

HOW CHRIS
FOUND RAFFI

"I SHOULD BE TELLING THIS IN BUCKY'S WORDS," BADGER BEGAN AS WE sat on the deck again in front of our cabin at Nuk Tessli, "but he was never very bright, and his memory couldn't be trusted. I have been able to put the story together well enough, though."

And this was the tale he told me.

WHEN CHRIS TOOK MAX TO THE TOOTH LADY, SHE STAYED AT THE SAME friend's place where she had picked up Ginger. She told her host Max's sad story.

"Now I need to find another dog," she said.

"You should give the SPCA a call," her friend commented, "but I saw something in the paper not too long ago. The article was about an outfit called Big Pooch Rescue. Why don't you phone them and see if they have anything suitable?"

Chris phoned the number in the advertisement and was informed that the rescue place was a little distance out of town. It was in the opposite direction from where we lived, but the man said he would drive and meet Chris partway. Chris thought this was very generous of him at the time—it was only later that she realized he probably did not want anyone near his place because he had things to hide.

Chris and Bucky eased into the pull-off where they'd arranged to meet the rescue people. A man and a woman were waiting beside a battered van encrusted with rust. One of its windows had been broken and sealed with an orange garbage bag. Chris thought it looked a bit rough and ready, but then her own truck was pretty beat up and rusty so she couldn't condemn the humans too much for that.

The people had two dogs with them. They said they would give Chris a deal if she took both. They quoted a price above that which the SPCA was charging.

Chris didn't have room for more than two dogs at a time so could take only one of them. The new one would have to get along with humans and with Bucky. The nearest dog was a female Australian Shepherd, one of those animals with a splotchy grey salt and pepper coat. The man held her on a tight leash, and when Chris drew closer, she lifted her lip to show her teeth and growled faintly. Chris might have been prepared to deal with that if the dog was just for her, but she always had tourists to consider, and many of these people had no experience with strange dogs. Besides, Shepherd was on the small side.

The larger animal was a Rottweiler mix much the same colour as Bucky, but skinny and long-legged. He looked quite young. He seemed friendly, but nervous.

"Why is his coat so greasy and dull?" Chris asked. "He's got an odd smell about him, too."

"We get these dogs from poor situations," the woman replied guardedly. "It takes a while to get them healthy again. We haven't had him long. He's had all his shots."

There was something a bit odd about these humans, a bit furtive even, but Chris could only think that people who rescued disadvantaged dogs would want the best for their animals. She had no idea that there could be anything fishy about them.

Anyway, she hauled Bucky out of the truck and introduced him to the new canine. Bucky did his usual thing of ignoring the new guy, but at least there was no fighting. Despite his shabby appearance, the new guy seemed fit and lively enough. So Chris handed over some Money, received some papers, and Raffi became part of our pack.

When Chris bothered to look at the documents she had been given, she could not make head or tail of them. A vet's certificate regarding distemper shots was included, but the dog on the paper was not named, and the paper was very crumpled. The dates were for six months previous.

"They said that they had not had the dog for very long," Chris said to her town friend. "And yet the certificate says he was vaccinated six months ago. If they've had him six months, how come his coat is in such a bad state?"

A few weeks later, when Chris picked up her mail at Nimpo, it included an article from the local paper, sent by Chris's town friend.

"Will you look at this," Chris exclaimed to her landlady. "Big Pooch Rescue has been taken to court on several accounts of animal cruelty."

"Who knows why those people do what they do?" the landlady said. "Maybe they thought they were doing the right thing but were just stupid. Maybe they stole the dogs and sold them. Maybe they fed the dogs improper food to try and save Money."

"It's all a big puzzle," Chris agreed. "I hope their other animals were not in too bad a shape and went to good homes. I would love to have taken them all."

The landlady laughed. "It would cost you a fortune in plane fares," she said.

So this is how Raffi came to live with Chris, and it is through him that we learn the next part of the Wilderness Dog Saga. Raffi told the story to Nahanni, and Nahanni—despite her unfriendliness—passed it in bits and pieces on to me. I have put her contributions together in the proper order to make them less of a muddle. As far as you are concerned, therefore, it is now Raffi who is continuing the Saga.

15

RAFFI

THE BIG FIRE AND OTHER STORIES

MY SHORT LIFE HAD SO FAR BEEN VERY CONFUSING, AND I REALLY DIDN'T know what to expect when I was put in the truck with Chris and Bucky. I was taken to Chris's friend's house in town and tied up for the night. I barked a lot and whined—I was frightened and alone. Bucky wasn't much help. Unless something affected him directly, he didn't much care what else was going on around him.

At least I got a decent meal. Chris prepared our food dishes and made us both sit before allowing us to eat. As I got to know Bucky, I was always surprised that he would do this, as he never listened to Chris on any other matter; but I guess food was important enough to him that he didn't mind going through this process. Once the food was put in front of me, I wolfed it down. One mouthful had an odd taste—"That's your worm pill," Chris said—but it went past my teeth too fast to spit it out.

"You'll soon put some weight on," Chris added, taking the empty dish away, "but I'm not going to give you too much to eat at once."

In the morning, Chris put us on leads and took us for a hike along a logging road behind the house. We each pulled in different directions, but Chris hung on tightly. Bucky kept trying to get at the remnants of a deer that some hunter had dumped the previous fall. There was not much left but dried skin. I must admit it smelled quite good, but even if Chris had not kept me away, Bucky would have prevented me from reaching it. As soon as he saw me looking at it, he growled and snapped.

Once back at her friend's house, Chris loaded us into her truck—Bucky in the back and me on the front seat. She first drove to some stores and picked up human food and dog kibble. Then she set off on the long road out of town, where we eventually arrived at the Cabin-in-the-Bog, which Bucky had already told me about in a sketchy sort of way. As it was obviously not our final destination, I didn't take much notice of it. I continued to be fed well and was beginning to feel a lot less nervous.

We stayed at the Cabin-in-the-Bog only two nights, and then we headed for the float plane base. I had never seen a plane before. I couldn't make out if it was a car or boat.

"Are we going in there?" I asked.

Bucky nodded in a bored way.

The ladder looked impossible for me to climb, but with a boost from Chris and the pilot I was able to scramble in. Chris couldn't push Bucky up by herself, and he usually growled during this process, so she would put a muzzle on him just to make sure he didn't nip anyone. He was calm enough inside the plane, though. I took my cue from him, and although the flight proved to be incredibly noisy, I did not find it alarming.

We bumped down onto another lake with a big whoosh, then turned and puttered slowly to a half-drowned wharf. A couple of cabins sat a bit haphazardly among the trees on the rocky land behind the wharf, and once we had docked, Bucky was pushed down the ladder. He immediately stuck his nose to the ground to find out which creatures, human or otherwise, had been by since he had last been there. I jumped down of my own accord but was still held by my rope; Chris did not let me run free until the next day. I had no intention of going anywhere, however. I was feeling so much better after a couple of good feeds, and wherever Chris was hanging out was where I wanted to be. My coat had even lost the stink and oily feel already. I wish I could have explained to Chris what had been done to me at my previous home to make me so unhealthy, but I didn't know how.

At first, Chris stayed close to home, and cleaned and fixed things. Then we started to go on hikes. On some of these, Chris carried tools on her back and whacked at trees or built piles of rocks; on others, she drove a canoe while Bucky and I ran along the shore close by. It had taken Bucky two years before he had decided he could swim, but now he loved the water and, where inlets or the river cut into the land, we would swim across. I enjoyed being in the water from the get-go.

"Your coat's beautifully clean and shiny now," Chris said soon after we had arrived at Nuk Tessli.

I really loved Chris. Somewhere in my distant past, I remembered sitting on a human's lap and enjoying it very much. I kept trying to do this with Chris but I could get only my front legs and head up there. Chris would laugh.

"You must have been a lap dog at one time," she would say.

One day, Chris slipped a kind of coat made of plastic and straps over my back. It was old and battered and smelled of another dog—

Bucky told me it was Max's backpack. He said that Chris would patch it up properly when we did some serious hiking. It felt a little funny and itchy at first, but I liked pleasing Chris and would do anything that she asked. Bucky thought I was sucking up needlessly, but that's the way I am.

After a while, the plane came in again, and some more humans stepped down onto the wharf. Bucky liked to meet the plane. He would sit on the edge of the wharf and watch it come in, tail wagging in anticipation of the pats he was going to get. Chris would stand behind him and, as the plane drew close, you could see people behind the tiny windows trying to take pictures of the two of them.

Chris was always very busy when tourists stayed with us. She would get up early, do a few exercises she called yoga (I like "downward dog" best!), have a bath in a bucket, partially cook dinner, and then have the coffee on and breakfast started by the time the tourists walked through her door. After their meal, the visitors would prepare sandwiches with Chris's homemade bread. They would get ready for their hike while Chris did the dishes. Then we would all go off for the day.

We dogs were fed only in the evening but, if Chris wasn't looking, we could get treats from the tourists' lunches. Chris asked them not to feed us—"They bug people too much, and Bucky often fights over food," she tried to explain—but we had no trouble picking out which visitors were a soft touch. We never begged from Chris—even Bucky now knew she would never give us anything during the day.

Once we got home, the tourists would relax—often swimming in the lake if it was warm enough—and Chris would finish making supper. She sometimes fed us before the humans, but Bucky started a sort of trick that Chris found very funny so she often used to hold our meals until after the tourists came in to eat.

The door of Chris's cabin had been constructed in two halves. The top half could open independently of the bottom half. She would open the upper part while the visiting humans were eating inside the cabin. By rearing on my hind legs I could see over the lower door.

Bucky would begin his performance with a sort of sigh. Chris's small smile told me that her sharp ears could pick the sound up even over the noisy chatter of her guests. She never said anything, but would wait in anticipation for what came next. After repeating the sigh a few times, Bucky would progress to a low moan. Sometimes the guests would hear him then. The calls became louder and louder, until Bucky was yodelling at the top of his voice. It wasn't really a howl and certainly wasn't a bark; it was a particular sound he made only at mealtimes. Some of the tourists thought this was hilariously funny; others thought Chris was being cruel to keep him from his dinner. (Couldn't they see how chubby he was?) But there was more to this concert than Bucky's unique song. As Chris stood up to prepare our food, we would both leap up so that our paws were on the top of the lower door and our heads stuck above it. Bucky had a problem with this because of his short legs, but I managed it easily. The tourists absolutely loved this and sometimes there were six cameras at once pointed at us during our finale.

That first summer in the mountains with Chris and Bucky proved to be an exciting one. It was very hot and dry, just as the previous one had apparently been, and there were many lightning storms. The humans constantly talked about the fires that had sprung up all over the province, and for weeks the air was filled with smoke. Apart from the general haze—sometimes like a brownish fog and sometimes so thick you couldn't see the sun—there were also the fire towers, which were made

Raffi and Bucky

from steam. When the hot winds fanned the fires in the afternoon, the brown smoke would roll over the ground, but the white steam from the burning forest would rise high into the sky. The fire towers happened only when the flames were out of control. At one time, we could see three fire towers in different directions around us. Two were south of our lake, but one was behind the North Ridge. It had first appeared close to the big mountains, but suddenly it had begun to move quite quickly to the east. Chris figured that the fire must have been raging at great speed along a high valley.

These conflagrations were big enough to make national news. Earlier that summer, Chris had finally been able to afford to have the Internet installed. First she'd needed more solar panels—a friend came and set them up for her—and then another man arrived with various bits of equipment, which he attached to the gable end of the cabin. It was all meaningless to me, but judging by Chris's delighted comments, it seemed she could write on her computer as if she were talking to someone—and they would very quickly reply. She could also pick up the news about the fires. It was all very puzzling. Just like magic. Maybe the computer was making sounds too high for a dog to hear.

The two Wwoofers who were helping us at that time were both women from Ontario. They had come to aid Chris during the busy part of the tourist season. One group of tourists was already with us, but because of the fire news, other parties were cancelling. Chris told the Wwoofers that she had been expecting the busiest season yet but it was now quite literally going up in smoke.

The closest fire was the one that was moving very quickly behind the North Ridge. Our current visitors were waiting to fly out. On that particular morning, the wind had dropped, and the smoke was too thick for the plane to find us. Around the middle of the day, a small breeze started to blow from the mountains, and finally the smoke thinned and our visitors could leave.

"Everyone in the whole area's been taken out except us," said Chris to her two helpers as the plane flew away. "There're no other humans for at least sixty kilometres in any direction—and a lot farther than that to the south and west. This is the most isolated from other humans that I have ever been."

It was so fantastic to see the blue sky over the mountains at the head of the lake again that everyone relaxed. It had been a very tense time. A couple of hours later, however, Chris made a trip to the outhouse—to do that, she had to turn her back to the mountains and walk the other way.

"Oh my gosh," she exclaimed.

We all ran to see what she was looking at. Behind us, an enormous black pall of smoke had started to crawl across the sky. What was worse, the bottom of the smoke was orange. The small breeze that had so nicely cleared the view must have also stirred up the fire. For us to be able to see the orange glow from so far away, the flames must have been huge. Soon tiny particles of ash started to fall like fine flakes of grey snow.

"It's pointless trying to get help or news on the Internet," Chris said worriedly to her Wwoofers. "It will take too long to get a reply. Let's hope the radiophone works. I can only get through one day in three most of the time so keep your fingers crossed." Chris was lucky and she was able to contact someone near the float plane base.

"What's happening?" she asked.

"We don't know," came the scratchy reply, sounding like someone trying to talk inside a tin can. "But it's obviously very big."

Chris gave a big sigh. "I think we're going to have to leave," she said dismally to the Wwoofers. "Problem is, most of our overland routes to the road are blocked by the fire. I know of one way that we could hike out that is clear at the moment, but if the fire travels with the speed it has done in the last couple of days, we would never be able to outrun it."

She pressed the button and spoke to the person on the radio-phone. "We'd better get out of here," she said into the microphone. "Can you ask the float plane company to send in a plane for us? We're clear right now but the smoke is thickening fast."

"Roger that," said the tin can voice.

Then followed frantic packing. Because fires had been threatening for so long, Chris had made a list of essential things, and another list of things that she would take if there were time and room. With three people, two dogs, and three backpacks, there would not be space for anything beyond what Chris considered the most important Stuff. The Wwoofers threw their gear together; they didn't have much anyway. We dogs, of course, needed nothing but ourselves.

The plane must have taken off as soon as we had called, for it was hissing down on our lake within half an hour. Chris expected it to have come the long way round via the mountains because the air was still comparatively clear in that direction, but it flew right through the black wall of smoke. We tossed everything inside and took off without delay, plunging into the foggy dark. The pilot was allergic to dogs (why that should be I don't know; I've never heard of dogs being allergic to humans). Because of this, Chris had been relegated to the back seat where she hung onto both me and Bucky.

Chris always hates flying, and it was obvious from her expression and body language that she now had the appalling worry as to whether she would ever see her home again. The air was thick with smoke and bumpy with heat. Suddenly we saw a flame. Soon we were flying over sheets of fire, many of which had straight edges where they were burning along a lake. The flames were higher than the trees. It was an inferno, a land in torment.

The plane was suddenly flung into the air like a leaping salmon.

"Hot spot," called the pilot. He seemed to be enjoying himself but for us it was very scary.

Then, just as suddenly, we exited the fire zone and plumped down again. The air was now calm and smooth and perfectly clear. It was as if the black smoke had been cut off with a knife: behind was a maelstrom, but beyond was a gentle blue evening, as serene and beautiful as one could wish for. We glided down to the float plane base without a single bump.

THE MAN WHO HAD INSTALLED THE NEW SOLAR PANELS EARLIER THAT year was called Dave. He and his wife, Rosemary, also lived off-road, although it was possible to drive to their place in summer. During the winter, they would travel in and out by snowmobile.

Once we had escaped from the fire, all of us, including the two Wwoofers, were invited down there to stay.

We first drove by the Cabin-in-the-Bog to pick up a few things, and then continued west along the highway before turning onto a dusty logging road. When this ended, we plunged down a narrow track so rocky and rutted the truck could not travel much faster than walking speed. Chris let Bucky and me run alongside. In spring, Bucky told me, the ditches beside the narrow road would be running with water, but now everything was dry. Down and down we went, the truck lurching like a rudderless boat in a storm. Thick bushes lined the track and they constantly scratched and squealed against the sides of the vehicle. After a long time, we came to a creek, and Chris stopped while we dogs jumped in the water and cooled off. She put us back into the truck after that, and it wasn't long before we rattled over a cattle guard and started to drive beside a fence. More lurching and swaying, and we suddenly came through a gate to an open field. Hay had recently been taken off it and the stubble was short and brown and aromatic of drying grass. We drove over a bridge: *bang! bang! bang!* went the loose timbers on its deck. A sharp right, and soon we climbed up a steep little trail to Dave and

Rosemary's house. Like Chris, they generated electricity from solar power, but their system was much larger. Two big banks of panels had been mounted on swivels so that they could be turned to the sun.

Dave and Rosemary had a dog called Chilko who ran free, but we had to be tied at this place. Rosemary was growing a lot of leaves and roots for humans to eat, and she did not trust us to keep off her garden. Besides, there were horses not far away and Bucky for sure would have chased them. I have to confess—I probably would have chased them as well, given the chance.

Later that day, Chris and Rosemary climbed onto an ATV and the two Wwoofers walked behind them, bringing Bucky and me on our rope leads. We went between the main ranch buildings (which belonged to someone else), then up a steep track that grew worse and worse. Chris and Rosemary finally abandoned the ATV, and we all walked together. We had been climbing high up the other side of the valley from where we had driven in, and we eventually came to the top of a cliff. The rocks were quite peculiar, looking a bit like giant pencils on end, standing squashed together.

"Wow," said one of the Wwoofers. "What a classic example of columnar basalt."

"Most of the Chilcotin is of volcanic origin," Rosemary explained. "Chris's mountains are different. They're at the edge of the continent and are made from granite that's been pushed up by the squeezing of the tectonic plates. But behind us are hills that were once active volcanoes. That was a very long time ago, though, before the last ice age even. As a result, basalt columns are common along the edge of the Chilcotin. They can be seen all the way to Williams Lake. It is this cliff that has given our valley the name 'The Precipice.'"

At the top of the basalt columns, we had a great view, not only of the valley with its tiny houses far below but also of the distant mountains beyond the far rim. The main reason for us going up there at this time, however, was not the view, but to try to judge the progress of the fires. Although it was late in the day, we could see three steam towers spread across the horizon.

"That's the one down the Klinaklini," Rosemary explained as she pointed. "The two over there are both parts of the Lonesome Lake fire. Nuk Tessli is somewhere in the middle."

The sun was going down and it painted the steam towers red. Looking at them did not really give us much idea of what was going on, as it was impossible to pinpoint their bases exactly. And this was the worst thing of all about the fires—the not knowing. From a distance, it was never easy to judge what was happening, and getting close to the fires was impossible because of the smoke. It was too dangerous even for helicopters to fly near the flames when the fires were raging this much; big fires created their own violent winds and you never knew which way they were going to blow.

The following day, Chris put Bucky and me into the truck and we bumped our way back to the Cabin-in-the-Bog. The Wwoofers stayed behind to help Rosemary with her garden.

Chris never liked being at the Cabin-in-the-Bog at the best of times, and now, with the fire worry and no indication as to how long she would have to stay there, she was in a miserable state. What was more, the local wind had changed; the clean, clear air we had encountered when we had landed at the float plane base was now thick and acrid with smoke. An army of firefighters had arrived at the nearby Anahim airport with all sorts of heavy equipment, including eighteen helicopters. The constant rattle and roar of these machines, and the thick brown smoke, made it feel like a war zone.

Chris had no Internet in the cabin, and the only way she could keep in touch with the fire news was by going up to the landlady's house. Day after day, she would walk up there and try to find out what was going on. At last, however, there appeared a sky that was grey with cloud instead of brown with smoke. A few spits of rain fell.

"There have been a couple of showers in the mountains," Chris told us after she came back from the landlady's house that day. "They're not enough to put the fires out—that won't happen completely until the snow flies, but the summer is drawing to a close and the nights are longer and cooler. With a bit of luck, the fires can now be kept under control. Nuk Tessli has been spared, and we are going to be allowed to go home."

We packed hurriedly, scrambled to the float plane base, and flew in on a bumpy wind just before sundown.

The wind and rain had swept the lake and the surrounding mountains clean. It was as if the fire had never been. When the wind veered again later in the summer, smoke would again creep in, but the danger was over. Now that everything was safe, it was hard to imagine what the fuss had all been about.

AFTER THE SUMMER OF THE BIG FIRE, BUCKY, CHRIS AND I TRAVELLED around on one of Chris's Book Tours. We stayed with Len and Miriam, where Bucky and Chris had first met. Bucky and I were tied in the yard where Bucky barked at any dog he saw walk by. Fortunately both Len and Miriam loved to take long walks, and they took us out when Chris was too busy. Although we had to be kept on leads, we were able to have plenty of exercise.

Once we arrived back at the Cabin-in-the-Bog, Chris tried to organize a flight home for the winter, but it was becoming increasingly difficult to find anyone who would put skis on their planes. The pilots told her that insurance had skyrocketed, and they didn't think the added expense was worth the couple of months' winter play. If she had been younger, Chris might have snowshoed in and made us carry packs. I'd learned from piecing together the Saga that

Lonesome and Sport used to do this with her, and so did Taya for a while. Chris would pull a toboggan packed with light things like her sleeping bags and the axe, and the dogs would walk in the track she had made with her snowshoes.

These were long and gruelling treks that might take up to four days; they were often extremely uncomfortable, being either very cold or too warm. Now, however, Chris had finally admitted that she couldn't do this kind of hiking anymore. She had sore knees and she was getting old. So we had to look for another way to get back into the mountains.

While we had been out in the big city on our Book Tour, Chris had exchanged her old truck for a van. It was by no means a new vehicle but it was still quite presentable. It was certainly far more comfortable for me and Bucky to ride in.

One day early in the new year, we packed all our gear and winter supplies into the van. Instead of driving out on the ice to meet the plane as Bucky had told me was usual, we travelled a long way, climbing first to the top of a snowy mountain pass and then zigzagging down and down into a deep valley. It was much warmer down there and very little snow lay on the ground. The road was bare and wet, and you could see patches of dirty green grass beside the roads.

We arrived at a place that was full of planes. Some of these were much bigger than the ones we habitually flew in. None of them had skis under their bellies, however. Why we were here was a big mystery.

A small building sat at the end of a string of airport structures, and Chris drove to it. Out back was a helicopter. I'd seen plenty of these things roaring overhead during the fire, but they are funny-looking machines when you get up close. They have propellors on top of their heads instead of on their noses, and the arms of the propellors stretch over the whole aircraft.

The pilot had Chris, us dogs, and all the freight stand on a big square that he said was a scale.

"If you're too heavy," he said, "we won't be able to get off the ground." He peered at a digital screen sitting on top of a pole beside the square. "Hmm," he said. "Borderline. We'll see. If we can't lift off you'll have to leave something behind."

Chris looked panic stricken. "I've packed so carefully," she wailed. "I can't imagine spending all those winter months in the bush without every single item I've brought."

"As long as she doesn't turn out any of my kibble," muttered Bucky under his breath.

We loaded all the freight and climbed inside. It was a lot cleaner, tidier and less battered than the plane we were accustomed to. The helicopter was used for a number of things, but its main purpose was to carry passengers who went skiing in the mountains—these people had a great deal of Money, so they were quite happy to pay for a cleaner, fancier aircraft.

The pilot asked Chris to sit in the back with us dogs beside her. We wore our ropes, and Chris hung onto them tight. The pilot pressed a button and the great propellor on the top started to turn. Soon it was whirring so fast you couldn't see it. The motor's whine grew higher—and suddenly, we were off the ground.

"Hooray," said Chris. "We don't have to leave anything behind."

The windows were much bigger than on a float plane, and you could see all around, even underneath our feet. Helicopters are very noisy when you are standing outside them, but inside this one it was remarkably quiet. Chris and the pilot could talk without raising their voices.

"I hate flying in planes," Chris told him, "I think the main problem for me is claustrophobia. I am out of control. But I actually quite like being in helicopters. I don't know if it's the more open views or what, but I just have the feeling I can open the door and step right out of it, even though my brain tells me that's impossible."

"It cuts through the wind more easily, and it's less bumpy as well," the pilot explained. I, however, who had no trouble at all with planes, became increasingly uncomfortable in this machine. I could not have told you why. Soon I was trembling hard. Chris tried to comfort me but without much success. Bucky was his usual bored self and he had curled up and gone to sleep.

First we travelled low over the little village that was near the helicopter office, and then we seemed to be heading straight for the mountain wall. Chris was as startled as I when we popped into a small gap—a plane could never have gone into a tight space like this. We were in a very steep-walled valley. The black rocks at the bottom gave way to white snow on the upper slopes. Up and up we climbed until we were higher than the mountain pass we had driven over that morning. It had been cloudy in the valley, but now we rose through the vapour layer. Above it the sun was shining. Still hanging onto our ropes, Chris freed a hand so she could take pictures with her digital camera.

"There's Monarch!" she exclaimed. Monarch Mountain was the name of the big peak we could see beyond the head of our lake. "I hadn't realized how much higher it is than anything else around here. It sticks up like a hitchhiker's thumb." Thousands of other snowy peaks were jumbled in all directions.

At first we stayed fairly close to various land forms, all rugged rock and clotted snow. Chris kept exclaiming and taking pictures. Suddenly the world fell away beneath our feet into a great canyon. Below were dark carpets of forest and white frozen lakes. Then we swung into another valley, but there were no trees in this one. Sometimes a few black sticks poked above the snow.

"This is where the Lonesome Lake fire was last summer," said the pilot. "It was so fierce when it came through here that it vapourized the trees and destroyed the soil down to the rock. It will take a very long time for the forest to grow back again." I remembered how the steam tower had moved so quickly behind the North Ridge. This must have been where the fire had raced.

Soon our lake was below us. The helicopter was not as handicapped by overflow as a plane would have been, and the pilot landed it right in front of the cabins.

"That's pretty much the first flight I have ever really enjoyed," Chris laughed. "I wish I could afford to fly by helicopter all the time." I, however, was only too thankful to have my feet firmly on something solid again.

"Good news for us," said Bucky eyeing the helicopter's landing place. "We won't have to carry the freight so far."

In fact we didn't have to carry it at all. Once the motor had shut off and the big propellor had wound down, the pilot dragged out a large net. He loaded all the freight onto it, took off in the chopper again, and lifted the net way above the trees. He brought it down gently, right in front of the cabin door.

"Wow," said Chris. "It's almost worth paying all that extra just to get the freight up to the cabin like this. What luxury!"

WE HAD A WONDERFUL WINTER. CHRIS CHOPPED WATER HOLES AND skied and snowshoed; we endured blizzards; we basked in fabulous sunny winter days; we also enjoyed the excitement of breakup. Chris was having such a good time watching the seasons unfold that the ice had been gone off the lake for nearly a month before we flew back outside, which we could do by plane at that time. As usual, she had to make the trip to town to buy supplies for the summer, but she had something else on her agenda as well. She had inherited some Money and she was going to buy some land.

"I've got to have an outside place of my own," she told her friends. "I've always hated the Cabin-in-the-Bog. It's too crowded with all those people close by, and it's such an uncomfortable building to spend any time in. It's impossible to keep the gaps in the logs stuffed and that makes it far too cold in winter and full of bugs in summer. I really need somewhere decent for when I have to spend time outside, and also to store all my Stuff."

We visited lots of properties, all large and fairly far away from anyone else, but Chris found fault with every one of them.

"Too close to the neighbour's house."

"No good water."

"Too shady—I'll never get up that north-facing road in winter."

One was in a different direction from all the others. There were neighbours, but their buildings were hidden by trees. Also, they were across the river and it would be quite a journey to drive round to see them. The other sides of the property were surrounded by government land.

"It's going to be hard for me to live so close to people," she said. "But this place at least has some space around it. Let's camp for the night and get the feel of it."

Chris set up her little tent and made a small fire on top of a knoll. She cooked her supper and the smoke from the fire had the added advantage of keeping the bugs away. Whenever she hauled her camping gear out of storage, it always reeked of old woodsmoke. Below the knoll the river was still wild with spring runoff. Beyond were mountains—not as big or as close as the ones at Nuk Tessli.

"But at least they are there," she said.

There was a dog across the river; even Chris could hear him bark. She sighed.

"Life is full of compromise," she said, scratching me behind my ears as we sat beside the fluttering flames. "But I'm getting older, and I've got to think of the future. My knees are giving out, I can't afford to keep hiring helicopters, and I won't be able to run Nuk Tessli forever." She sighed. "There's no cabin on this property either. I'll just have to build again." She pulled a long face at that thought, but pushed it out of her mind: "I guess we could do a lot worse. I think this is where we are going to live. We'll be here only during the winters—we'll still go into the mountains in the summer. And"—she smiled when she said this—"we'll be able to get rid of that awful Cabin-in-the-Bog!"

Then she turned to me and continued on a more serious note. "It is quite scary to think I will actually be a landowner. The mountain property belongs to the government and I have only been renting it. Owning a place is a whole different ball game. I've never had Money. All my life I've scrimped and stretched every penny. Thanks to my inheritance, I suddenly have a fortune, although to buy this place I will have to spend almost all of it. That's a pretty big commitment." She paused for a moment. "I guess we should think of a name for it. The second person to live here was called Ginty Paul. She was an eccentric spinster like me! The first and only other resident here was her father. Ginty died about twenty years ago—plenty of time for the pack rats to really take over! However, in memory of Ginty, who by all accounts really loved the place, I think I'll call it 'Ginty Creek.'"

Such philosophizing was beyond me, but I liked the way we all sat around the fire together. We could not spend more than one night at the campsite, though, because this summer's tourist season was already upon us. The first visitors would arrive in a week.

Before we flew into Nuk Tessli, however, we drove down the bumpy road to the Precipice to visit Dave and Rosemary for a couple of days. Bucky and I ran down the rough bush road for a while. Sometimes we caught a whiff of Bear—they were very common here in the spring. That was the only time we were let loose, however. Down at Dave and Rosemary's we had to be tied up again.

To compensate us for having to be chained so much, Chris always gave us a good long walk in the morning. Dave and Rosemary's house was on a hill, and we would head down a steep trail to the little river that ran below. When there was no livestock nearby, Chris would sometimes let me off the lead. (Bucky, however, could never be trusted at any time.)

Our first morning down there was a gorgeous late spring day. Although the sun was already bright on the basalt cliff, the bottom of the valley was still shady and cool to the point of being nippy. The rancher had dug trenches to channel the water from the river to irrigate his hayfields, and at this time the ditches were full and flowing fast. The grass beside them nearly covered my back and was saturated with dew.

It was glorious to be able to run, and the cool wetness spurred on my excitement. I tore around in a circle. Chris prepared to jump over an irrigation ditch. Her timing was totally wrong. When she was still in mid-air, my head connected with the inside of her right knee, and I knocked her clean over. Fortunately she didn't fall in the ditch—then she would have been really mad. She managed to hang onto Bucky, and she climbed awkwardly to her feet, but she was walking very strangely. I was still having a good time, but it seemed as though our morning hike was to be cut short. Very slowly, Chris limped back up the steep trail to Dave and Rosemary's house. She fastened us to our usual tree and hobbled to the garden hose to fill our bucket with water. Dave was in the yard.

"What have you done to your leg?" he asked.

"Not sure," Chris said. "But it got a good whack."

Chris went inside and sat down. When she tried to move an hour or so later, the leg simply would not work.

Dave and Rosemary's home was three and half hours' drive from the nearest hospital where Chris would have to go to get an X-ray. Rosemary drove her down there the next day. The doctor said a small chip of bone had been broken off. Chris had never broken a bone before. The chip was lying against the top of the tibia and would heal by itself, so she wouldn't need a cast, but she wasn't supposed to walk on it for three months. She would have to use crutches.

"Three months!" Chris wailed to the doctor. "That's my whole tourist season!" We had been due to fly back into the mountains in two days' time. Tourists were supposed to arrive five days later.

Back at Dave and Rosemary's, Chris spent a lot of time inside. Rosemary was the one who came out to feed us and take us for walks, and she told us that Chris was busy on the Internet. She had to try and arrange help for the summer. Fortunately a man called Peter, who was working at the ranch, had a bit of slack time for a couple of weeks. The Cows and Calves had already been pushed up to their summer grazing, and haying would not start for a while. Chris also managed to arrange a bunch of Wwoofers and a hiking guide to help her throughout the summer.

And so, a few days later, Peter, Bucky and myself, and Chris with her crutches, presented ourselves at the float plane base. This time it was Chris who needed the boost to climb the ladder into the plane. Once we had landed at Nuk Tessli, Peter had to carry all the freight to its storage places; his second job was to rearrange all the rocks along the trail to the outhouse so Chris could crutch herself back and forth.

It was a lovely summer for the rest of us. Not too buggy, not too hot, but lots of sunshine. Peter left, and the first tourists, the guide, and the Wwoofers arrived. We would all set off for the day, either working on trails or hiking with the tourists. Chris was left behind with the cooking and the dishes. As you can imagine, although she was very grateful for all the excellent help, she was not too happy with this arrangement.

"Now I know what it's like to be a housewife," she grumbled gloomily to everyone. "I can't figure how anyone can be happy with a life like that."

We came out of Nuk Tessli a little earlier than usual that year. The golden leaves were still on the aspens around the float plane base. I expected that we would go to the Cabin-in-the-Bog straight away, but even though Chris said we still had Stuff there, we bypassed it. Instead, we drove along the highway quite a way and laid claim to yet another cabin. It belonged to some more of Chris's friends and they were happy to rent it to her for a cheap price. The two Wwoofers who had been with Chris during the last part of her time in the mountains planned to stay with her at this new place for a few days. They were going to help her start to build a new home beside the river where we had camped before I broke Chris's leg.

Every morning, we all drove to work. The humans cut down and peeled trees, shovelled soil and scrounged among some of the old barns that were scattered around the place for usable lumber. There was not a lot of this because most of the buildings had been shoddily erected, and they were also absolutely riddled with Pack Rat. There were so many of these little furry animals, and they had been there so long, that the buildings reeked. The scent was so strong that even the humans wrinkled their noses at it. One of the buildings had a wooden floor where Pack Rat poop was so thick that it was like walking on popcorn kernels. Bucky and I had a fine old time chasing the perpetrators around the high timbers and among the huge piles of garbage that were in the barns. They always stayed too high up for us to get them, though.

The soil that the Wwoofers dug away for the new cabin was dry and silty. The very second morning that we came to work, Chris exclaimed in amazement.

"Look at that!" she said. "Every square centimetre of newly dug ground is absolutely covered in pack rat paw prints. Those barns are at least three hundred metres away. How did they find this place? And why did they come?"

"They're obviously checking it out for future reference," said one of the Wwoofers.

"It looks as though they must have had a wonderful party," laughed the other.

After five days, the crew had built a foundation and a floor, and started to put up the walls. The Wwoofers were due to go back to

Badger in the pack-rat palace. The pack rats are hiding in the roof.

Europe, and Chris took time off to drive us all to town, where she also bought more supplies. She then worked alone for a little while. She first went into the forest and found a few more trees suitable for building. She had stopped using the crutches but was still wearing a leg brace. She soon found the brace so restrictive while climbing over fallen logs and the like that she took it off as well. The leg seemed to have mended perfectly. She had long ago forgiven me for the accident.

She dragged the logs back to the building site with the van and peeled them. Then, who should arrive, but the guide who had come to Nuk Tessli during the summer! It was great to see him again. He and Chris put extra supports in the walls and started on the roof. The guide stayed ten days, but before he left, two more old friends arrived. They were none other than the two females who had been with us when we had been evacuated from the fire! How fantastic was that? After they had left Nuk Tessli, they had gone to a place called Ghana to teach school for a couple of years.

Work went fast with the two new helpers, but now the weather was getting quite wintry. The cabin that we were sleeping in could not be heated properly. The water had been turned off, and we had to fetch it in a bucket from the owners' house, which stood on a hill nearby. Sometimes it was so cold that there would be ice on the bucket in the morning, even when it was stored inside, and again in the evening when we came back from work.

"Remember what you emailed to me?" Chris said one evening as she broke the ice

Pack rat

on the water pail. "You said, 'It is so hot in Ghana, we can hardly stand it. We would love to come and help you build your cabin. We can't wait to be cold!' Well, cold is what you've got." This was just the start. We didn't know then, but it was to be one of the coldest winters on record.

Chris was going on yet another Book Tour. This time, however, we did not go with her. We stayed with the two women while they continued to work on the cabin. Their job while Chris was gone was to install the insulation.

The ground had been snow covered for quite a while before Chris left, and the day she drove away there was a fresh fall that was as high as my hocks. The Wwoofers had planned on having a well-earned day off before driving all our supplies to the new place and moving in, but during that time it dumped more snow, and then the temperature crashed. They first had to dig their way out of the cabin we had been staying in, just to reach the ploughed road, and when they arrived at the turnoff to our new place, they could no longer drive along it. They skied the whole four kilometres, dragging some supplies with a toboggan, while Bucky and I ran alongside. Many of the vegetables left behind in their car froze solid. The Wwoofers survived those days by wearing many layers of clothing. Humans have poor resistance to temperature changes.

The metal roof over the main part of the building had been finished before Chris left, but the porch was covered only with a tarp. The women built a giant doghouse under the tarp using bales of insulation. Fortunately, the weather warmed, and although it snowed again, Bucky and I were quite comfortable.

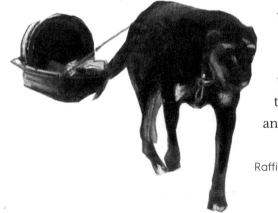

Raffi

We helped fetch water from the river. The route down there was quite steep. While Chris was still at home, she made Bucky and me carry milk jugs of water in our backpacks. The Wwoofers kept a hole open in the river where it ran close to the bank and when the snow was deep enough, they harnessed me to the toboggan and I dragged up a whole bucketful at a time.

The bush road had to be ploughed before Chris could get home. She needed to drive in because she had piles of winter food, much of which would freeze if left overnight at the highway. A man came with a big, dirty yellow tractor and pushed the snow out of the way.

"What a treat!" Chris exclaimed to the Wwoofers when she drove into the yard. "At the Cabin-in-the-Bog and Nuk Tessli, I always had to deal with an icy cabin that might take a couple of days to warm through. I would have to chop a hole for water, and break trail with snowshoes to go to anywhere, even just to the outhouse. It's so wonderful to be welcomed by a warm cabin, two buckets of water, a pile of wood split, tramped-down trails, and my mail picked up from the post office. In comparison, this new place is decadent!"

The inside of the cabin, however, was far from finished. The two women had insulated the walls and ceiling. The wall insulation had been faced with wood already, but the ceiling batts were covered only by a thin plastic skin. The lumber that would be used to cover it was stored on one side of the cabin, and this took up almost half the floor space. A crude shelf against the opposite wall held cardboard boxes of food and kitchen supplies. A big ugly stove squatted in the centre, and almost all of the rest of the floor was crowded with Stuff. A bed platform lay under a window, and jammed next to it was a space for Chris's small computer. She'd had the Internet installed even before the roof was finished. Funny: she had lived all those years at Nuk Tessli with no Internet, but now you'd think she could not live without it.

NOT LONG AFTER CHRIS RETURNED FROM THE BOOK TOUR, WE TRAVELLED back down to the Precipice, where Dave and Rosemary had invited us down to their valley for Christmas. There was too much snow for Chris to drive down the bumpy road. Dave, however, had a big truck with chains on, and he was able to meet her at the top of the steep part. More snow was falling as we set off and, even going downhill, Dave's truck was having terrible trouble, slithering back and forth across the narrow road.

"The truck will never make it back up again," said Dave. "When we come out again, we'll have to travel by snowmobile."

We loved visiting the Precipice. Rosemary was an excellent cook and all kinds of good treats came our way. The rancher and his wife invited us all for dinner and we had a great time. We ate more turkey and gravy and leftover scraps of pie and whipped cream. The weather stayed relatively warm and snowy, but the evening before we were due to leave, the sky cleared and the temperature dropped.

If we dogs had not been with her, Chris would simply have ridden behind Dave on the snowmobile. We could not run alongside because the hill was too steep and the snow too deep. Dave would have to go too fast for us to keep up, otherwise he would bog down and get stuck.

A kind of sled called a skimmer was harnessed onto the snowmobile. Chris was given extra clothes so she looked as though she had been blown up like a balloon. She sat in the bottom of the skimmer with her back to the snowmobile. She dragged me in beside her, and I lay on top of her legs. She held onto my collar with one hand, and the other grasped a rope which was tied to Dave's waist. He could not look behind him as he was driving, and the fierce noise of the machine would hide Chris's yells if anything untoward happened. With the rope tied in place, however, if the skimmer turned over or Chris fell out, Dave would feel the pull of the rope, and stop.

Problem was, there was no room for Bucky. Dave tried to lift him onto the snowmobile in front of him, but Bucky growled and snapped. It wasn't going to work.

"We'll have to try the dog crate," Rosemary said. She fished it out of the storage shed. "I'll give Peter a call."

Peter was the man who had flown home with Chris when I had broken her leg. He was still working at the ranch. He drove up with another snowmobile that was also pulling a skimmer, and Rosemary strapped the bottom half of the dog crate onto it. "We'll do it this way," she said. "It will be easier to sit Bucky in the lower part and then screw down the top afterward. He might not go inside otherwise."

I thought we would have trouble getting Bucky settled, but he seemed to think the crate was just another car, and he always liked riding in cars. Dave fastened the top of the crate down, and off we went. Dave and Chris and me first, Peter and Bucky behind us. The machines whined, the skimmer banged on the frozen ruts, and fumes and snow were blasted over us. I struggled and tried to get off, but Chris would not let go of me. I relaxed a bit; Chris would never put me in harm's way and I figured this would be survivable.

Bucky was not so lucky. We hadn't even got across the hayfield at the bottom of the valley before his skimmer tipped over, the dog crate flew into two pieces, and Bucky was running free. Chris yelled at the top of her voice, but Dave could not hear her. She yanked on the rope around his middle, and he slowly came to a halt. Bucky was

Raffi and Chris in the skimmer behind the snowmobile waiting to be towed up the hill from the Precipice.

hard to catch if he wanted to be free, and I didn't see how we were ever going to get him back into the crate. But would you believe it? He came when Chris called, and then he hopped right into the bottom half of the crate and allowed the men to fasten the lid again.

Once again the whining motors were fired up, and now we started to climb the rough trail. We were half-suffocated in fumes, buried in a blizzard of snow, and flung about so hard our spines cracked. A rim of ice was forming around Chris's face (courtesy of the wool hat and scarf she was wearing), but she slit her eyes and kept watch over Bucky's crate. Through our self-made blizzard we could see the yellow glow of the light in front of Peter's snowmobile. The crate slewed and tipped alarmingly from side to side: it looked as though it would turn over again at any moment, but somehow it always righted itself again. Finally we reached the ploughed road where our van was waiting. The snow packed tightly upon us was so fine that it cracked like an eggshell when we moved. How wonderful it was to stretch our legs and have a good run along the road.

THAT WINTER, WE DIDN'T HAVE TO LOOK FOR SOMEONE TO FLY US INTO Nuk Tessli. Chris planned on staying at the River Cabin to finish the inside. But she plodded along her daily tasks in misery. She constantly moaned that she had never enjoyed building, and she really missed being in the mountains. More snow fell—a great deal—until it was at the level of her chest. This was the normal amount we could expect at Nuk Tessli, but it was very unusual here. She did steal a day or two occasionally to tramp around on snowshoes. Because Cow was over the river, she had to keep Bucky tied—something neither Bucky nor Chris enjoyed.

The river froze enough so that we dogs could cross it. The neighbours' dog could, too. There was some kind of hump of vegetation in the middle of the river, all covered in snow. The farm dog would come from his house and pee on it, and I would go from ours and do the same. Chris laughed because no matter how much the snow kept falling, the hump in the river was always yellow.

By the time the spring came to Ginty Creek, the new River Cabin was a little better organized inside and Chris felt that we could spare some time to explore the surrounding country. Apart from the ranch across the river, the rest of the property was bordered by government land, so we could go anywhere we wanted. However, that land was full of logging roads, old fences, and cutblocks, and I often heard Chris say sadly that this human stain on the country made it a poor second to the wildness of Nuk Tessli. Even the few flowers that eventually showed after the snow went did not give her the same pleasure as the ones she found in the mountains. She called them aliens.

"In the mountains," she would say, "everything belongs."

Alongside the river, a short distance from the cabin, were hills that dropped precipitously to the river. They were amazingly sandy. On the windward sides, almost nothing grew. When the wind blew it was impossible to walk up there, as sand was blasted up the cliffs into a blizzard of silt. The disappearing snow revealed that these hills were actually sand dunes. The walks up there gave Chris views of the mountains that she enjoyed. She knew that if she climbed those mountains she would be able to see Nuk Tessli, but the peaks were difficult to reach, even after the snow had mostly gone. Bucky and I were much happier with our lot. The scents that told us of the life along the river were endlessly fascinating. Moose and Wolf were plentiful that winter.

Because it had been a big snow year, the river was very high at the peak of the spring flood. The yellow hump of snow soon washed away—so did other lumps and bumps, and even chunks of the bank below the cabin.

The extra snow also meant that the ice went out late from the lakes both near the cabin and high up in the mountains. The green leaves were already fully out on the aspens before we could fly into Nuk Tessli to start our summer tourist business. Three spring Wwoofers had been helping us at Ginty Creek and we took them into the mountains with us. The snow around the cabins was amazing. The previous year there had been hardly any when we arrived at the beginning of summer. This time it was so deep that we had to cut steps in the drifts to enable us to carry the freight up into its storage spaces.

BUCKY WAS A KILLER. HE COULDN'T RUN ALL THAT FAST, BUT ANYTHING that he got in his jaws was instant toast. Once he was simply snoozing on the deck. It was spring and the migrant birds were arriving and squabbling over the territories that they would use to build their kennels and rear their young. Three juncos zipped in front of Bucky's nose. He barely moved, but with a snap, he snatched one of them out of the air. Chris was trying to keep bird records for an ornithologist. If she found a dead bird and she knew the reason for the death, she was supposed to add it to the information. She was very embarrassed to keep having to write, "Dog ate it."

Chris made use of Bucky's mercenary behaviour on occasion. Sometimes she caught Pack Rat in a trap and he wasn't killed right away. Chris tried to keep Pack Rat out of her house, but her carpentry work was not good enough and he often found his way into the attic. Bucky was an efficient executioner.

One winter, Bucky killed Otter. Grown-up Otter can be as big as a dog, but this one was small. It was very thin and was close to death anyway. It must have been starving. This was before my time, when Max was still in the pack, but Bucky boasted about it to me. Max managed to grab it and prance around on the ice with it, keeping

it away from Bucky. Chris saw what was going on from inside the cabin and ran out to see what the dogs had caught. Max wasn't going to let her have it either. He ran off into the snowy forest and buried it, but Chris was too smart for him. Her nose might be useless, but her eyes are quite good. She paused long enough to strap on snowshoes and followed Max's tracks. He had pushed Otter under a leaning log and was tamping snow down on top of it with his nose. Chris had no trouble reading the marks in the snow and she easily dug it up again. She let Bucky and Max have Otter anyway, but first she gutted it and chopped it up and cooked it. Bucky said it was absolutely delicious. Chris boiled and cleaned the skull and added it to the collection of bones, mostly skulls, that she keeps on a shelf. There are Bear, Wolf, Beaver, Fox, the lower jaw of Caribou, and a host of smaller Birds and Mammals. I've never been very sure what they are there for. I can only assume she stores them in case she runs short of food, but I have never seen her chew on any of them.

WE WERE PRETTY BUSY WITH THE USUAL RUN OF TOURISTS AND WWOOFERS that year, and the summer passed much as it had done before—although without the fires. Some of Chris's friends arrived during a gap between other visitors. They were experienced hikers and had

Wolf, harbour seal and grizzly skulls on the windowsill.

been to Nuk Tessli before, so they mostly explored on their own. On the day that they were to fly out, therefore, Chris felt she could leave them to their own devices and take off for the mountains for a day hike alone, which was what she really loved to do.

Bucky always ran loose when he was not packing, and the three of us set off in high spirits. We crossed the little meadow behind the cabins and started up the creek. We had not gone very far before Bucky, who was up ahead, started barking. There was a great crashing sound in the bushes as a large animal crossed the creek—Chris froze in alarm. I knew she would not be able to smell the creature so she would have no idea what kind of danger she was in. Her hand hovered over her bear spray. Bucky's yelping voice was not following the large animal across the creek, however, but running after something else up the trail. I hesitated for a moment, but I could not resist the chase and raced after him. His yapping continued upstream—and then turned and came back down. As I caught up with him I saw that he was chasing a big Moose Calf.

All three of us were now galloping along the trail going downstream. Chris was standing right where we left her. She had to step aside to allow Moose Calf to get by. It was as tall as she was and bellowing for its mother. Chris was yelling at us by this time. She tried to grab Bucky and missed—she whacked at me with her hiking pole. I faltered and almost stopped. But the chase was too exciting, and off I went after Bucky.

Usually if we ran after something, we would soon give up and get back to Chris. We learned later that she had continued on her hike, expecting that we'd eventually track her down. Bucky didn't stop chasing, however, and neither did I. Moose Calf ran right down the creek and plunged into the lake. He started swimming to the other side. Bucky plunged into the water after him. I did, too. Moose Calf swam and swam, and so did we. We were almost across the lake when

Moose Calf suddenly gave up. We did not catch him—he simply sank. We swam around a little bit, but he didn't come back up. Bucky and I turned around and paddled slowly back to the cabins.

Chris's friends were still there. They had observed Moose Calf's drowning and were not sure what to do. Bucky and I were pretty tired by now, so we decided to stay by the cabins. Shortly after that, the plane came to pick up the humans and we dogs waited there alone. Chris came back, tired and happy after her day in the mountains and glad to find us safely at home. Her mood changed abruptly, however, when she found a note on the table.

"I don't believe this," she said, reading the note. "You guys actually drowned that moose!"

She turned to Bucky. "That's the last straw," she said. "Raffi would never have done that alone, but you never listen to me. You simply don't know how to stop killing. It's bad enough having to keep you tied outside. I don't want to have to deal with that kind of hassle in the mountains. You're going to have to go."

It turned out that Len and Miriam were due to visit later that year. They lived near Vancouver, if you remember, and it was through their neighbourhood SPCA that Chris had found Bucky. When they arrived, she asked them if they could take Bucky back with them, and return him to the SPCA. Chris learned of his fate via her magic computer.

Miriam would have handed him in, but Len was more softhearted, and he persuaded his wife that they should try keeping him. Miriam and the cats weren't too happy about it, but Len persevered. Both humans enjoyed all sorts of outdoor activities and they often took Bucky running with them. Len belonged to a running group: a couple of years after Bucky had gone back to the city, Chris was giving a slideshow in the area and a lady came up to her, beaming, and said, "We run with Bucky." Apparently he was much loved down there.

Chris knew that Miriam and Len often went hiking for several days so she sent down Bucky's old backpack so he could at least carry his own food. He was, needless to say, always kept on a lead.

Miriam and Len also liked to bicycle. When Bucky got too old for vigorous exercise, they would sometimes put him in the little bike trailer in which they had towed their kids when they were small. Chris showed me a photo of him in there. He was really too big for the trailer but he looked perfectly happy.

One day Chris received an email that told her Bucky had become sick and died.

"He was seventy-seven canine years old," she said to me. "He really landed on his feet. Miriam and Len took on a troublemaker and gave him a good end to his life. I simply didn't have the patience."

But that was all in the future. After Bucky left us that summer, I was alone with Chris. When we came out of the mountains in the fall, it was just the two of us who drove to Ginty Creek.

As always, one of the first things that had to be done when leaving the mountains was drive to town to buy food. We came home from that trip with a great young female (human!) called Sarah. She helped Chris wall in the porch. She was too frightened of Bear to walk anywhere on her own or even with me for company, so the three of us would often go up onto the dunes together. Chris and Sarah exclaimed over the fall colours, which they maintained were splendid that year.

Bucky riding in a bike trailer
when he lived in Vancouver.
Photo by Miriam Soet

Sarah left when the Book Tour started, and Chris took me along with her. We became very close during that time, and I would have been quite happy for it to stay that way. Chris, however, felt she needed another dog to help carry her Stuff on backpacking trips. Shortly after Christmas, we drove to town again. It was raining in the city. Wet dirty snow piled up on the streets.

Chris tied me up at her friend's place and disappeared for quite a while. When she came back, tugging at the end of her lead was a wet, bedraggled, disgruntled-looking Nahanni.

16

HARRY

RAFFI IS TAKEN ILL

"NAHANNI!" I SAID. "SHE WAS THE ONE WHO CAME OUT OF THE GREAT White North and got eaten by a cougar, isn't that right?"

Badger nodded, but was uncharacteristically silent. He sat staring into the nothingness that surrounded us.

"You've told me about her," I persisted, "but what about Raffi? There must be a reason he is not with us today."

"Yes there is," Badger sighed. "He got a twisted stomach and had to be put down."

"A what?"

"A twisted stomach. It happens to large dogs with wide chests, particularly Rottweilers, and is most common when dogs reach forty-two canine years of age. Dogs who inhale their food instead of chewing it properly are also at risk. Raffi had all those things going on in his life. Nahanni told me the story on one of her more friendly days, before she got eaten.

"Chris and her current Wwoofers at the time (a couple from Austria) had been to Bella Coola for the day. It was the end of April—the leaves were not even on the trees here yet, and it would be over a month before they could go to Nuk Tessli, but it was extremely hot. You have to reach Bella Coola by a mountain road that goes high over a pass, then drops down and down into a lush valley by the sea. It was where she had taken Raffi and Bucky that time she caught a helicopter ride into Nuk Tessli. The weather was now very different. It was even hotter down there than at Ginty Creek. Chris had shopping and business to do, and she also took the Wwoofers to a couple of interesting places. Every time they stopped, she had her friends take Raffi and Nahanni out of the vehicle and give them a walk and a drink, but of course the dogs became frustrated at being tied up so much.

"It's a long drive to Bella Coola—it takes almost as much time as going to Williams Lake. So they left early, spent the long, hot day there, and it was almost dark when they came home. Chris let the frantic dogs out of the truck at the highway so they could run along the bush road to the cabin."

"Just like I love to do," I put in.

Raffi. *Photo by Dylan Spencer*

Badger humphed at the interruption, but he continued with the Saga.

"Raffi and Nahanni tore down to the river to have a swim to cool off. Chris waited a short time before she gave them their dinner, but the damage, it appeared, had been done.

"The next day, when Squirrel came to the bird feeder, Chris called Raffi to chase Squirrel away as he usually did, but he was in his kennel and didn't want to move. She persuaded him to come out and took him for a short walk—he followed her reluctantly and then went and laid down again. She'd had a phone installed by then, and she called the vet.

"'Bring him in right away,' she was told. But of course there is no 'right away' when the vet's takes four hours' driving to reach. She loaded Raffi into the van and drove as fast as she could. She left Nahanni behind with the Wwoofers so there were just the two of them in her vehicle.

"She told the Wwoofers the story when she came back home. At the vet's, Raffi was taken into the back for an X-ray. Chris was told to wait—it was nearly three hours before they got back to her. A lady vet showed Chris the X-ray pictures. A large balloon of air was trapped in Raffi's gut. 'We can operate,' the vet said, 'but there is no guarantee of success. It will very likely twist back again the next day. It is also a very expensive operation.' The vet didn't say any more, but it was obvious that she felt the right decision was to put Raffi to sleep. Chris was terribly upset. She walked up to Raffi. He lay on a mat, looking puzzled. He couldn't understand why he hurt, why Chris couldn't make him better, and why she was saying goodbye. She was broken-hearted when she came back to Ginty Creek.

"Nahanni was never close to Chris. She had no interest in comforting her, even if she had been able to do so. She enjoyed being Top Dog, though, which is what she always felt she should be.

"Chris was due to give a few more slideshows before they went into the mountains that year, and Nahanni went with her. At every town big enough to have an SPCA, she went and looked at dogs. In previous years, it had been easy to find large canines. Now the only ones that were available seemed to be too small, or Huskies. Chris didn't want to be bothered with another Husky who would probably have to be kept chained up most of the time—it's hard to stop that kind of dog from roaming. Now that she was spending winters with Cow nearby, she didn't want the responsibility of a dog who would cause trouble with the ranchers.

"After she and Nahanni had been on the road for a while, she came to Salmon Arm."

"And," I interrupted triumphantly, "that's where she found you!"

"Yes," said Badger. "That's where Chris found me." He paused for a minute, then looked at me, not unkindly, and smiled.

"My work is now finished."

"What do you mean?" I asked, puzzled.

"You now have the full Wilderness Dog Saga up to the present day," Badger replied. "There are no more stories for me to tell. It will be your duty to pass the Saga on to the next members of our pack."

At first I was quite taken aback. I had been begging Badger for so long to tell me the Wilderness Dog Saga that it did not occur to me that it would come to an end. I was going to miss Badger's accounts of all the animals that had been in our pack. When I mentioned this to Badger, he simply said, "Now you will live your own story."

Part Two

GINTY CREEK

17

HARRY

THE SECOND FIRE

LIFE AT NUK TESSLI THAT SUMMER BEGAN TO UNFOLD AS IT HAD DONE many times before for Chris, and quite a few times for Badger, but it was all new to me. However, I had heard so much about it that none of the events seemed all that surprising, at least at first.

Chris cleaned the place up, made a number of small repairs, and then the first of the summer's Wwoofers arrived. Chris canoed up the lake with them and selected trees for firewood. Usually she did the falling and bucking, but many of the Wwoofers wanted to learn how to use the chainsaw and she would spend time teaching them. When they had experienced the different moods of our lake—the winds could be very wild at times there—she could let them go off on their own. Soon they would return with a precarious canoe-load of firewood and toss it out onto the wharf. It then had to be carried up the steep little trail to the woodshed. Chris often told her helpers that she used to do all this work alone, falling, bucking, splitting, loading the canoe, paddling the wood home, unloading and hauling it up the trail to the woodshed. While she was doing the last job, Lonesome, Sport, Taya or whoever was with her at the time would sit on the deck, head on paws, waiting for her to take them for a hike. The job would take her weeks; no matter what other work she gave the Wwoofers to do, firewood was the task that she appreciated them doing most.

The other main job the Wwoofers helped her with was either brushing out old trails or making new ones. Through the forest, once she had decided on the route, Chris marked the trail by blazing the trees. (In a deep snow winter, the blazes, which were at human head height in summer, would sometimes become buried.) In the open spaces where there were no trees, rock piles called cairns were built. Above the treeline, where stones and boulders lay everywhere, these little structures were easy to construct. In the bogs among the forest, however, there were often no rocks for quite a distance. Again, Chris was thankful when she had a group of strong young people to find and carry them. It was sometimes boring work for them, so after a while the Wwoofers would get creative and build tall, precarious monuments, always trying to balance that last wobbly rock on top. These sculptures generally fell over, but when Chris had to rebuild them, she didn't mind so much.

"At least I don't have to carry the rocks," she said. Her structures were never as imaginative, but they were less likely to fall over.

WHEN THE TOURISTS CAME, THEY ABSOLUTELY ADORED ME BECAUSE I am so handsome. They tended to push Badger into the background.

And yet Chris had a soft spot for Badger. He had formed a special bond with her.

Chris was now walking quite slowly compared with most humans. She had sore knees and hips, and she used hiking poles to move along. She could still cover a lot of ground as she had a great deal of stamina, but most hikers were impatient with her. They had arrived fresh from the city; they still had a kind of frantic city energy about them and they wanted to gallop everywhere. Chris would keep everyone together for most of the day, especially when we were above the treeline where there are no trails, but when we picked up the path on our way home and she knew the tourists couldn't get lost, she would encourage them to go ahead at their own pace.

Badger and I always ran ahead with the tourists, but after a while I would realize that my canine buddy was no longer behind me.

"We were worried when we didn't see Badger anymore," the tourists would say when Chris eventually arrived home. "But we see that he has come back with you."

"He's started doing that," said Chris with a small smile. "He rushes on with you guys and I plod along at my own pace, but suddenly there he is, sitting in the shade under a tree beside the trail. He never stays close. As soon as I notice him, he runs ahead and disappears again; then, there he is a few minutes later, waiting under another tree."

Chris had never looked for demonstrable affection from either of us and she had accepted Badger's initial standoffishness as just part of his character. I could see that she was very touched by this gentle recognition of friendship.

THAT FIRST SUMMER I SPENT AT NUK TESSLI WAS THE FOURTH IN A SERIES of very dry years. Lightning storms flashed and rumbled, and forest fires erupted everywhere. The big mountains at the head of the lake were often obscured by smoke. Chris was constantly on the Internet.

"I'm checking out the fire maps and trying to predict the wind," she told the Wwoofers. "Weather forecasts are not a lot of use as the data are recorded a hundred kilometres away and mountain weather varies considerably from one valley to the next. Fires are the most worrying part of my life here. If they get into their extreme phase, nothing can stop them."

When the wind came from the mountains, the sky usually stayed clear. If it came from the Chilcotin, following the route the plane took when it came in from Nimpo Lake, it very often brought a blackening of the sky and a thunderstorm. Late one afternoon, cloud built up in the east and began to smother the heavens. Thunder grumbled, and soon lightning zigzagged through the clouds. Gradually, the storm travelled right overhead and then passed west. It was by no means the loudest thunderstorm we had experienced that year, but it lingered a long time, and not a drop of rain fell.

The next day, the wind blew down the lake from the mountains and cleared the heavens of clouds. At first, this seemed a good omen; it was always welcome to see the sunshine and a blue sky after a day of gloom. Several fires near and behind the mountains had been burning for weeks; according to the data Chris found on the Internet, a couple were quite big. Smoke was often dragged in front of the peaks. On this day, however, it seemed to be much thicker than it had been before.

"It's hard to make out," Chris muttered, "but I think there's a new fire and it's much closer to us than the others..."

She attempted to contact the fire service by radiophone and by email. Eventually she got through on the radiophone and was told that they were very busy with the other fires—thousands were burning in the province, but they would check out her report as soon as they could. This conversation took place in the morning, but it was quite late in the afternoon when a helicopter landed in the meadow behind the cabin. We ran over and waited at the edge.

A man jumped out and walked over to Chris. She probably already suspected what he was going to say, but as the words were spoken, you could see that it was like a blow to her heart. "The fire you reported is fifteen kilometres away and directly upwind. It's not that extensive at the moment but it's very fierce. If it behaves like the other one did five years ago, which travelled thirty kilometres in two days, it could be here within hours. You are going to have to leave."

"It's just like Raffi's fire," I whispered to Badger. "We're being evacuated again."

Four tourists had arrived just that morning. "We haven't even unpacked properly," they said when Chris told them the news. "It won't be difficult for us to put our gear back together."

"I don't even have an emergency list this time," Chris moaned. "The other fires have been burning a long time but they are all too far away to be of immediate danger so I never bothered to put a list together. I'll just have to try and remember everything important."

She frantically threw Stuff into boxes, hoping there would be space in the plane for it all.

The plane arrived promptly; this time the smoke was not on our flight path and our journey to Nimpo was uneventful. Once again, it was evening when we landed. It wasn't clear and limpid as it had been the night Raffi and Bucky had flown out five years before, however. Smoke from yet another fire—this one at the top of The Hill to Bella Coola—filled the air above the float plane base.

All the resorts Chris visited or spoke to on the phone were full of firefighters and she had a hard time finding accommodation for the tourists. She eventually managed to sort out somewhere for her clients to spend the night, and it was dark by the time we drove to Ginty Creek. A full moon was shining; because the sky was thick with smoke, the moon was coloured blood red. No stars were visible at all in the choked blackness.

The following day, Chris lost no time hooking up to the Internet again. Just because we were out of the mountains didn't mean that we were safe from fires.

"Goodness," she said as the fire map came up on the screen. "The highway between Williams Lake and Bella Coola is closed by fires in four different places, some east and some west. No one on our part of the Chilcotin can go anywhere, even if we want to. I hope we don't have to evacuate from here."

She clicked a few more buttons on the keyboard. "I wonder how accurate these fire websites are. When the BC Wildfire Service is so busy, their maps are not always up to date; in any case they don't show fires smaller than ten hectares in size. A small fire can erupt into a large one within hours. All this smoke could be coming from anywhere. The biggest fires are a hundred kilometres away but thick smoke often travels twice that distance. Or there might be a smaller, newer fire not yet recorded just over the hill. We'll just have to hope for the best."

Hoping for the best, however, was not Chris's forte. Her face was full of worry lines. But then, if the fire weren't there she would probably find something else unpleasant to anticipate. Fear-of-What-Might-Happen should have been her middle name.

As it was my first summer with Chris and Badger, I didn't know any different, but Badger explained that it was strange to be at Ginty Creek in August. It was unusual to see the leaves full on the trees—normally we left when they were only just opening and arrived home again when they were ready to fall. The ponds on the property had all but dried up. Although Chris was obviously desperately worried about the fires, a small part of her brain could not ignore the starry yellow carpet of water crowfoot that was blooming in the peaty soil of the ponds, where the water had drained away. Out came her camera and she twisted into the usual contortions to try to get the best possible picture. Dozens of baby Western Toads hopped about among the flowers. I was interested in their movement and thought at first that they might be a kind of Mouse, but they had a funny smell and I didn't try to bite them.

The pattern of our exile repeated itself almost exactly as it had done (according to Raffi's account in the Saga) during the big fire of 2004. Once again, we were out for ten days until the temperature cooled off and it rained a little, and then we were told we could go home. This time we flew back in with two Wwoofers. One of these was a German girl but the other was Badger's great friend, Sarah, who had helped Chris finish the River Cabin's porch. The highway to Williams Lake was now open again and the volunteers were driven up by Sarah's parents. Sarah had been travelling the world since she was last here, and, oddly enough, she had worked for a while at the tourist dogsled place where Nahanni had come from. She and the young German woman were going to help Chris with the remaining tourists of the season.

It was evening, windy and spitting rain when we landed at Nuk Tessli. As we taxied in, to our surprise, we saw a group of men sitting on the wharf. Very few people visited Nuk Tessli unless Chris invited them. The men wore sooty clothes and hard hats. They were fire-fighters, and they explained that they had been setting up sprinklers around the cabins. A powerful pump sat on the wharf and hoses snaked everywhere among the rocks around the buildings. The winds had been kind while we had been away, and the fire that had caused such concern, and which was still burning, had not entered Chris's valley.

"But if we get we get one of those powerful west winds, like what happened with the 2004 fire, your place could still be in danger," one of the men commented. "We've been flying in to run the sprinklers every day. If the fire does come, there is a very good chance that we will at least save the buildings." Chris grimaced at the thought of having a view full of burned snags, but she didn't say anything.

The men had finished their work and were waiting for a helicopter to pick them up. When the chopper came in, it was as big as a bus. It flattened the vegetation in the little meadow behind the cabins with its own private wind. We watched as the men climbed aboard. The roof propellor whined and began to spin, and soon the great machine hopped up into the sky.

"Bucky and Raffi had a helicopter ride," I said to Badger as we trotted back to the cabins. "I wish we could have one."

"As a matter of fact, I did ride in one once," Badger said with a sly smile.

"You never told me that part of the story."

"It didn't quite fit in with the other part of the Saga." Badger said nonchalantly. He tried to look as if this was planned but I strongly suspected that he had simply forgotten to add it. I thought it wise not to say anything in that regard, though.

"Well?" I prompted. "Aren't you going to tell me?" I looked directly at Badger—and saw the twinkle in his eye. Of course he was going to tell me. He was just pretending to be an old curmudgeon.

18

BADGER

SUCCESS LAKES

IT WAS WHEN NAHANNI WAS HERE. YOU SEE THE TWO BIGGEST MOUNTAINS at the head of our lake?

There are two small lakes right in between them. Climbers fly to the lower one by float plane so that they can scale the mountains. Somebody must have managed to complete the climb and call the lake after the triumph, for they are known as Success Lakes. You can't fly out of them—they are too small for a plane to take off while loaded. The only way out is to walk.

Some years before, Chris had hiked from another direction to a point not far away from Success Lakes, and she figured that if we flew in, we could walk out on her old route. Friends were going to

join her—these were the same people who had visited when Bucky and Raffi drowned Moose Calf. The friends drove to the float plane base, and their plane stopped at Nuk Tessli on the way so they could pick us up.

From the air, Success Lakes looked very tiny. The upper one was even smaller than the lower one, and it was bright turquoise. Chris loved to give lectures, whether her audience wanted to hear them or not, and I had learned that this was a phenomenon caused by a suspension of rock flour in the water. Rock flour is made by ice flows as they grind away the mountains, and we could see part of a small glacier tumbling down the black rock face of the mountain above this lake. Most of the glacier was hidden in cloud.

The plane had to spiral at an angle to lose height between steep rocky walls before it could touch down on the water of the lower lake. We unloaded quickly. It was already spitting rain and the pilot

The mountains at the head of the lake. Monarch Mountain is on the left, Migma on the right, Success Lakes in between.

wanted to get out of there before the weather socked in. He lost no time in roaring away.

The humans thought the upper lake would be more interesting to camp beside, as it was closer to the glaciers. We would have to find a way up the valley. Nahanni and I had both carried camping gear before, but this was to be our first major backpacking trip. We expected to be away for ten days so we had very heavy loads.

Chris had told our friends that the hike she had done from the other direction had been over trackless country, but the ground had been fairly open and not too difficult to walk across. She didn't think we would have any problem reaching her former route.

"It should take us only a single day to connect with it, and another four days to where we're going to be picked up," she said. "We have enough food to spend extra nights along the way."

But the best laid plans of Dogs and Men "gang aft agley..." (We sometimes heard Mouse singing this song while building his nest in the attic.) The problems started at once. The bush behind the lake was very thick and full of windfalls. There was nothing to compare it with around Nuk Tessli. Neither Nahanni nor I had carried packs through anything like this, and we found it much too difficult. We were always getting hung up and the humans had to come and rescue us. We made very slow progress. When we came out of the trees, we faced a steep boulder field. Our bulging packs kept hitting rocks and knocking us off our feet so that we rolled down the slope, crashing into boulders. After a while, one of Chris's friends carried Nahanni's pack on top of his own, and Chris dragged mine along in her arms. Even so, we travelled painfully slowly.

Eventually we came to the upper lake, but we were once more surrounded by thickly tangled bush. There was simply no place to set up camp. A small clear spot at the upper end of the lake looked

like it might be a good spot to spend the night, so although everyone was tired, they decided to struggle on.

Chris had always been a slow hiker and she could not keep up with the others. Nahanni and I were both wearing our packs again by this time, but Chris constantly had to untangle us from obstacles. I found some relief by going into the water—I could actually make progress that way. Chris was a bit alarmed at first to see me swimming with my packs on, but the air trapped in them made them float, so it was actually quite easy.

The clearing was only three kilometres from where we had landed that morning, but the country was so bad it took us the remainder of the day to get there. When we finally staggered into the open space, we realized it was covered in stones and boulders. Chris's two women friends were already putting up their tent, but the man was nowhere to be seen.

"John has twisted his foot," said his wife, Susan, grimly. "He stepped on a rotten log; it broke and he tumbled into a hole. He's sitting by the creek with his foot in the water, hoping the swelling will go down."

Chris took our packs off and we went to look. John's foot was almost the size of his head. He didn't think it was broken, but he wasn't going to be able to walk anywhere for quite a while. In the planning stages of the trip, John had talked about bringing a satellite phone but at the last minute had neglected to do so.

This was very wild country with almost no human impact. The city people were worried that without the satellite phone, we had no means of communicating with anyone. But Chris did not think we should be concerned.

"We're directly under the route of the standard flightseeing tour over the glaciers," she assured them. "We'll be able to signal a plane when it flies overhead. It won't be able to pick us up, but the float plane company knows where we intended to go and when we were supposed to finish our trip. We have ten days' food, don't forget. We're not going to starve."

The stony space was tiny and not comfortable to walk or lie on, but when we'd arrived, I'd seen Chris's eyes gleam at the profusion of mountain fireweed that grew great magenta bunches along the creek. Given her history, I knew she would take the first possible opportunity to follow along the water to see what else was growing there.

"I bet those guys won't stir for hours," she whispered to us as she prepared a quick breakfast at first light the following morning. She often commented that she could never figure out why people wasted such a big part of the day by staying in bed.

We had to fight through the bush at first, but as we were heading away from the lake, we soon broke through it into clearer ground. Now we could see the path that the creek took as it tumbled down from the little glacier. Most of the ice was still hidden in cloud and all the mountains around were similarly capped or wrapped in scarves of vapour.

"Nobody will risk flying in these conditions," Chris said, smiling a little. "I don't feel so guilty about leaving the campsite."

We followed the little creek up and Chris found it to be an absolute garden of wildflowers. She ecstatically bent into all sorts of positions so she could take pictures of plants with the jumble of ice behind. We explored for some hours, but when we arrived back at camp it was to find that the others were only just making breakfast. Like most city folk, they timed their meals by their watches and ignored what might be more practical in their surroundings.

Later that day, Chris and Susan headed in the direction of the point Chris hoped to reach, but their plans were foiled. The country proved to be far too difficult. They had left us dogs in camp but they told John and the other woman of their woes when they arrived back some hours later. They had scrambled up steep slopes and squeezed around rocks. But after every few steps forward, their way would be blocked by cliffs, precipitous moraines and enormous boulders with gaps between them that would have swallowed Nahanni and myself. Even if John could have walked, Susan said, the dogs would have found the route impossible. Chris knew that climbers usually hiked out that way somehow, but they were obviously more skilled at dealing with such inhospitable terrain than we were.

On day three it poured with rain and we all sat miserably under a tarp. It was not a very good shelter because the wind was so strong, flapping the plastic and blowing the rain underneath. Day four marked Chris and Susan's second attempt at finding a route out, but they had no better luck than the first time. There was no way they were going to get out of there on foot.

The morning of the fifth day was fairly clear, and it wasn't long before we heard a plane. Everyone jumped up and waved like mad. The pilot saw us—he went round in a circle and waggled his wings.

"I hope he realizes that we needed help and are not just saying hi," John said.

The humans had already come to the conclusion that a helicopter was the only way they were going to get out of there. "The nearest one's in Bella Coola," Chris explained. "The flight from there should take an hour. Add onto that the time it will take for the plane that we saw to land, for phone messages to go back and forth, and an available pilot to be found, and the quickest that help can get to us will be in a couple of hours."

Chris and her friends hastily packed their gear. Nahanni and I were tied—Chris wanted to make sure we were right there when the chopper came in. We waited. And we waited. The two-hour deadline was soon long gone and a good chunk of the day filtered away. The weather started to deteriorate again. Cloud crept around the mountain masses and began to lower. We had almost given up when we suddenly heard a battering rattle coming up the valley we had walked along with such difficulty. Through the gap in the mountains popped an RCMP helicopter. It was too small for four people and two dogs. The pilot decided to take Chris, Nahanni and me home first; he would then come back to pick up the others and drop them beside their vehicle, which they'd left at the float plane base.

We pushed ourselves and our gear inside, took off with little ceremony, and touched down quite quickly right in that meadow behind the cabins where the firefighters had landed. The space seems quite big when you are on the ground, but it was amazing how small it looked from the air. The pilot was impatient. He did not switch the motor off. Chris grabbed us and ran away from the machine, ducking low. Our bags were dumped onto the ground. The motor bellowed louder as the pilot put on the power to take off again. Nahanni was so frightened she wriggled out of her collar and ran. I had a small tremor of satisfaction to think that, for all her self-aggrandizement, I was superior to Nahanni in the fear department. Sure, the noise was awful, but I knew Chris would keep me safe from harm.

19

HARRY

GOODBYE NUK TESSLI

SUMMER AT NUK TESSLI ENDED. SMOKE CAME AND WENT ACROSS THE mountains, but our high valley remained fire-free. We flew back out to Nimpo Lake and drove along the highway to Ginty Creek. The van seemed noisy and stinky and terribly fast to us after we'd been travelling at hiking speed for so many months. (The plane doesn't count. It was fast and noisy and stinky, but because we were so far away from the ground, we seemed to be moving quite slowly.)

The leaves had completed their summer cycle and were now looking sad and half dead on the deciduous trees. They were on the verge of changing colour and falling off. The grass was pale brown, the old stalks frost-bleached already.

It now became apparent that all the messing about Chris had been doing on the upper property was because she wanted to build a very big new cabin. Not just in the hole she had completed in the spring, but above ground as well.

"What's wrong with the old one?" I asked Badger.

"Who knows?" he shrugged. "I guess she simply doesn't have room for all her Stuff."

A German Wwoofer called Birgit arrived, and she and Chris prepared the first upright log posts. Using a mix of ropes and pole scaffolding, they started to raise some of the higher timbers. Another woman came for a couple of days. She had bought her own wilderness property and wanted to learn how to build. When we first started, it was incredibly hot, but on Birgit's last day it turned bitterly cold. Birgit, Chris and a young local woman called Aileen raised a huge pole that was going to form the top of the cabin. Aileen had helped on concrete-pouring day and also when the ceiling beams had been lifted onto the structure. Chris and Birgit had built scaffolding for the three women to stand on, and they laboriously inched the pole up using blocks and tackles and ropes. Nonetheless the raising of the pole took several hours, because it was very heavy.

"You are right," I muttered to Badger. "This cabin is *huge*."

"It's still a lot smaller than most humans' houses, though," Badger said. I thought of the enormous homes I'd seen in Vancouver and had to concede he was right.

Birgit had to leave after a couple of weeks, and who should arrive next but our old friend Sarah. Not long after she first met Chris, she had visited Nahanni's old home in the Great White North. While there she had adopted an old male Husky whom she called Tundra. He was pure white like Nahanni had been. She brought him with her to Ginty Creek. He was pretty doddery and cranky, but on the whole we got on well enough.

We dogs didn't have a lot of entertainment laid out for us, because the humans were so busy building. Sarah and Chris worked frantically to put a roof on the cabin. The frame for it had to be built first, and then huge pieces of metal were screwed onto it. The work was delayed by more snowfalls and bitter winds; Chris became more and more frantic. Aileen came when she could, but she was busy with her husband on their ranch: when she got out of her tiny rust-bucket of a car, she would smell delightfully of Dog, Cow and Horse, and freshly butchered meat. It was apparently the season for slaughtering.

The reason for Chris's higher-than-usual stress level soon became apparent. She was due to go on yet another Book Tour. She often said how desperate she was to finish the roof before she went, but in the end she had to leave before the last pieces of metal were screwed into place. We watched Aileen and Sarah finish the job alone. Because the building was so high, the ladder could not reach far enough to install the last two pieces, and there was nothing for them to stand on. So the two young women hung from the roof with ropes to complete the job. Aileen said she would email pictures of their aerial gymnastics to Chris.

Badger and I were delighted to find that Sarah was to be our dog sitter while Chris was away. We went for lots of great hikes, but Sarah also did a considerable amount of work on the big new cabin. Chris had often praised her for being such a good carpenter. The outside shell was mostly in place when Chris left, but Sarah framed the inner structure of the walls, preparing them to receive the insulation. She also put insulation and plywood on the floor. Once in a while the hammer would miss the nail and hit her finger, and she would yodel like a coyote.

When Chris arrived home, she felt it was too cold and miserable to do much work on the new building for a while, but come March, when the days were longer and brighter, she knocked the plywood off a couple of holes in the walls and fitted in some big windows. There were no doors in the door holes, and the wind whistled through the building with a vengeance, so even after Chris had layered in some of the wall insulation it was still very cold inside.

Then, who should turn up again but Sarah—this time with her parents. Sarah's dad was an electrician, and Sarah was his apprentice at the time; she would later become fully qualified herself. The two of them ran all sorts of cables inside the cabin's walls. They were wiring the place for the solar-power system that would eventually be hooked up. This was not going to happen for quite a while, but the wiring had to be done before the inner walls could be finished, which is what Chris worked on after Sarah and her family had gone. She was able to get the inner walls completed just before we went back into the mountains.

THAT WINTER HAD PRODUCED VERY LITTLE SNOW, AND IT WAS FOLLOWED by another very hot summer with fires everywhere. This time, at Nuk Tessli, we were spared a lot of the smoke and worry, but Dave and Rosemary at the Precipice were told to get ready to evacuate and the Chilcotin highway was again closed in several places. It seemed as though we were destined to be threatened by summer fires every year. However, the season was to end in a way that none of us expected. In September, it started to rain.

It was a relief, at first, to see that water pouring from the sky. The temperature dropped and the parched earth breathed again. You could see Chris relax as the constant anxiety about forest fires was eased. A few days later, it rained again. Then again. They weren't gentle showers either; they were downpours. The soil surface near the door turned to mud, the little mountain creeks filled, and we dogs had puddles to drink from everywhere along the trails.

When Chris welcomed her last visitors of the year, she told them she had never seen anything like it, especially in September. I well remember one hike with these tourists, because there was snow on the ground which made walking over the rocks very slippery for the humans. Their claws are too short to be of any use, and besides, they usually cover them up with boots. The underbrush was turning colour, and Chris and the tourists oohed and aahed at the beauty of the snow on red berries and yellow leaves.

This was about three weeks into September. As soon as the hikers had flown out, Chris went through the usual ritual of sorting and packing and crankiness, getting everything ready for heading back to Nimpo. The shutters were up on the cabins, all water containers were empty and inverted, and so many boxes were stacked in the porch it was hard for Badger and me to squeeze into our kennels. The only chore not yet completed was the dismantling of the laptop and the satellite modem. They would be flying out with us, but the radiophone was no longer working, and the electronics needed to stay connected until the last minute in case the pilot needed to contact us.

On the day we were due to fly out, it rained again. It poured. Clouds were weighed down almost to lake level. No plane was going to be able to get to us in this. Chris put the kettle on the stove and lit a small fire to make her foreign-leaf water. All her food was stored or packed, but as the day progressed and the rain continued to deluge, she filched a bit of this or that from boxes and kept sliding wood into the stove. There was nothing we could do but wait. We couldn't go for a hike in case there was a break in the clouds and the plane came in. At least we didn't have to be tied. Badger and I liked planes—either they brought interesting visitors or we were going to get a ride in them, so as soon as we heard their motors, we ran to the wharf and wagged our tails.

Chris tried sending an email, for she knew that the weather might be quite different where the float plane base was situated, but no one replied. The Internet was still new to most people around Nimpo Lake and very few bothered to check their emails on a regular basis. The rain continued all day.

The next morning was hazy with water vapour but it was at least halfway sunny. Chris felt sure the plane would come, and she figured it was safe to take all the Stuff out of the shelter of the porch and down to the wharf.

"I sure hope it doesn't sock in again," she muttered. "These boxes are heavy and I don't fancy having to lug them back up to the cabin."

As we followed her to the wharf, we heard an exclamation. We ran down to look. "The level of the lake is up half a metre!" she said. "This is unprecedented. I wonder why the lake didn't rise when we had all those other heavy rains before?" Then she answered her own question. "It's been a lot warmer this last couple of days than it has been for a while. All the other rains must have fallen as snow higher in the mountains. The whole lot must have melted at once." She looked across the water. "This is a big lake. Half a metre extra in height means an awful lot of water. I wonder what's happening downstream?"

We didn't know it at the time, but these were prophetic words indeed.

Eventually a plane droned over the ridge, swooshed onto the water, and chugged its slow way to the wharf. Apparently it had been foggy at Nimpo that morning, which was why it had come in later than Chris had expected. The freight was soon loaded, we all climbed in, and the plane took off. It circled round, and we bumped our way through the mountains back to the float plane base.

Nimpo always seemed gentle and peaceful to us after we'd been in the mountains for a long time. There was less wind, the scenery was less dramatic, and of course there was Chris's obvious relief at getting her feet on the ground again. Chris piled the Stuff and us into the van, and there was that temporary feeling of strangeness as the motor caught and we started to move over the ground by machine.

Before leaving Nimpo, we parked outside the bakery. Chris prided herself on making excellent bread but, having been away from Ginty Creek for four months, she knew there would be almost no food at the River Cabin—the first thing she would have to do was drive to Williams Lake to shop. Bakery bread would fill a few gaps in her diet until she had time to make her own.

The husband of the woman who ran the bakery was standing near the van. "Have you just come from your place?" he asked. (He meant Ginty Creek.)

"No I've just flown out from Nuk Tessli. I'm on my way there."

"I don't know if you'll get through. I heard there's been a washout just this side of the bridge. Might be just a rumour, though."

We started driving. Everything seemed calm and quiet. Winter-brown grass lined the roadsides. The sun was still hazy but at least it was trying to shine. We saw no other traffic, but that was not unusual in this empty part of the world.

Suddenly, we rounded a bend and encountered a cop car angled across the road. This was definitely out of the ordinary. We stopped and Chris got out. We could hear a loud roaring sound punctuated by cracks and whooshing noises. The police officer said something to Chris, and through the van windows we could see Chris's eyebrows go up and her jaw drop. She walked a few metres along the road. When she turned her face was still open with astonishment.

"This hole must be as big as a house!" she shouted to the police lady. She had raised her voice to combat the roar of the flood and her words carried to us easily. "This is amazing! Half the road has fallen into the river. Tons of water is smashing into what is left!"

Boulders groaned and knocked below the water's surface, and with another crack, a tree snapped in half and tumbled into the flood. Chris looked at the van and the bit of road that remained. She walked over to the police lady so she didn't have to shout anymore.

"Maybe I could squeeze by," she said. "I live only about six kilometres away. I really need to get home."

But even as they watched, another big chunk of road slid into the river with a loud whooshing rattle.

By now, other Nimpo people were starting to drive up in their cars, all hoping to travel east along the highway. They stood around in disbelief. One by one, they shrugged their shoulders and drove away.

At that point, two figures could be seen walking halfway up the high bank above the remaining piece of road. They were wearing red and yellow safety vests. As they drew closer, Chris recognized them.

"It's the guy in charge of the road maintenance service," she said. "I think that's his wife with him."

And so it proved to be. "Well, if they could walk this way, I can sure walk the other," Chris said determinedly. "Six kilometres is nothing for us."

"You can't leave your vehicle here," said the policewoman.

One of the Nimpo people who was about to head back to his house overheard this and offered to take the van back to his place. He could drive it, and his wife would drive their car. Chris rummaged around in the van for what she felt she could carry—the road services man and his wife were slithering down the bank and soon they stepped onto the highway by the police car. From their end they had not known the extent of the flood but now that they had seen it, they said they would go back to their truck. They confirmed that Chris would be able to walk back with them. They even offered to carry a few things, too. Chris snagged ropes onto our collars and let us out.

The bank of the hill above the washout was saturated and very difficult to walk on. The sodden gravel and mud was poised ready to slide into the river, which continued to roar and whoosh and snap trees below us and eat more rattling, hissing chunks out of the road. After the hill, we could see that the next section of highway was completely underwater. It wasn't washed away yet, but the water rolling along it was brown and swift and it would have been too deep to drive through. Already broken trees littered the surface. We had to make a detour through swampy forest, and then climb another, smaller hill. Sitting on a dry piece of road beyond that was our rescuers' yellow truck.

"Looks like we're going to have a bit of trouble with the ditch," shouted the man above the noise of the water. "It was nowhere near this deep when we came across a couple of hours ago."

The ditch was between us and the highway. It was no more than three human paces wide, but it was brown and deep and fast. On our side a few spindly aspens trembled as the raging water tugged at their roots.

"Okay, dogs, you're on your own," Chris said.

She unclipped our ropes, fastened them together, and tied one end to the firmest of the aspens.

The roaring level suddenly grew much louder and I worried that a bigger wall of water was coming down on top of us, but the increase in noise was actually made by a small helicopter. It had been flying up and down the road, checking on the damage. It landed beside Chris's friend's truck. The rotors of the chopper kept turning and a man jumped out, ducked beneath them, and ran across to the ditch.

"Hold the other end of the rope," Chris yelled, flinging it across the ditch. "Keep it tight."

Chris's friend stepped in first. The bottom of the ditch was invisible under the thick brown water. Slowly, he lowered himself into the flood, hanging onto the rope with one hand. The water was up to his waist, but he made it across, thanks to the tight rope. His wife was smaller, but she also managed to wade through safely. Now it was Chris's turn. She hung onto the rope and began to feel her way with her feet. The current was very swift and the brown water piled against her stomach. Just as she was about to take the last step, the man holding the rope reached toward her with his hand. Which was a good thought, but in doing so, the rope was allowed to go slack. Over Chris went. Fortunately she fell more or less onto the road.

"My computer!" she wailed. It was in her backpack. There was no time to check it now, but the water did not seem to have gone much above the bottom of the pack. The camera slung around Chris's neck, however, had become submerged and drowned.

The man in the helicopter had not landed to help us across the ditch—fortuitous though his arrival was—but to tell his co-worker that he should move his truck fast as the road on the far side of a bridge, about a kilometre farther on, was also in danger of going out.

Badger and I were still on the wrong side of the ditch.

"Come on, pups!" Chris yelled.

We were both of us expert swimmers, but this fast, furious stream was terrifying. There was no alternative, however. First I, then Badger, flung ourselves into the water. Even though it was such a short distance, we were whirled downstream for quite a ways before we were able to scramble our way up onto the road.

The helicopter had left and the highways man was impatient to get going. Chris flung Badger into the back of the truck (I could jump in on my own), and she hopped into the cab with the other humans.

"Don't bother to take me all the way in," she said. "It will take an extra half hour there and back, and you might not be able to cross the other place where the highway is washing out." So we were dropped off at the end of our road and the pickup truck roared away.

Chris was not going to be able to carry all her Stuff at once (some of which was our kibble), and the dog packs were still in the van, so we could not help. The hazy sun had long ago been swallowed by cloud, and it looked as though it was going to rain again.

"I'll have to take the computer on this trip," she said. "Can't risk getting that wet—if indeed it survived my dunking."

She topped her load with a few other items, including the two loaves of bakery bread and the small bag of kibble, and we started to walk.

Our road is about four kilometres long. When it leaves the highway it first travels away from the river, and as we hiked the bellow of the raging water faded away. We did not hear it again until we came closer to the cabin. The roar gained strength again, loud and rattling and banging. The cabin was invisible until we were almost upon it, and the river was so wild and noisy, we wondered if our home was still going to be there. But it still stood on top of the high bank as before. Down below was a very different picture than what we were used to, however. The whole gravel bed was a wide, raging sea of water, brown and thick with silt, and undulating in foam-topped waves.

Daylight would be gone soon. "We need to get the rest of the Stuff," Chris said, "but I'd better get water first. It will be too dark to find it when we get back."

She took a couple of small water jugs and started to go toward the river.

"That's going to be no good," she said, stopping short. "It would be like trying to drink brown porridge. We'll have to get water from the creek."

We walked past the old barns to where a small stream, usually dry in summer, now raced between its banks to join the river. The water was clear but it smelled very swampy. We dogs didn't care what we drank, of course. I couldn't think why Chris didn't just lap from puddles as we did. Mind you, she had a long nose (for a human) and was further handicapped by having such a short tongue, so maybe that was why.

Chris took the wheelbarrow when we plodded back along our road to where we had left the Stuff. It was very hard work for her to push the loaded wheelbarrow up and down the hills and through the big puddles and mud to the cabin. It was indeed dark by the time we reached it, and we were all very tired. We went to bed, but none of us slept much. The river roared and pounded, trees cracked like rifle shots, and constantly there was that great hissing, rattling *whooooosh* as more bank fell into the water. Badger and I barked at all these strange noises, and Chris got up several times, worried that the river was eating its way too close. We knew it was nerve-racking for her: her night vision was so poor she didn't know what was happening.

In the morning, however, the sun was shining. The river still roared and roiled, but the worst of its fury was spent and, although it was still very wild, it had begun to shrink. Flood debris had already been left along the banks. We walked to where we should have been able to have a proper look at the river. Before the flood, we would have been able to go right down to the edge in this spot—this was where we used to go to collect water. Now our way was barred by a cliff as big as a house. An enormous chunk of land, complete with several trees, no longer existed there. A long section of old fence that used to run beside the river had also disappeared.

Chris wanted to see what damage had been done to the highway, and we walked the four kilometres back to the bridge again. The bridge must have been very strong because, although it was visibly quivering with the more violent onslaughts of water, it was still there. Most of the road leading up to it was gone, however, and by climbing up a bank we could see that a huge canyon had been cut right across the road on the far side of the bridge. There was no sign of the yellow truck, so our rescuer must have been able to cross it before it had washed out. Walking the other way, back toward Nimpo, we could not even reach the place where the yellow truck had been parked. Swift-running water poured over the road. We could see that the flood had been even higher during the night than when we had last walked this way; washout marks and fresh gouges were everywhere.

The only things to benefit from all this wet, as far as I could see, were shaggy mane mushrooms. They had erupted everywhere at the edge of the road, their fragile heads pushing up hard-packed dirt and gravel. Their caps were pale and scaly, and on the older ones they spread like floppy sunhats revealing a black lining underneath.

Chris said she had never seen so many anywhere before. She had dug out an old camera from the Stuff inside the cabin and at once busied herself taking pictures of them. Is that crazy or what? No matter the disaster, the only thing she raves about are silly-looking plants.

"WELL, OUR CABIN'S OKAY, AND WE'RE WARM and dry," said Chris. "But the little food we have is not going to last very long. We're cut off from our van at Nimpo which contains a few more supplies, but even if we had the vehicle, we would not be able to drive anywhere to shop for more."

Drinking water was also a serious problem for Chris. The river still looked like chocolate milk, and the creek tasted strongly of Beaver swamp.

Rain started again before long and she tried to collect water that ran off the roof, but that tasted disgusting to her as well. Humans' stomachs are not as tough as ours, and Chris had to boil the water for a long time before she felt able to risk drinking it. Even then, she pulled a big face at the taste.

The computer had survived the flood and had been hooked up at once. The Internet was full of news about the devastating floods in Bella Coola.

"I figured they would be in for it," Chris muttered. "That's where the water from Nuk Tessli goes."

But Bella Coola was three hours' drive away and Chris could find no information about our area online. Fortunately the land line phone was still operating. It made strange noises and sometimes cut out altogether, but it continued to function. Chris spent hours with this instrument at her ear trying to find out what was going on, and trying to arrange food, or a back road vehicle, or *something—anything!*—to try and prolong her stay at Ginty Creek.

"I want to work on our new house," she complained. "But I don't even have enough gas for the chainsaw." In the end, there was nothing for it. She phoned the RCMP station at Anahim Lake for help.

At first the lady sergeant couldn't believe that Chris was stranded. Chris, it appeared, was the only local person who could not drive to the local store. The cops are all city people, in the district for only a couple of years at a time, and few are in sync with the remoteness of the country away from the police station. In the end, the lady cop said she'd send a helicopter.

"I tried to get her to fly food in," Chris complained to us. "She said that was not going to work and we will have to be flown out."

"Wow!" I said to Badger. "Did you hear that? I'm going to have a helicopter ride after all!"

But waiting for it was no fun.

We were ready for it at first light the next morning. "I will have to keep you guys tied up," said Chris. "I have to stay by the phone for word and they could come at any time. I can't have you busy chasing a rabbit or something." But fog covered the land at sunrise, and it did not clear for several hours.

Then Chris received a phone call telling her that we dogs could not travel inside the chopper unless we were in a crate.

"They don't need a crate," Chris protested. "They're experienced fliers."

"We didn't have a crate when Nahanni and I were rescued from our mountain hike," Badger growled.

Chris was listening on the phone again. "I have one crate," she said.

I nudged Badger. "That's the crate I travelled in when I was flown from Vancouver," I said. "I wonder if the stuffed toys are still in it."

Eventually, Chris put the phone down in disgust. "Regulations!" she said. "They said they might have to make two trips. There will be room for only one crate at a time in any case."

It seemed as though we were spending half our lives waiting for aircraft to pick us up. At last there was a very distant beat above the noise of the river, more of a pressure on the ears rather than an actual sound. I heard it first, then Badger, and finally Chris. She had piled the things she was going to take with her near to where the helicopter would land, and now she pulled us to the same spot, holding firmly to our ropes.

The machine noise grew louder and suddenly the chopper hovered and sank slowly on spindly legs, like a crane fly. A passenger in a policeman's uniform climbed out. He would go back on the second trip.

"You know," said Chris, dragging the crate over to the chopper. "I think both dogs could squeeze into the one crate. They will be terribly squashed, but they're good friends and it is just a short flight."

I had no trouble hopping up the helicopter ladder and into the crate. It was indeed roomy (the stuffed toys had been removed) but I didn't think there was space for both of us. Suddenly I felt a great push on my rear end. Badger was being heaved into the crate behind me. He thought he was going to be put in a bigger space and as soon as he saw the tiny part of the crate that was left to him, he tried to turn and get out. But Chris and the RCMP officer were already slamming the door. Badger was bent like a pretzel. Both his tail and his head faced the door. I had so little room left I could hardly breathe. Neither of us could move an iota.

Chris climbed up beside the pilot. The Stuff would come with the other police officer on the second flight. As Raffi had told us, Chris wasn't as bothered in helicopters as she was in a plane. She almost looked as though she was enjoying herself. The motor fired up, the rotors whined, and we popped off the ground like a hatching mayfly. Chris snapped picture after picture. We saw them later on her computer. Once in the air, we followed the course of the devastated river. It was now four days after the flood, and the water level had dropped considerably, but a long stretch of highway had been destroyed. Badger and I couldn't see anything at the time—we could hardly breathe. Thankfully, the flight took only about ten minutes.

We landed in the yard of one of the resorts at Nimpo Lake. It was a short distance to where the kind gentleman had stored Chris's van. We now had access to the food that had been flown out of Nuk Tessli, which was just as well as the store was running out of supplies. The van food wasn't going to last all that long, either. No supply trucks could get in until the highway was drivable again.

Chris was given a cabin belonging to one of the resorts, paid for by the rescue services. It was very quiet—the only people staying there were other strandees. All the rest were trying to travel between Bella Coola and Williams Lake. They commiserated with each other when they met. Chris said she was grateful that she did not have to pay for the cabin. It had running hot water and a shower and a flush toilet—luxuries she had lived without for decades, but she was not happy.

"I want to work on my house," she complained. "I was hoping to move in before Christmas. I have to leave on a book tour in just over four weeks. I wonder how long I'll have to stay here."

We hated it at the resort, too, as we had to be tied all the time and Chris's crankiness spilled over onto us.

Ironically, the weather was now gorgeous. The sky was blue, the trees were golden, the lake a mirror.

Every day, we would walk up a small hill to the restaurant, where Chris was able to check her email. She would tie us up outside the door so we could enjoy the comings and goings. We often met the other strandees, all hoping up to get online and bemoan their fate to their friends.

One day, after we'd been living in this miserable idyll for a week, a huge flatbed truck carrying an enormous bulldozer drove by. Everyone inside the restaurant ran to the door and cheered.

"That truck means that the bypass must be open," Chris said excitedly. "I wonder when we will be allowed to drive it."

Apparently a new track had been bulldozed through the bush to join some old logging roads; these would form a long bypass that would avoid the broken section of road near our home. Soon, we would be able to drive to Williams Lake and buy supplies.

This bulldozer, however, was not going to repair our washouts; it was heading the other way, toward Bella Coola. Some machines had already been brought in by sea to work at the lower end of the valley; this was the first of many that would start repairs from the eastern end. The Bella Coola valley, where hundreds of people were still stuck, was a much bigger priority than our small community.

A day or two later, we were told that private cars could drive the bypass, and we headed east along the highway until just before the first washout. We had to wait for a pilot truck to guide us around the long bypass. It was early in the morning and still pitch dark; the only visible light, powered by a generator, illuminated a sandwich board on which was a single word: *FLOOD*.

At last the pilot car gave the signal and we slowly lined up behind it and bumped onto the new road. It was bizarre: after all that rain, the logging road was already a sea of dust. It was so thick it was like driving through a bag of flour, and we could barely see the tail lights of the vehicle in front. When we encountered the heavy equipment (crews were working day and night), their giant machines loomed out of the dust fog like great shadowy dinosaurs, pausing while we filed by.

Daylight was in full swing by the time we reached the highway again. The bypass had taken us two hours. The trip to Williams Lake was uneventful after that, but both driving and shopping make Chris cranky, and although she was relieved to have a good quota of food and supplies, she was not in a very good mood when we had to line up behind the pilot car again and wait. Another long, dusty drive and we were back at the Nimpo resort. The bypass had solved most people's problems and some of Chris's, but we still could not get home.

Rumours kept flying around that there was an old bush road that would take us to the back of Chris's place and thus avoid the washouts. It would be too rough for Chris's van, but Aileen (who had helped build Chris's new house) had a four-by-four with excellent clearance, and she said she would try to find this lost road. So we loaded up the vehicle with extra gas, two chainsaws, and four dogs (two were cattle dogs from Aileen's ranch) and gave it a go. We started up several old logging roads heading in the right direction and cut out all the windfalls, but they simply disappeared in overgrown cutblocks. Finally, we met a man on the highway who told us that the road we were looking for took off from the bypass.

We lined up to wait for the pilot car and followed the dusty convoy. At the highest point, we branched onto another old road. We could see the mountains across the valley that were visible from our home, but Ginty Creek was hidden in the forest far below. This road took us to another dead end and we thought we had been misled again, but a track worn by ATVs looked as though it had been used more recently, and with some trepidation, we lurched along that. Down and down we went, winding, rearing over banks and dropping into hollows, straddling rocks and wallowing in bog holes. Chris was amazed that anyone could get a truck over country like that. At last the country flattened out.

"I know where we are," Chris said suddenly as we came upon a wider dirt road. "This goes to my neighbour's place four kilometres away. If we go along it, we should reach the junction to mine."

And it proved to be so. Within ten more minutes, we were home. How thrilled Chris was to be able to unload her Stuff after all those agonizing weeks. It was already late in the day. Would Aileen be able to manoeuvre her vehicle up that rough, steep track and back to the bypass in the dark? Chris gave her some food and a can of gas as a bit of security, Aileen drove away, and we were alone. Chris could hardly believe that we'd actually made it.

We had no idea how the road repairs were progressing. When Chris had phoned or emailed the road maintenance service while she was stuck at Nimpo, no one seemed to know. Even though the nearest washout was nearly four kilometres away, we could hear the heavy vehicles grinding back and forth as they pushed earth around. As soon as we'd eaten breakfast the next morning, we walked to the highway to see what was going on. Most of the muddy areas had dried up and the smaller puddles had disappeared.

A good part of the road surface close to the bridge was now driveable, although it was single lane and surfaced with gravel. Chris watched a digger moving shovelful after shovelful, trying to fill the canyon on the far side. Then, to her amazement, a pickup truck nosed its way into the washout, dipped down, and climbed out onto the bridge. Chris scrambled to the edge of the cut. It was now no more than a wide, shallow ditch.

"I live here," she yelled to the driver of the digger. "When can I drive through?"

The driver looked startled. He was a stranger and probably had no idea that anyone resided nearby. He shrugged his shoulders. "Any time you want, I guess."

"Why on earth couldn't the road services people tell me about this?" Chris said to us as we walked home. "Surely they must have a record of the work that's been done. It means we can now drive in from the east. Only problem is, the van's still at Nimpo in the west. That section of the road is going to take a lot more fixing than the little washout. But it's only six kilometres long. We can easily walk that. Then we can probably get a ride with a construction vehicle to Nimpo."

The next day, we set off early. Chris had us both on ropes. She still had no decent water, and she was carrying three large empty twenty-litre water jugs on her back. They looked like big balloons. The river had dropped right down, but the damage to this section of road had been extensive. The water had turned the highway into a new riverbed and most of it had been washed away. A human being standing in the bottom of the new channel would not be able to reach the level of the highway even with his or her arms outstretched. The sodden hill we had struggled over before we swam the ditch had mostly disappeared. And no wonder the phone line had been intermittent: some poles were knocked sideways and one was hanging completely free, its base washed away. It was amazing that the line had kept working. Prior to the flood, only a few glimpses of the river had been visible; now whole sections, littered with great heaps of tangled broken trees, ran beside what was left of the highway. The power of the water had been awesome.

Soon we came to where the heavy machinery was working on this side of the bridge. The drivers were city people brought in for the job, and they were all astounded to see an old lady with two scruffy dogs on ropes and a backpack bulging with water jugs in what they thought was the middle of nowhere. Getting a ride to Nimpo, however, was not going to be that easy. Chris flagged down and spoke to all the drivers, but it appeared that no one was heading to Nimpo until the end of their shift at 7:00 P.M. So we walked. And walked and walked. We walked all the way to the bypass—probably twenty kilometres in all from our cabin. We were all very footsore because we kept to the hard surface of the highway.

"I can't let you guys loose," Chris said. "It would be just my luck that someone would come and you would be running off somewhere. You'll have to stay on a lead."

At the bypass, Chris sank down gratefully on her pack. She knew that, when the next convoy came through, we would be able to catch a ride to the van.

It was late afternoon by the time the truck that picked us up deposited us at Nimpo. That was one hurdle out of the way, but our day was not over yet. We could not drive directly home, but would have to travel all the way over the bypass, then turn around and come back again to our turnoff. This took several more hours, and it was dark when we drew close to the washout east of the bridge. A barrier partially blocked the road. A generator operated flashing lights along the barrier, and it lit a sign saying: *Flood. No Admittance.*

"Ha!" said Chris. "You can forget that!" She squeezed by the barrier and drove cautiously to the washout. It was even less steep than it had been the day before. She nosed the van into it, dropped into the bottom, and slowly climbed out the other side. "We made it!" she sang. And very soon, all three of us, and the van, were home.

WE MOVED INTO THE NEW HOUSE AT ONCE, AND SHORTLY AFTERWARD Chris took off on her Book Tour and left us with dog sitters. They were adequate but not very interesting people as far as we were concerned, and when Chris arrived home just before the winter solstice, she was appalled at the mess they had made. Not that there was much to make a mess of. A sheet of plywood did duty as a kitchen counter and most Stuff was still stored in cardboard boxes on the floor. But food was caked on pots, inside and out, and candle grease and soot were plastered everywhere.

"Oh well," she said. "At least you were obviously fed properly. I hope they took you for lots of good walks."

Like all the other homes Chris has moved into, her new cabin was far from finished. Indeed, as I am writing this several years later, the house is not completed yet, at least to Chris's satisfaction. It seems pretty palatial to me, though—and, you've guessed it, a lot of Stuff is still in boxes that have never been unpacked.

Before Chris left on the Book Tour, the ugly old stove from the River Cabin had been brought up and a new Internet connection had been installed. There was no phone in the new place—Chris still had to walk down to the River Cabin for that. This place was some distance from the river and she hauled water from the restaurant at Nimpo Lake every time she went for mail, but once the snow was deep enough, she shovelled big bowls full and sat them hissing on the ugly iron stove. She picked away at interior tasks on the house in the coldest part of the season, and did more work outside when the snow melted. All too soon, it seemed, it was time to go into the mountains again.

My second summer at Nuk Tessli was a wet one and the bugs were bad, but at least there were no fires. Chris never liked rainy weather as a rule but often commented that after such a long streak of smoky and worrisome seasons, this wet spell was a relief. Friendly Wwoofers and tourists came, and there was a lot of exploring to do. Chris still raved about flowers, and Badger and I enjoyed our encounters with Moose, Caribou, Mouse and Ptarmigan. We also kept curious Bear away from the buildings.

When we came out of the mountains at the end of summer, Chris hired a big noisy machine and had a well dug at Ginty Creek—she now had running water *inside* the house—the first time, she told anyone who would listen, that she'd had that luxury for over thirty years. When the water was installed, she could put in a sink and a drain, and construct kitchen shelves. She made other storage places around the main room, and also in the outer room, which was a sort of porch-cum-shop, and which was where Badger and I had our insulated kennels. She let us inside her living area when it was really cold but we liked the outer room, as it had a dog door and we could come and go whenever we wanted. Another person came to put in a much larger solar-power system. Chris could now run a few electric tools like a drill and a vacuum cleaner as well as just the lights and the Internet. And finally, ten years after she first exchanged Money for Ginty Creek, she bought a washing machine.

"I'm sixty-nine years old," she related happily to everyone when that happened, "and it's the first time in my life I've owned a washing machine!"

WHEN THE LEAVES POPPED OUT ON THE ASPEN TREES IN THE SPRING after the Big Flood, there was the familiar bad-tempered shopping and packing—all the usual preparations for flying into the mountains for the summer. Once there, Badger and I had our habitual great time, but Chris did not seem to be enjoying it as much anymore. The summer was full of people, either Wwoofers or tourists, and she had little time for herself. She and Badger were getting old, and they no longer had the energy for really long hikes; indeed, when she had days off, she rarely did much except relax or go for short walks near home.

"Without our winters," she often said sadly to us, "we never get any solitude up here. Nuk Tessli has become less like a lifestyle and more like a job."

The following year, the ice went out really late from all the lakes. We could not fly into Nuk Tessli until mid-June. A big wind had gone through there during the winter and a tree had landed on one of the outhouses, splitting it in two.

Badger and I did not realize it, but our lives were going to change drastically that year. Chris certainly behaved differently. She cleaned a couple of the cabins, but not the third. She cut the fallen tree from the trail, but did not buck it up and carry it to the woodpile. The chimney had been pushed off Cabin Two's roof by sliding snow, as it often was, but she did not replace it. Once more, she seemed to be waiting.

About two weeks after we had arrived at Nuk Tessli, a man flew in on a plane that was loaded with building materials and brand new tools still in boxes. These things were not for Chris, however. They belonged to the visitor. He was not a Wwoofer and he was not a tourist. His name was Doron, he was from a country called Israel, and he had come to buy Nuk Tessli. The land was still owned by the government, but Chris could sell the cabins and the business.

Chris and he worked together for a couple of months. He was a cheerful person and he particularly loved me. He didn't have a lot of patience, so he found Badger a bit slow. I could sympathize with him—I found both Badger and Chris too slow most of the time, but they didn't mind as they still had that little secret bonding thing going.

A bunch of Wwoofers arrived, but again they were not there for Chris. Doron had brought young people all the way from Israel to help him. They rarely spoke English (although they could all do it well)—Chris often felt quite out of place being the only one at the dinner table who could not understand the conversation. She told us she had begun to think of Nuk Tessli as "Little Israel." She had become a foreigner in her own home.

There were a few English-speaking visitors—tourists who had been booked before the sale had taken place—and Chris took them on slow hikes to see the flowers. But her knees hurt and she walked everywhere with two poles. Back at Nuk Tessli at the end of the day, the cabins were noisy and lively with people. Chris found this difficult to deal with, but Badger and I enjoyed all the extra attention.

Chris's favourite place to see the flowers was up the trail behind the cabins, where she had taken me on my first alpine hike. I had been there many times since, of course—with Chris and also with the tourists and Wwoofers who did not need a guide. Everybody loved to have me along. They knew I would keep them safe from Bear. Indeed, once I had quite a dramatic altercation with Grizzly. He was a young male, and he charged at me, but I was more than nimble enough to keep out of his way. The tourists had a great show of Mr. Grizz and me lunging at each other. Finally, Grizzly ran away. The very next day, we encountered Mr. Grizz again in a different place. He did not hesitate this time; as soon as I barked he galloped up a steep hill and over a ridge. I had proved once again that I was superior to even the most dangerous animal in the country.

Chris wanted to make one last trip to the flower meadows and the mountains behind them. It was too far for her to hike in one day anymore. If she carried a camp, however, she would have to put the heavier stuff on our backs. If I was packing, Chris always kept me on a rope: I was still plenty skinny and I could wriggle out of my pack if I wanted to, and she would not risk letting me run loose. Two hiking poles and a dog on a rope over rocky uneven ground was not a good combination. If I was too close to Chris, the rope would wind around her poles; if I stayed a little farther away, it would snag on rocks. When Chris mentioned this predicament to Doron, he and some of his friends decided they would carry Chris's camp to the edge of the alpine. She and Badger and I would be able to walk up with nothing at all on our backs.

We left very early, as Chris likes to do, and we arrived at our campsite, which was at the edge of the treeline, ahead of the others. The land fell away below us into the forest. Nuk Tessli Lake shone silver far below; the familiar panorama of mountains soared behind. Soon the hikers plodded out of the trees and dropped Chris's gear in front of her. Chris thanked everyone profusely. This last trip into the mountains was very special to her. She had told Doron she was going to have a knee operation after she left Nuk Tessli, and she didn't know if she would ever be able to come up here again. She could not have done this hike without everyone's help.

As the hikers disappeared, you could see Chris relax. Being alone was very important for her and, because of the Wwoofers at home and the busy crowd at Nuk Tessli, solitude was something she had rarely been able to experience for months. She set up her little tent and collected brush for a tiny fire. She built this some distance from the tent, where the ground was full of boulders. She moved some of the rocks aside before making the fire; when the fire was put out, the rocks would be replaced. This is what she did almost everywhere we camped. No one would ever know she had been there.

Having established our home for the next couple of nights, we started to explore. This was very familiar country to Chris and she slowly walked over every inch, constantly taking pictures of flowers.

"They really are at their best this year," she said almost reverently. "It is as if they made a special effort for me, so I could say goodbye."

The next morning we were away by sunrise. We hiked along the whole ridge behind the camp; each small peak had a different array of the scruffy-looking plants that Chris found so inexplicably exciting. Badger and I had Marmot and Mouse and Pika to keep our noses active. There were whiffs of Bear, both Black and Grizzly, but these creatures did not come close.

The weather was not great, being cloudy, and a strong wind buffeted us and blew our fur backwards. Sometimes it drove spits of rain into our faces, but it was never really wet. On the second evening, the wind died and Chris sat beside her little fire, imagining the crowded, noisy cabins far below.

"It's hard to describe why being alone in a place like this brings me so much joy," she said as we lay with heads on paws beside her, tired after running around on rocks all day. "It is as if my soul is free.

Nuk Tessli from the camping spot on the last hike in the mountains.

I can encompass the whole enormous space about me, right to the most distant peaks, and at the same time feel connected to the wiry, scruffy vegetation and coarse rocks by my feet. It all has a kind of vibrant energy that I simply cannot put into words. People often say I live 'remotely.' I may be remote from cities, but I am close to this gorgeous and relatively untouched world that has been my backyard for twenty-three years. How many city folk can enjoy such a perfect comingling of spirit?"

"Do you know what she's talking about?" I muttered to Badger.

"Humph," he said, which meant he didn't know either.

The following morning, Chris lit her fire and breakfasted at first light. She wanted to climb a nearby hill to watch the sunrise. The clouds had left the sky during the night and there had been a stiff frost. Many of the flowers and grasses were rimmed with rime, which sent Chris into even greater paroxysms of photographic delight. Badger and I rolled our eyes at each other, but we followed her to the top of the hill. The sky in the east grew lighter. The big mountains in the west were massed and grey. Buried among them was the lake from which Badger and Nahanni had received their helicopter ride. Nuk Tessli, far below, was hidden under a layer of fog. Suddenly, a flash of pink hit the highest peak. Chris was ecstatic. She jumped around snapping pictures, putting this rock or this natural bonsai tree in the foreground. As the light travelled down the mountains and turned from pink to orange to yellow to white, she took the same pictures over and over again.

"What a perfect end to my time at Nuk Tessli," she said. "What a wonderful way to say goodbye."

We made our way back to the camp and Chris began to put our stuff together. Because we had eaten all our food, we did not have a lot to carry down, and we could manage without help. Badger would carry a light pack—my bags would be put into his. Chris would carry the rest on her back. I would run free so she would not have to bother with a lead and have it tangling her poles. Before we set off down the mountain, Chris sat for a while looking down toward Nuk Tessli (which was now clear of fog) and across to the mountains that serrated the far horizon like teeth on a dog's jaw.

"You guys have only seen a fraction of this country," Chris said to us. "I look over this wild landscape and remember all the creeks and ridges and lakes I have been to, tucked among the folds and creases of those mountains. And—yes—I remember the flowers." She laughed and tickled our ears. "I know you guys think I'm nuts!"

She continued: "And I remember all the times I've hiked with you and all the other dogs that have come into my life. Nahanni with her pink nose and unhappy ways, and the cougar that was the end of her. Raffi—lovely Raffi—with his terrible twisted stomach. Bucky and all the problems he caused. Max the TV star who, like me, was afraid of flying. Ginger who ate humans' poop and then licked their faces. Taya with the wonderful table tennis bat ears. Sport, poor boy, with his somewhat limited brain and his itchy skin. And of course Lonesome, the one who started it all. She was with me before Nuk Tessli, when I lived at my first cabin near Lonesome Lake.

"I've been privileged to have this great way of life for nearly thirty years. It certainly hasn't always been easy. I've been frightened and uncomfortable more times that I could begin to count. I've always had to struggle to find Money. But as Rudyard Kipling said, 'no price is too high to pay for the privilege of owning yourself.'

"It's going to be different living full-time at Ginty Creek. All this time I've been known as the weird woman who built cabins alone in the bush. Now I will be just an ordinary old lady with a road and running water and a vacuum cleaner. Soon I will be forgotten. But," she said, smiling a little wistfully at us, "no one can ever take those wonderful years away from me."

"Who's Rudyard Kipling?" I whispered to Badger.

"Who knows?" Badger shrugged, equally *sotto voce*. "Perhaps he was one of the tourists. I never can remember any of their names."

She strapped Badger's pack onto his back and hoisted up her own. Badger wasn't carrying much weight, but she knew he would be reliable. It was to be his last backpacking trip ever, and as Chris had often said, if her knee operation wasn't successful, it might very well be hers as well.

Slowly we walked down to Nuk Tessli. Life there was busy and indifferent. A couple of days later, we climbed into a plane, flew out of the mountains, and drove to Ginty Creek. This was now to be our full-time home.

WE STILL HAVE FUN. CHRIS RECOVERED FROM THE KNEE OPERATION, BUT it didn't really help her lameness. Badger is getting older and slower, too, but I can run as fast as ever, and I'm even more handsome.

Our principal job here is to keep Range Cow off the garden. Deer and Moose hang about as well, but Cow is our most common neighbour here. Bear often visits in the spring, but Badger and I let him know that this is our territory now, and so far he has respected that.

People brush against the edges of our lives in ways they never did before, both friends and Wwoofers, but they are good people on the whole, and Chris manages to get a lot of time alone. We even go back to Nuk Tessli sometimes. Chris is still able to take slow hikers to see the flowers. I go along, but

Badger

I chase Marmot and Pika and Bear alone. Badger always wants to come, but his legs are too stiff, and he has to stay at the cabins with the volunteers. He is taking courses in Hebrew and doing very well. Chris enjoys the flowers and the views and the people she meets, and the quick summer snapshot of Nuk Tessli, but the evenings there are now spent in crowded, noisy buildings, and Chris never has time for those contemplative moments that are, for her, the essence of living in the wild.

Our existence at Ginty Creek is much easier physically. We can drive heavy supplies, including firewood, right to the door, and we have running cold water in the house—no more hauling buckets.

But when the west wind blows and brings the groan of the logging trucks toward us from the highway, Chris sighs for the silence and solitude and untouched beauty of Nuk Tessli that was hers for so many years. She knows, however, that she had to let it go.

ACKNOWLEDGMENTS

THOSE WHO HAVE READ THIS FAR WILL REALIZE THAT I HAVE INDEED learned humanspeak and, like Lonesome, the craft of writing. It was Chris who helped me find someone to make it into a book. Thank you, Harbour Publishing, for making it work.

Thanks also to Miriam and Len for hosting us all in the big city and for giving Bucky his final home. The various SPCAs deserve our gratitude as well for taking in all the unwanted animals, making them healthy, and giving them a better life.

Thanks to Nick for his great help building the third cabin at Nuk Tessli, and for the background on Taya. Kudos also to all the other Wwoofers—the human kind—who have been marvellous fun as well as very useful over the years. Sarah deserves a special mention, as she was a wonderful help building our house at Ginty Creek. She still visits us often and has become a good friend.

I must also acknowledge all the participants in this Saga for their contributions: Lonesome, Sport, Taya, Max, Ginger, Bucky, Raffi and Nahanni. Special thanks of course to Badger for faithfully recounting the Wilderness Dog Saga and for passing this history on to me. I am grateful as well to you, Badger, for being such a good buddy all these years.

And finally, I must thank Chris for rescuing all of us from our various backgrounds, many of them abusive, and giving us the chance to be our canine selves.

Check us out on our website: www.wildernessdweller.ca.